A FOOL AND
HIS MONEY

by the same author

LIVES, LIES AND THE IRAN-CONTRA AFFAIR

A FOOL AND HIS MONEY

LIFE IN A PARTITIONED
MEDIEVAL TOWN

ANN WROE

JONATHAN CAPE
LONDON

First published 1995

1 3 5 7 9 10 8 6 4 2

© Ann Wroe 1995

Ann Wroe has asserted her right
under the Copyright, Designs and Patents Act, 1988
to be identified as the author of this work

First published in the United Kingdom in 1995 by
Jonathan Cape
Random House, 20 Vauxhall Bridge Road, London SW1V 2SA

Random House Australia (Pty) Limited
20 Alfred Street, Milsons Point, Sydney
New South Wales 2061, Australia

Random House New Zealand Limited
18 Poland Road, Glenfield
Auckland 10, New Zealand

Random House South Africa (Pty) Limited
PO Box 337, Bergvlei, 2012 South Africa

Random House UK Limited Reg. No. 954009

A CIP catalogue record for this book
is available from the British Library

Papers used by Random House UK Limited are natural,
recyclable products made from wood grown in sustainable forests.
The manufacturing processes conform to the environmental
regulations of the country of origin.

ISBN 0–224–04067–7

Phototypeset by Intype, London

Printed and bound in Great Britain by
Mackays of Chatham PLC

To Pierre Vincent: priest, organist,
friend, and son of Rouergue

Contents

Cast of characters

THE MARQUES FAMILY

Peyre Marques, cloth-seller
Alumbors Marques (formerly Rostanh), his wife
Johan, his son
Guilhema, his daughter
Gerald Canac, his son-in-law
Bartelemi Marques, his uncle
Huc Rostanh, his brother-in-law, cathedral canon
Ramon Griffe, priest, his minder

BUILDERS, NEIGHBOURS, CREDITORS, FRIENDS

Deodat Segui, merchant, Bourg consul
Johan Manha, City consul
Huc del Cayro ⎫
Stefe Cayrosa ⎭ builders
Johan Gasc ⎫
Galhart Guisardo ⎭ master-builders
Marti Barbier ⎫
Marot de Namaria ⎭ labourers
Dona Guizas, lime-kiln operator
Peyre Valeta, count's treasurer

Guilhem Camboulas ⎫
Bernat Camboulas ⎬ local rascals

Huc Serras ⎫
Johan Gabriac ⎬ border-dwellers

Berengar Seyrac ⎫
Peyre Jalenca ⎬ trespassers

Helias Porret, notary

Johan Girma ⎫
Berengar Natas ⎬ creditors

Aymeriga Guasanha ⎫
Guirbert Engles ⎬ Marques's tenants
Andreas Formis ⎭

Pons Aldebal, sergeant and tenant

Alamanda Fromenta ⎫
Huc Farcel ⎬ friends and neighbours
Bernard Rigaldi, lawyer's clerk
Bernard Claustras ⎭

Peyre Combas ⎫
Peyre Corbes ⎬ sergeants
Ramon Valeta
Johan Brau ⎭

A note on currencies

The principal system of currency in Rodez was livres, sous and deniers. As in the old British money, 12 deniers made one sou, and 20 sous made one livre. Rodez added a complication: these coins were sometimes weak local issue minted by the count (livres, sous and deniers *rodanes*), and sometimes livres, sous and deniers *tournois*, a stronger and more centralised currency which was also the official currency of account. Unless otherwise specified, the *tournois* currency is the one used here. The denier was also worth two obols, or halfpennies.

Readers will also encounter florins, francs, marks and other foreign coins. These were interlopers, but in time of war any coin was acceptable if its pure-metal content was high enough. Rates of exchange were too variable to mention.

Introduction

THIS BOOK IS about a divided town, with a political frontier running through it. We know such frontiers well in the late twentieth century. We know that they can run through villages, houses, even kitchens; and that they can divide people of the same race, the same language, the same religion, the same family. Racial and tribal frontiers, the sort that produce ghettoes in cities, are of another kind; they may often be natural or voluntary. Political frontiers are always imposed by the authorities for reasons of power, rivalry or convenience of rule; and men have then to decide whether to live with these artificial constraints, or find a way round them.

The story focuses on the strange case of Peyre Marques, a merchant who forgets where he has buried his gold. When, in 1370, two workmen discover a hoard of coins while unblocking a drain, Marques's pathetic situation becomes for us the centre of a detailed canvas that takes in the history of the town and lights it up against a background of compassion and brutality, cruel justice and individual acts of kindness, shadowed by the ever-present threat of attack.

Peyre Marques, the chief character in this book, is the man I have singled out to tell this tale of partition. He is the thread that runs through the whole fabric: together with his wife, his son-in-law, his neighbours, his tenants, his brother-in-law and his creditors. These people lived with partition every day, and partition in turn worked on them; they were its victims and in some ways, also, its perpetrators. They are the guides we need.

The story of Marques was preserved quite accidentally. We know about him only because a pitcher of gold was found buried in the floor of his shop. His son-in-law took it away, and ownership of the money was disputed in court. The result was a full-scale inquiry — detailed character references, anecdotes, gossip — about a man who was perfectly ordinary: just a middling businessman trying to support his family, stay solvent, keep his wife happy, keep his wits together. For that reason alone, this case is precious. History keeps memorials of the great, the saintly or the vicious, but we may pine for the chance to hear about men and women more like ourselves: common folk. Marques was preserved, in effect, in the tittle-tattle of his neighbours. Reading the documents about the jug of gold, we hear the ancient equivalent of lace curtains being moved aside.

To the modern eye, Marques — with his confusions and obsessions, his steady loss of business acumen, his sharp long-term memory and vagueness about the present — seems likely to be one of the earlier recorded sufferers from mental illness, possibly Alzheimer's Disease. That may provide another reason, together with political partition, for twentieth-century readers to involve themselves in such a distant story. But we shall never know for sure what Marques suffered from. All we can say is that his case is like an archaeological section that allows us, by concentrating on a tiny area, to go down deep through the layers of medieval life and the peculiar pressures of a partitioned place.

The background to this story, beyond partition, is war: the Hundred Years War, fought for sovereignty and land between two powers which were both essentially foreign to Rodez, England and France. This war had been going on, in an intermittent succession of truces, pitched battles and wild skirmishes, since 1337. The Treaty of Brétigny, in 1360, gave King Edward III of England lordship over all the lands he had formerly held as a vassal of the King of France, including, at the furthest eastern edge, 'the City and castle of Rodez and the *pays* of Rouergue'. This, and the broad area stretching westwards to the sandy Atlantic coast of Aquitaine, fell under the charge of the Black Prince, Edward's eldest son, who thus became the suzerain of Rodez. But in 1364 the new king of France, Charles V, re-opened hostilities; and the Count of Rodez, Jean I of Armagnac, who had always been opposed to the Black Prince for his own local reasons, began to gravitate to the French cause. By 1369, the town could be counted in the French camp — but only just.

These grand strategies, however, hardly touched men like Marques. Two other problems bothered them more. The first was that the war had become an endless series of guerrilla eruptions, interrupting trade and travel, terrifyingly unpredictable. The people of Rodez, though physically almost untouched by fighting, were scared of it almost all the time. The town stockpiled food and weapons, and watch duties were organised to involve as many people as possible, even down to teenagers and friars. But the main effect of war, an indirect one, was crippling taxation. It could be said that Marques was ruined by the war between England and France as surely as any traveller who met

3

with mercenaries on the road. And that, too, is part of the story.

The case of Peyre Marques is found in court registers which go into considerable detail. It is possible to hear him talking (in his own words), to hear his neighbours talk, and so to derive a great deal of information about him, his wife, his relations, and the main characters. It is possible to reconstruct dialogue and even to recover chance remarks, and I have tried to do this wherever possible: but only when the material allows it, and where no violence is done either to fact or to the integrity of the actors. History may need the zip of fiction, but any *frisson* it delivers must come from the fact that what is related really happened, or was really said. So if dialogue occurs in this book, it is as it was spoken then and recorded at the time, and it is not in any way invented; if incidents are recounted, that is because they took place, and I have added nothing to embroider them.

There remains what might be called the careful use of imagination. We are dealing in fact, not fiction; so there is much we can never reconstruct, including what the characters looked like, precisely how they dressed, how most of them talked, the rooms they lived in, their private thoughts. All this must remain unknown. Yet it is no offence to historical truth to describe such things as the blossoming of a pear tree, the stench of rotting meat, the heft of a building stone or the breathlessness of a running man, if these things (as they do) come into the evidence. And they can transport us very quickly. Similarly, if we know the path a man travelled to go home (as in one case we do), and what lay along it, it seems no offence to historical truth to retrace his steps. And if a man makes his opinions clear, it seems fair enough, from time to time, to try to derive from that a little of his character and his state of mind.

Of course, no re-telling of history can be absolutely truthful. Inevitably, certain matters are emphasised, others left out; events may be made more important, or poignant, or funny than they actually were. There is no way round this — round the fact that we live in the twentieth century, with all the judgments and attitudes that modern life implies, and the people whose lives we are reconstructing lived in the fourteenth — except to note that attitudes may not be so different as we imagine. We sometimes suppose, for example, that medieval people were inured to death and less affected by it. And often the evidence will support that. But one witness to a court case, in 1296, when asked how he knew that the accused, one Berengar, was not yet twenty-five years old, replied: 'Because on the feast of St Michael next coming it will be twenty-five years since my own father died, and then Berengar was still less than a year old and being suckled.' That painful memory was keen enough.

We sometimes imagine, too, that it was a time of casual brutality, when men and women were not particularly squeamish about capital punishment or mutilation. But one court witness around 1350 remembered a man being hanged in a village outside town, rather than on the town gallows, 'at the request of his friends, so that they shouldn't see him'.

In short, the voices in this book are often surprising, and the attitudes unexpected. It may seem unnecessary to get in so close to examine the effects of partition on the way a medieval town organised itself. A strictly academic view might do the job just as well. But towns are the sum of the people who live in them. The advantage of approaching so close to fourteenth-century Rodez is that, when one does so, the medieval crowd splits up into its individual elements;

each man or woman can be seen as the neighbour in our street, the passenger on our train, the worker in our office, a human soul, despite the mists of the past.

The place,
the sources and the story

I NEVER MEANT to go to Rodez. When I first hit upon the idea of spending three years between Oxford and Somewhere Nice Abroad, I hoped it could be the picture-postcard part of southern France: plenty of vineyards and orchards, cypress trees, the Mediterranean near at hand. But the academic map of medieval France, just like the political map, revealed it as a huge collection of overlapping fiefs in which certain professors already sat in jealous possession. I wanted to study the Albigensians, but was told these were 'spoken for'; to look at the hinterland of Toulouse, but this was already someone's intellectual back yard; to scratch around a little in Perpignan, only to find that both town and region were a domain already conquered, plundered, and carved up.

My supervisor, Peter Lewis at All Souls, suggested I go first to the Bibliothèque Nationale in Paris to look up the printed catalogue of town records, the *Inventaire Sommaire*. It was a wet spring; Paris, which I never liked because I had learned my French in the south and had an accent Parisians

7

mocked me for, looked frowsy and unlovely; and the *Inventaire* proved disappointing. I wanted to go to the south-west because I knew it and liked it, had friends there, and could think of nothing more appealing than studying under that intense sun, among the red Roman tiles, in an atmosphere thick with garlic, Gitanes and Ricard. But it became slowly clear that I would not be going there; the treasures were going to be hidden in harder places, even places that, at first sight, I might not like much.

Rodez certainly had treasures, as far as I could judge; pages and pages of fourteenth-century town documents. When I broke the news to my friends in Montauban, the grandfather proffered me a ready explanation. 'Of course it has lots of stuff left. It's such a God-awful place that no-one would want to go there even to sack it.' He turned to his neighbour for confirmation; the neighbour, underlining his words with a wide sweep of ash from a spent cigarette, replied in a growl. 'Rodez? Bé, c'est un assez sale coin.'

My friends agreed to drive me up there in the same cramped 2CV, with flapping side-windows and an armchair for a back seat, in which we had made a joyful pilgrimage to the Roussillon the year before. This journey was different indeed. The road ran north-east and uphill away from broad red fields, peach orchards and baking river beds; it became narrow, winding and grey. The hills closed in; the dry-stone walls began. We crossed limestone moors, bare except for heaps of stones, solitary thistles and sheep that carried the wind in their fleeces. In the villages not a soul stirred. The houses became tall, with slate roofs dark as the rain. Their shutters were no longer to keep the sun out, for there seemed to be no sun in these high valleys. They were evidently closed to keep secrets, like grim old mouths.

Over the two years I spent there, I approached Rodez in a variety of ways; but each time there was the same sense of a journey deep into the interior. If I went by train from

Paris I would always seem to reach Cahors, where I had to change, in the middle of the night. The little two-coach train to Figeac, where I had to change again, did not run after ten; I remember half-sitting, half-lying in the waiting room, stiff with lack of sleep, until the buffet opened in the morning for coffee and bread. From Figeac, another small train travelled on to Rodez. By now the track ran in the mountains, through impossibly narrow cuts and rock walls glistening with water, round improbable bends, into gardens full of cabbages and marigolds, under washing lines, up the backs of grey stone barns. Geese honked on the verges, and trees pinioned to cliffs of rock brushed against the windows. This, at least, is how I remember it, as if it were a train in dreams.

On one summer journey it stopped midway, and we were told that another train would arrive in a couple of hours. I had no idea where we were; the stop seemed to have no name to it. Nothing lay beyond the station but steep meadows high with grass and ox-eye daisies, with a lane on one side and a lazy river on the other. I left my suitcase, which was on the point of disintegrating, and walked out into the sound of birds and flies.

At the top of the lane, under a cliff, was a shabby little bar the colour of the cliff-stone, with dark green paint and awnings, where I was served a bright red grenadine by a surly man with a tea-towel over his arm; and then I walked out into the hayfields. For an hour I sat in company with the shining river and the flies. Once a grey horse came out of nowhere, swishing his tail and tearing thunderously at the grass with a swivel of long teeth. It was an hour when time sat suspended, like a still leaf from a branch: present, past and future coming seamlessly together between the coughs of two small trains.

Journeys like these became a way of acclimatising myself to the isolation of Rodez, like a diver habituating himself to the pressure of the sea. But the town itself remained mysterious. Its history seemed as hidden as its personality. Rodez did not put on airs; it had no pretensions. Its first claim to fame, the huge red sandstone cathedral, was a peculiar mishmash of styles, Gothic, fanciful, fortified and classical; nothing matched on it, and it sat, uncompromisingly, right in the middle of the town. The town's medieval walls had mostly been demolished, and its older buildings had often been bashed about a bit, or hollowed out to take modern shops. This was twenty years ago; they tell me that the place has now transformed itself, with everything that is old carefully done up and repainted. But Rodez seemed less ambitious then. Around 1974 the town adopted a motto for itself: 'Rodez: Ville Moyenne'. An average place which, like an average woman, would occasionally try to tart itself up by, for example, 'pedestrianising' with livid bricks the alley that led to the Codec supermarket; but which was generally content to stay much as it was.

The alley by the Codec supermarket led also to the archive building; and it was there I uncovered my first secret, the passion of many Rodez folk for the history of their place. At the back of the archives was a grassy yard. This yard was the preserve of one Canac (a name I was to encounter again), a taciturn, dark-skinned young man who wore blue overalls. Canac's job was to fix the erratic plumbing and to move the many objects in the archives that were too heavy for others to shift: bundles of nineteenth-century newspapers, pieces of farm equipment, huge paintings of *notables*, bits of stone. But he spent most of his time sitting on the back step, cigarette in hand, surveying the yard, which was strewn with pieces of column and column base and bits of reddish rock. I asked him about them once. 'They're Monsieur Trémouillé's collection,' he told me. Then, wonderingly: 'You know, it's really old, all that stuff.'

How old was that? Trémouillé himself, who haunted the

archives like a busy wasp, had no doubt: these artefacts were Roman, and he turned them up continually. You would see him trotting through the town and up the archive stairs, a cardboard box under his arm, in his scoutmaster's shorts and socks turned over at the top, with his hair crew-cut like a boy's. Out of his box he would tip small mounds of treasures: bits of pot, slivers of column, murky corners of glass. Each piece, with its reddish dusting of mud, would be lifted lovingly between dirty thumb and forefinger to be brushed and scrutinised. These were the bits and pieces which, I was soon to learn, the people of fourteenth-century Rodez turned up in their gardens too, and decided belonged to the Saracens; but Trémouillé knew better. 'Romain! Romain!' he would mutter, bending over them, giving the word its long southern twang, like a breeze of anisette in the Forum. You could stop him sometimes in the street, in mid-trot, box under arm; he would invariably find time to say 'Such beauties! And Roman!' before he fled away.

Apart from Trémouillé, searching for physical signs of the town's past was a hit-or-miss affair. Sometimes, out in the country, I would notice a place-name that spoke of old aristocracy, but find there was little more to it than that. Châteaux could be seen from the road, half-ruined, or blighted by outcrops of stained cement holding aerials and washing. The shutters were often down, the hedges uncut; they were pieces of old extravagance that pleaded not to be looked at. I went with a friend to trespass on one once, through a scrubby wood and a meadow of long grass. We came out, unexpectedly, on an avenue of limes standing in the same long grass, with a small temple at the end of it. Somebody had smashed the temple, but it still contained paintings of nymphs and shepherds between grey triangles of damp; and we stood for a while there, uncertain whether to feel monarchist regret or Jacobin relief, while the blue Dyane sat brazenly at an angle in the middle of the drive.

But I wanted humbler evidence, too. Going home to my basement flat in the evenings, I would pass certain low arched doorways below the level of the street, sometimes closed with iron grilles, smelling of potatoes and drains; and I would surmise that these were perhaps medieval shops, burrowed into the hill like rabbit warrens. In the cathedral, I would search for medieval remains among the later layers of pious ornament, such as the Christ praying in the Garden on a mat of greengrocer's grass; and it was always a thrill to find those older pieces, whether gargoyle or carving or tomb, like a touch from far away. But to know the folk of medieval Rodez, as to know their modern counterparts, was going to require much more time and much more digging than that.

The people in the archives, researchers and staff alike, were unfailingly friendly. We were all having fun. Even Madame Fabre, who fetched the documents to the reading room and battled constantly, against the barrage of noise from the school playground outside the window, with her *rhumes* and her *migraines*, seemed positively to enjoy complaining. I would find her often in the ladies' room (which was guarded by a bust of Voltaire) pouting, sighing, adjusting her earrings, and washing down tablets with the iron-tasting tap water. The documents were *putains*, her colleagues *cons*, her children probably the death of her. Beyond the tiny window, out of which she directed her glances and her sighs, lay a grey crowd of rooftops; beyond them the Place de la Cité, lofty, haughty and austere, surrounded by tall grey buildings and loomed over by the cathedral. The square's centrepiece was a statue of a local bishop killed on the Paris barricades in 1848, who now held back with imploring hand the crowds of pigeons that wheeled round him. The motto on his pedestal, *Que mon sang soit le dernier versé,* 'may my blood be the last to be shed', seemed to sum up the martyrised air of the fashionable in Rodez, trapped like Madame Fabre in a *ville moyenne*, their high heels impossible in the steep streets, as the wind blew out their hairpins.

The chief archivist himself, a sweet and shy young man, stayed most of the time in his office, for the reading room was a rambunctious place. The deputy archivist, Noël, was a communist. This was in the days when communism still had some glamour in it; and Noël, with his sharp face and little tufted beard, gleaming eyes and polo-necked sweaters, was the closest Rodez could come to political fanaticism. Even he made a joke of it. Just before noon, when the archives closed for two hours for lunch (a hiatus I always found impossible to fill, though by the end of my stay I could almost spin a coffee and a sandwich out so long), he would appear in the reading room, tap the clock, and announce that it was noon, 'Moscow Observatory Time'.

Much of Noël's pleasure came from bearding the two elderly conservatives who haunted the archives, Dropy and Fournial, and making their lives wretched. Dropy was a waspish, impeccably courteous man with a finely chiselled face; he had once been a jeweller and watchmaker, which showed in his delicate hands. He was now an inveterate follower of minor aristocracy, and courtesy dictated that before he attacked the shelves, looking for the counts of Panat or Villefranche, he should offer everyone in the room an aniseed drop from the tin that rattled in his pocket. Noël would always decline, ascetically, but would then hang at his sleeve with sharp jibes about kings and revolutions, as Dropy lifted the books one by one to his weak eyes. When he was tormented enough the two would fall to passionate argument, rules of silence notwithstanding.

Fournial received the same treatment. He had the face of a benevolent toad, with slobbering mouth, and a huge stomach barely contained within the suit he always felt obliged to wear. (In summer the jacket came off, the tie was tugged down, the shirtsleeves rolled up, and a great red handkerchief was mopped across the brow.) Fournial was searching for his ancestors, convinced that there was some nobility there. In the morning he worked fast, licking his thumb extravagantly with each page he turned; after lunch he became progressively slower, sighing, snuffling, until his head dropped and he snored, with a trickle of saliva running down on to the table.

Madame Fabre would look on with distaste, one eyebrow raised; Noël would pass with remarks about the decadence of crypto-monarchists. And indeed everything Noël said to Fournial, sleeping or waking, was calculated to ignite a spark and start a political fight. Fournial was also a not-so-secret smoker; and the arguments between the two of them, out in the corridor among the glass cases containing the town's medieval charters of privileges, were characterised by Noël banging on the glass to emphasise freedom and socialism while Fournial stood, one arm suspiciously contorted, holding behind his back a Gauloise that was slowly burning down to the stub.

To this rowdy place, with its big school table round which we all sat, the documents were brought; and they were as good as the *Inventaire Sommaire* had suggested. In fact, they were far better, for the *Inventaire* could only scratch the surface of what they contained. Most of them were in good shape: the vellum still supple, the paper of the account books, of wonderful thick quality, only slightly yellower than records from three hundred years later. (This was despite the fact that, one hard winter, Canac brought a pile of registers down from the attic with the snow fresh on them.) I soon came to distinguish, and sometimes to appreciate, the handwriting of the fourteenth-century clerks: the notaries' crammed, with copious shorthand; the town treasurer's with a strong, generous, lovely script, evenly inked and effortlessly level; most precious of all, the occasional painstaking script of someone not too used to the act of writing. Here, for example, was Peyre Rollan's declaration of his properties to the consuls for tax, written with care on a very small piece of paper. Rollan was a knife-maker.

Gentlemen, God give you good life always gentlemen I have a house in the carrieyra del Bal which is next to Duran Gasto and Johan Seyrac and Duran Gasto's garden the hospital of Peace of the Virgin Mother of God has 17 sous from it. Gentlemen I have a garden in Gorgon, it's held from the prior of St Amans for a rent of 6d.
Gentlemen I am your servant P Rollan
I recommend myself to your mercy.

Most of the script could be read with no difficulty. There was little if any crossing out, even in the town registers, though sometimes on vellum the surface would be painstakingly scratched away, and a correction written over. But there was no sense of stuffy officialdom in these records; though they were carefully done, they were alive. There were sketches, doodles and poems; pieces of straw set in as markers; fragments of seals on fragile strips of ribbon; stray bits of paper containing the medieval equivalent of reminders; marginalia, and rude remarks. To plunge into these documents was to be caught up completely in their world; I would leave every day with my brain spinning and a jumble of small pieces of a picture in my head, some of which would slowly begin to come together and cohere.

About half these documents were written in highly abbreviated (and often careless) Latin, for which I was prepared. The rest were in Occitan, a Romance dialect nearer to Catalan than French, which is still spoken in the country regions round Rodez. This I had not met before. With a smattering of Spanish and several dictionaries (my decent French being almost no help at all), I made my way in it well enough, but from time to time it defeated me. Frustratingly, the words I could not translate were always the most interesting: natural objects, household items, slangy phrases tossed at a woman in the street. Sometimes it was the grammar as much as the words that foxed me: with all the words translated, the whole phrase still made no sense. I once took a word to Monsieur Delmas, the archivist, unable to work it out; it was something small boys would trespass for. He thought about it for some time, and eventually told me it was either pears or magpies' nests. We never did any better; I had to leave it at one or the other.

In the end, I decided to take lessons. These were offered in the Institute at night; I went along, eager to understand not only what my medieval characters were saying, but what was being shouted out around me in the marketplace. If I went into the Bourg square when the country folk came in from their smallholdings (just as they came in in the fourteenth century), Occitan was all I heard. The black-hatted grandmothers offered baskets of dandelion leaves, dried flowers, untreated fruit (which was wizened and wormy) and little *crottins* of goat cheese laid on straw mats; they knew the French for these things, presumably, but Occitan was the only language they cared to speak.

The lessons, however, were not a success. We were a strange set of students, of all conditions and ages, some smartly dressed, some in workers' overalls; most of the class knew Occitan pretty well to speak, but wanted to know the grammar and how to spell it, which was by no means straightforward. At the very first lesson, we came to the word for 'cradle'. One student objected; that was not the word he knew. The teacher went round the class, discovering, with mounting astonishment, that almost every village used a different word. At that point, I gave up. Perhaps I should have persevered; giving up meant that a few phrases got away entirely. I can still take an educated guess at what they mean; but for the purposes of this book, I could never render them convincingly into English. So I have had to let them go.

Translation of speech posed problems of another sort, too. To hear men and women talking across the centuries is a thrilling thing; it closes time up instantly, like the snap of two interlocking springs. The tiny word *be* (meaning 'well', or 'you know') was a case in point: used then, and used now, at the start of any remark needing a bit of thought, or scorn, or underlining. The word *putana* (whore) was another. It cropped up constantly in my documents as a favourite term of abuse, and its popularity had lasted, certainly among my colleagues; *putain de voiture, putain de crayon, putain de porte*, they would mutter to themselves of any inanimate object that caused them annoyance.

The word *putana*, like *arlot* (which meant the same but was applied only to men, and not to women, giving a satisfying slur of effeminacy) was never translated out of Occitan by the medieval notaries. Yet this was rare. Because most of my characters' remarks were from their testimony given in court, they were almost all put into Latin and indirect speech, except for dialect words or slang which the notary could not translate. (A favourite example of mine came from a court case of 1290, when one furious man had chased another into a house: *Bernardus tunc intravit et dixit Quo loco est larlot?*)

Recovering the original words that were said, or the turns of phrase, was rather like diving down through many layers of water and mud; even when they were recovered, it was difficult to sift out differences between one man talking and another. There were wonderful exceptions: the judge who, for every question, delivered an answer bristling with references to the precise section in the relevant chapter of his law books; the eighty-five-year-old who could not stop talking; the nervous confusion of a woman who had been burgled and could not get the story straight; the bluntness of sergeants. Wherever I thought I could catch the tone, I tried. But there was still no substitute for the occasional flow of original Occitan, leaping as if in full colour from the page: usually street obscenities and blasphemies, but just occasionally — as in the lament of the chief character in this story — a long impassioned outpouring straight from the heart.

The words conjured up scenes, and these in themselves were often intriguingly incomplete. Suddenly I would be in a medieval kitchen, looking out of a window as a man with a knife ran past down the street. I would be in a meadow with a courting couple, down near the river, and my idyll would be disturbed by a man running up to report an accident, a messenger fallen from his horse. I would be in bed, when suddenly I would hear the screams of a neighbour's wife and rush to the window; but it is dark, there is nothing to see, and I return to the warm sheets. I would hear someone knocking at the door on a rainy evening, and let in a strange woman; in the morning, I would find my small store of cash missing, together with a favourite cloak. Scene after scene appeared in this way, like a succession of snapshots or incidents in dreams. For a few lines I would be completely in the world of these people, with their sense of time and place and the objects and people they knew; and then the page would turn, the case would change, and they were gone again.

Clinging on to characters was an effort, but it was worth it. If I kept sharp, I could start to add on small details to the names in these scenes: where they lived, what they did, their relations, sometimes even a suggestion of what sort of people they were. As in getting to know the town outside, there was no substitute for human contact. I could never

know what the medieval faces looked like — none was ever
described — and I had to strain to hear the voices; but a
certain continuity of character seemed to link the pages I
was reading with the life in the streets around me. The
medieval sergeants took on some of the bustle and
officiousness of the modern policemen and janitors, for
whom no detail was too small to make a meal of; the women
took on the prim intentness of the bargain-hunters in
Codec, picking over the packets of biscuits; and the older
witnesses took on the growling, suspicious tones of the
gnarled *montagnards* who manned the benches at the edge
of the market, chewing their words for flavour like an old
cigarette. Past and present ran together again: the two
worlds were so deeply embedded in each other that it was
sometimes hard to tell where one ended and the other
began.

Going home one night, past the potato-smelling basements on the steepest slope of the hill, I saw a man sitting
down to dinner in the window of a café. I had considered
this café for my interminable lunch hours: it offered soup,
main course, cheese or fruit for a *prix fixe* of 20 francs. Each
table had a red-and-white checked oilcloth, set with jugs for
vinegar and oil, and a white ashtray; there were perhaps six
tables there, and I only ever saw one occupied. The man
who sat there was perhaps in his sixties, with a pink face,
round eyes and thinning hair; and as he sat, the waiter came
up to tie his napkin gently round his neck. I could never
work out whether the gesture was one of deference to a
boss, or protectiveness of an innocent; it could have been
either. Neither man gave anything away. But the elder man
bent his head carefully over the bowl of soup, as if eating
was something that he too had to draw out for as long as
possible. And this image began to impose itself on another
character I had met.

The story of Peyre Marques was unlike anything else I

discovered in my documents. To begin with, the evidence was in two parts, one part of which was not in Rodez at all; it turned up in Montauban, back where I had started, in the archives of the counts of Armagnac. And both parts were concerned less with the facts of a case (which might have been a theft, but was left curiously vague) than with the character of a man. This was a man who, despite past successes and prosperity, could no longer look after himself. Something was happening to him, something which he found terrifying and his neighbours found inexplicable: he seemed to be losing his wits. For page after page of two registers, people debated whether or not this was so.

All historians are detectives by nature. We cling to our facts, every shred of evidence, and we like to clear up our cases. The Marques case was supremely frustrating on that count. Neither register was dated, and neither was complete. I could try to fix the date from internal evidence, such as when A was consul, when B moved, when C died; and from the script, which told me at a glance that the registers had been written up late in the fourteenth century. But I could not find the end of the story.

I looked everywhere; for if the register was already scattered in two places, why not three or four? Time and again I took the bus to Montauban, back down the mountains, under the steep river-cliffs, into the broader country. I came to know every turn of the road: the grassy lane where an old woman once got off, laden down with newspapers and a live hen in a string bag; the white wooden goose at one particularly sharp bend, advertising pâté de foie gras; the wedding-tier spire of the pink church at Caussade, and the dog asleep under drifting streamers in a café doorway. The pimply bus boy would get off for a beer here, jangling the money in the bag at his crotch; and I would sit watching the plane trees, their leaves somehow larger, brighter and lusher than in Rodez, and wonder where on earth I could search next.

I went to these lengths because I felt I had got to know someone, and cared about what had happened to him. I wanted to know, too, about the other people in the case and what had happened to them: the son-in-law, the wife, the creditors, the neighbours, even the cowboy builders. But history defeated me. Like friends made on holiday whose interests and conversation can fill a whole summer, but whose paths never cross ours again, the characters in the Marques case engaged me, obsessed me, and left me.

Did it matter? The purpose of my research, after all, was to find out how a partitioned medieval town worked. Every piece of evidence helped in that regard. Besides, the effort to get to know the fourteenth-century characters, as to get to know the people in the modern town around me, would never be rewarded by knowing everything. In the end, I would remain an outsider. I would never quite catch everything they said; I would never learn convincingly to discuss local preoccupations (in the modern town, it was politics and rugby); I would never eat with any pleasure the savoury tripes that were heaped on my plate. And I would never know whether Peyre Marques, in 1370 or thereabouts, had ever actually owned the pitcher of gold that turned up under his shop. But that disappointment did nothing to spoil the journey I had taken.

1

Huc del Cayro
and the town at war

THIS STORY BEGINS with the clang of a shovel, and a clatter of gold coins. The coins were found in a jug, hidden in a drain. The drain was in a square in a town which, if you could hover over it like a bird, was perched on a high hill in the loop of a river in wild limestone country in south-central France. The town was Rodez; the river was the Aveyron. The year was 1369 or 1370, though nobody can say for sure.

On that day, a man on a pack-horse was travelling towards the town. He may have had salt meat in his saddlebags, or cheeses, or iron nails. He may have been wide awake, alerted by the stumbles of his beast on the rough stones of the road; or half-asleep, lulled by the sense that his destination was close. The landscape he travelled in was vast. The far bare hills were known as *segalas*, ryelands, thin, bitter soil producing bitter bread. After each harvest these uplands lay fallow for two or three years to recover, turning into a wilderness of broom and thin grass. In winter they would lie under snow, criss-crossed by padding wolves and, it was said, by more sinister beasts. Shepherds in their huts had sometimes seen them, materialising silently from the white land and the white sky.

Occasionally the rider would plunge down into woods, woods so thick that he was forced to lie on the neck of his horse to keep the scraping branches from his eyes. The trees were oaks and chestnuts, food for the thin local pigs and their scrawny masters. Somewhere below lay the river, curved deep into gorge and rock and wood; somewhere, still out of sight, lay the town he was making for. From time to time he glimpsed it, only to lose it again round the hills and twists of the road. At moments it seemed close, a canter away; then it was distant, unreachable, a town in a vision that would blink and disappear.

An ancient account of the miracles of St Amans, the patron of Rodez, told of a merchant travelling in like this from the south-west, weary and longing to be home. He had seen the river winking below him at the base of the cliffs, the hills around the town, the town on its peak. His mind was already wandering to the warmth of a fire, the hugs of his family, the stories he was going to tell them. Then, quite suddenly, his cart hit a rock bigger and more vicious than the rest. His pitcher of wine, bouncing, turning in the air, plunged down and smashed on the rocks below. The merchant, in tears, knelt and prayed to St Amans; and the saint restored the pitcher whole, as if it had never broken.

A prayer to St Amans, as to St Christopher, was good insurance on journeys out of town; for the devil haunted this country. There were places locally where he had leapt over gorges; his fossilised hoof-prints marked where he had taken off and landed. In the wilds of these high plateaux, on the edge of these dizzying drops, echoes could be tossed around like the looping cry of a falling man. Local shepherds had a style of singing — indeed, they still have it, though it is rare to hear it — that could carry for miles across valleys, bearing news, or warnings, or simply musing on the bitterness of life. One such song, from the time of the war, might have been whistled by our traveller on the windy road: the song of a girl who, given a ring by a passing knight on horseback, dropped it into the Aveyron from the Mirabel bridge near Rignac, down-river, and let another knight dive down for it; and both were lost.

> *Al' pon da Mirabel*
> *Catarina lababo.*

> On the Mirabel bridge
> Catarina was washing.

> *Venguero a passa*
> *Tres cabelhes d'armada.*

> Three mounted knights
> Came riding past.

> *Lo premier li diguet*
> *'Ne ses pas maridada?'*

> The first said,
> 'Aren't you married?'

> *Lo segon li donet*
> *Uno polido bago.*

> The second gave her
> A shining ring.

> *Mas lo bago del det*
> *Tombet al fon de l'ayo.*

But the ring from her finger
Fell in the water.

Lo trosieme sautet,
Foget lo cobussado.

The third jumped down,
Leapt over the parapet.

Mas tornet pas monta,
Ne trobet pas lo bago.

He never came up,
Never found the ring.

Al' pon da Mirabel
Catarina plorabo.

On the Mirabel bridge
Catarina wept.

The Aveyron was still a wild river, flowing strongly with
plumes of foam among the rocks; and it had a place in the
town's heathen past. It was here, at a spot called Laguiole,
that St Amans had performed his vital miracle, the conversion of Rodez to Christianity. The name Laguiole meant the
idol's whirlpool; the river there still flowed green with
strands of weed, and tall trees overhung it. St Amans, it was
said, walking by the bank some time in the fourth century,
had found the people playing viols and drums to a small
stone statue raised on a column. This was the idol called
Ruth, after which they had named both their town and
themselves. The saint withdrew to a little chapel, conjured
up a small black cloud, and with a single bolt of lightning
exploded the stone god. One piece fell into the river to

make the idol's whirlpool; another fell into the meadow to make a great pit that men could still see and wonder at, though it was now full of cabbage plants and regiments of bean-sticks; splinters fell into the rocks to make holes, cracks and crevasses, permanent signs of the vigour of the saint.

As the traveller came on, the river ran loudly beside him. It was narrow, but hard to cross. There was (and still is) a little pack-horse bridge at Laguiole, with barely room for a loaded beast and niches for men to pass. This bridge had been started in the 1320s because the crossing was too perilous: 'travellers have often crossed from earth to heaven, and to the perpetual mansions'. By 1370 the stonework was in bad repair again, the sides and balustrades crumbling, the road-stones loose. The traveller picked his way above the swirling water, noticing the sections of hewn stone that lay already, tumbled askew, on the deep bed of the river.

More meadows appeared here, spread with bright drying cloths. Bare-legged men and women, trampling cloths in the water, stared at him as he passed. Behind them were fields just large enough for an ox-drawn plough to negotiate; and the traveller as he rode could watch the muffled plough-men haranguing their beasts in the cold, wreathed in white breath, or the stooping summer workers with their sickles and broad-brimmed hats.

The town was now above him, looming almost unseen at the top of high red cliffs. Some years later, bushes were deliberately planted at the base of the town walls to stop children tumbling down into the river. Rodez had only one approach, on the western side of town, that was at all easy to negotiate. A traveller coming in on any but that western road faced a nerve-racking zig-zag route, some of it up steps, the mules and ox-carts desperately held to the path, the men sliding. People had dug allotments and little gardens on the slopes, and the plots could be made to produce cabbages and bent fruit trees; but the red soil was held in with walls, and each heavy rain brought a slithering descent among the bushes and loosened stones.

Coming closer, the traveller found himself under a ring of walls, the stone raw and new. Men were still working on them: hammering, shouting, pointing. Just above them he could pick out the tops of individual buildings among the huddled roofs, overhung with smoke as if they steamed after rain. In 1370 the cathedral was still half-finished, with a pre-fab bell-tower made of wood, and a wooden crane poking out of the top of it. It was either this, or the spires of smaller churches, or the high barbicans (sometimes daubed with 'nice colours' of paint, or battened with bright bits of tin) that caught his eye and the sun.

If he had looked up, on that day in 1370, he might also have seen a ladder set against the roof-beam of a house, and a man on high scaffolding directing the setting of stone. The wind — never anything to stop the wind in Rodez — ruffled his hair and billowed the shirt on his back. The man was Huc del Cayro, mason and wall-builder. The house belonged to Peyre de la Parra, a lawyer of standing; it was a lucrative commission, a clue that del Cayro was expert at his job. And indeed he was good, and knew he was. A few years later, he became a building inspector; and when bids were taken in 1380 for the building of one small upper wall ('with one or two arrow-slits if the consuls want them'), del Cayro dropped out of the bidding early as the offers fell, knowing what his work was worth and not prepared to undersell himself.

As he worked, two men came running up. One was Johan Manha, a consul, in his red-and-beige consular robes and his consular hat, which the Rodez wind would do its best to remove from his head; the other was Deodat Segui, also once a consul, therefore also to be respected. Manha, much the older, was the more out of breath; Segui was the more insistent; but both men gasped out to del Cayro that he should grab his tools and come at once.

It was not how del Cayro had expected his day to go; but he stopped work, climbed down, gathered up the tools he needed, and went with them. In another street, the traveller and his pack-horse made their last weary steps to the door of a lodging-house.

We have said that this happened in France; but that is not quite true. In the fourteenth century Rodez, ruled first by the counts of Rodez and then by the counts of Armagnac, was in one of many fiefs that were in loose association with France. The counts sometimes helped the king of France in his wars against the English, and sometimes careered off by themselves. Had you asked del Cayro and Manha what country they were in, they would not have said France; indeed, they might have found the question puzzling. France, they knew, was up north somewhere. It was not to the east, for Avignon and Montpellier, according to the town accounts, were not in it. Nor was it to the west, where the area was *Gascuenha, Albiges, Quersi* or *Lemozi*, rather than *Fransa.* To the north, the far hills were those of *Alvernha,* Auvergne; beyond this, possibly, opening out in woods and fields from those black mountains, France began.

And what was France? The king lived there, with his *parlement,* in a city called Paris, crowded with the spires of palaces and churches. Sound money was meant to come from France: francs, *louis d'or, parisis, reals,* those heavy impressive coins that money-changers laid out on their baize tables, but that men like del Cayro seldom had to jingle in their pockets. From time to time, too, emissaries would go up there, to return dazzled and exhausted.

Manha, as it happened, had been to France that very year. He was renowned for his travelling, but the longest journey of his life had been to Paris to ask King Charles V to ratify the town's privileges (and so, with luck, escape tax). He and a colleague, Berengar Natas, who will also feature later, struggled up over the mountains, pack-horses carrying their trunks, on a gruelling midwinter round-trip of sixty-eight days and eight hundred miles. They took a servant with them, and a lawyer to help with procedure. And they ran out of money; at the end of the journey they had spent 22 livres, the equivalent of their keep for twenty-two days, on tips for porters and presents for royal doorkeepers. The paperwork alone 'for writing the letters, and for sealing, and for the seals on the duplicates, and for registering the letters in the Chambre des Comptes and all that this entailed' came to 90 livres.

Manha and Natas also bought a cloak costing 17 livres, almost twice the price of their consular robes in Rodez. (What possessed them we cannot say; maybe it was only the winter cold in strange hotel rooms; but they were both cloth merchants, and knew good stuff when they saw it. Charitably, or timidly, the accounts did not say which of them ordered it, or who it was for.) At any event, when they fell into debt their instinct was to seek help from people who spoke their language. They borrowed money from Peyre Gras, a merchant of Montpellier, rather than from Parisians.

No local, in fact, could speak French. A line running roughly from La Rochelle to Lyon separated the *pays d'Oc*, the country of Occitan-speakers, from the lisping and pointed speech farther north. Frenchmen came to the town occasionally, and one wonders how they made themselves understood; it may well have been through interpreters. Little by little, French was beginning to creep in as the language of an élite and governing class, though still far away and seldom heard, like the cry of an exotic bird. Occitan, by contrast — the people of Rodez called it *romans* — was the language of life, rough, slangy, full of variants. When del Cayro came upon the job Manha and Segui wanted him to do, which involved unblocking a drain, he found it bunged up, in his words, with *bueg, mortier, arsila am peyre freial* (mud, mortar, clay and broken stones); he tried to shift it *am sas aysaias*, with his tools. The notary had no idea how to put such things in lawyer's Latin, so he did not try.

Another, more pressing consideration kept del Cayro from going to France; and that was war. For more than ten years bands of mercenary soldiers under the notional command of the Black Prince, the eldest son of Edward III of England, had been rampaging through the region. The prince was anxious to consolidate his new-won power as ruler of Aquitaine; the warring bands were there to help both him and themselves. This was no campaign of set-piece battles or organised offensives; it was guerrilla warfare and general marauding, punctuated by sieges of any towns that showed resistance. The soldiers were undisciplined and hungry, billeted in woods and fields, their ranks increasingly swollen by local miscreants; their campaigns, ostensibly about sovereignty, often seemed to have no purpose but the spread of terror. Rodez, in its mountains, was almost the last place they came to. From the dark plains of Picardy, through the Norman orchards and the vineyards of Gascony, the English wave petered out almost at the doorstep of the town. And the town waited.

For much of the time the war was distant: somewhere 'out there' towards Villefranche in the west, or the higher mountains to the north. The great war heroes of either side — Bertrand du Guesclin, Constable of France after 1370, and Robert Knowles, commander of the English — barely rated a mention in the Rodez records, where they were called 'De Clequi' and 'Quanola'. But their movements could not be ignored. Much of Manha's time that year, as a consul, was spent obsessively watching the borders of the region, the hill-forts and the outlying towns, to try to tell where the English were heading. Spies were sent to Entraygues, twenty miles due north, 'to see if the English are going to cross the river Olt', to Villefranche (forty miles away) 'to find out what's happening', to far-off Limoges 'to see whether the city is destroyed or not'. Messengers were despatched in every direction, often on foot with a spare pair of shoes in a bag, to bring back news of the enemy.

In these months, the region lost its character of isolated towns in difficult country and became vulnerable and small. The consuls of Cahors, Villefranche and Figeac (which was captured by the English in 1371) kept sending disconcerting messages, convinced that Rodez was the next town to fall. Rodez itself seemed uncertain how to behave, whether boldly or with circumspection. There was a curfew and a watch, for which every male over the age of fourteen was enlisted at 4 *blancas* a night, with a fine of 10 sous for not turning up; but at least twice a year, during the fairs, the night watch would be manned by strolling fiddlers and the whole town would be lit up with a lantern in every window, flickering across the hills.

The men of Rodez were hardly ever called on to fight in this war. In 1355, when the English reached Clairvaux to the north-west, miscellaneous weapons — crossbows, slings, pikes — were handed out to certain townsmen, who handed some of them back in, having lost most of them in 'practices', a few weeks later. In those nerve-racked days cotton wicks, rather than reeds, were put in the watchmen's torches, so that they would burn more slowly and give light all night. But the enemy never turned up. By 1369 the closest the town had come to battle was to send a contingent of ten crossbowmen (in bits of borrowed armour), four carpenters and a pack-horse with their food to the siege of Castelmary, where the English were holding the castle. They were fortified with strong drink before they left; and a supplementary mule, with more food, had to be sent five days later, as if there was nothing to do at Castelmary but sit around and eat.

All this seemed relaxed enough. Yet by 1370 deputies who set out to attend the increasingly frequent and bitter regional meetings about war levies sometimes returned *naf-ratz*: literally shipwrecked, comprehensively beaten up, by fighters in a war they purported to be surprised by. It was closer than they thought. Manha and his colleagues became convinced that the English were *entorn*, surrounding them, and close; they also thought them *embosquat entorn*, hiding out in the woods that lined del Cayro's horizon from the top rung of his ladder. No-one could say where they would turn up next, or how fast. 'The English are riding, no-one knows where', read one chilling message from the consuls of Entraygues; at which bundles of straw were set alight and roaring on the tops of the watch-towers, signalling 'English on the move'.

Many, or most, of these 'English' were not Englishmen at all. They were crews of roving mercenaries, local bad boys, Picards, Flemings and Bretons: the names of these last, Jan or Fulk or Alaric, were ones the people of Rodez had never heard before. These men stole horses, drove cattle away, set fire to isolated farms; but would occasionally show up too at official musters, unshaven, boasting motley pieces of weaponry and giving gung-ho guerrilla nicknames ('Adventurer', 'Blackbeard', 'The Bastard') when they were asked to provide them.

One of these adventurers, Merigot Marches, languished in gaol in Rodez for a time. His brother Auci was incarcerated with him. It was an uncharacteristically bad moment for them, as Merigot showed when he provided his reminiscences later for Froissart's *Chronicles*. 'Pillaging and robbing is a great life!' he laughed:

How we used to enjoy it when we rode out on the off-chance and found a rich abbey in the fields, or a rich prior or merchant, or a mule-train from Montpellier or Narbonne or Toulouse . . . all loaded with cloth of Brussels or Moustier-Villiers, or with skins from the fair at Lendit, or with spices from Bruges, or silk cloths from Damas or Alexandria! It was all ours, we could demand whatever ransom we liked for it. Fresh money every day! The peasants would bring us grain and flour, fresh-baked bread, oats and straw for the horses, good wine, cattle and fat sheep, hens and game-birds . . . we were treated like kings, and when we went out on a raid the whole country quailed before us. God, that was a fine life!

And it had its effect. In time, any stranger of violent disposition was called 'English', and these strangers became the stuff of nightmares, both for children and for consuls. It was easy then, as it is easy now, to be seized with sudden unease on the wide moors round Rodez, or in the deep-shaded gorges of the rivers. An overhang could take on the appearance of a face; a cave could swallow up whole legions of armed men; their smell was in the mustiness of narrow places, their English presence a chill between the shoulder-blades. Possibly some real confrontation had happened there; often it had not. The word 'English' was attached in those years to defiles, ravines, jumps and pillars of rock, and is there still, as if the invaders left behind a topography of demons.

Occasionally the *routiers* reached places less than ten miles from the town. By October 1369 they were at Marcillac, a place of vineyards scattered with pear and plum trees, where many of the richer folk of Rodez had their country houses. Marcillac produced a brackish dark wine that is still drunk now, as it was then, to wash down stodgy sweet bread and stews of bacon and cabbage. On the steep terraces stone houses were built to hold almost nothing but a wall cupboard, a winepress, treading vats and jars; they might be used for one week a year to press the juice from the grapes. That week in October, as the thrushes arrived with the first gusts of cold and the leaves reddened — all signs that the grapes were ready — Manha and his colleagues sent out a warning to the pickers that the English had arrived, too.

And it was not only the wine harvest that needed protecting. Rodez, with several thousand mouths to feed and poor land all round it, had to be sure it had food in case of siege. So grain was hoarded, and mill-stones were dragged up the hill from the banks of the river to equip little portable mills (which were never used) in the centre of town. The town banned exports of grain, sales of grain to foreigners, and even the practice of taking a bag of grain on a journey as a sort of ready cash in case of emergencies. Any carrying of grain outside town, officials declared, 'causes a shortage and hurts the *res publica*', and there was a fine of ten silver marks for disobeying.

Grain meant mostly rye and oats, for wheat did not grow well round Rodez: white bread was something to remark on. And foreigners, to be blunt, meant outsiders, anyone who came in and left again. The war had contracted this idea of where foreigners began. Almost two centuries before, it had been four leagues away, or about fourteen miles. Two generations before, it had narrowed to two leagues, which was taken as the longest comfortable distance for a daily commute. Now, in 1370, even people from one league away were vaguely resented. They brought things in to sell, true enough; but they also took other goods out, possibly more of them, running down the public provisions.

Supplies came in, along the difficult roads, from tiny settlements such as Valady, Palmas or Moyrazès, fourteen miles or so away. One girl called Guiralda (whose case ended in court) walked from Rodelle, fifteen miles to the north across the empty limestone moors, with nothing to sell in Rodez but a tray of eggs, which was snatched away by a boorish fellow as soon as she arrived. All food deliveries, from the footsore Guiralda to mules weighed down with grain to bellowing herds of cattle driven down from the bare heights of the Aubrac, were menaced by gangsters hiding out in the hills.

Nevertheless, though del Cayro may have grumbled about the price of eggs or the cost of bread, he had reason to be grateful for the war. Indirectly, it had made him rich. In 1351, the Prior of St Martin-des-Champs had arrived from Paris and had ordered 'before dinner' (rather peremptorily, the implication was) that the town should build up its defences. The royal order was general; all towns in the region had to have proper fortified walls. Languedoc still contains dozens of fortified towns, many rising seamlessly from the rocks on which they sit. Whether the walls deterred the English is a moot point; most towns, when it came to the prospect of siege, surrendered quickly for a quiet life. They did deals with the *routiers* to let them in, like rowdy children, in groups of so many at a time; within five years, in 1375, Rodez was cutting its own deals of that sort. The long sieges, by contrast, were usually rural affairs, struggles for control of some near-deserted pinnacle of stones.

But the royal orders had to be obeyed; and they kept del Cayro busy. In his youth, he had shifted stone and laid mortar with the rest; gloves were provided in those days only for masters of the works, 'because the mortar hurt their hands'. Now, closer to middle age, he was engaged on the endless task of keeping the walls standing. The main sections had been built fast, but by 1370 many connecting bits still remained to be finished; indeed, it seemed to officials that the work might never be done. Besides, the local red sandstone was friable and the *amour propre* of the town government considerable; even the finished walls needed constant embellishment, crenellation and repair.

Del Cayro's working days were hectic, even as an overseer. Building stone came from wherever men could get it, and the closer to home the better; many residents on the edges of town lost their gardens and fruit trees to men who suddenly appeared from nowhere, quoting vague permissions and digging furiously for sandstone. Sand came from the banks of the Aveyron, dug out by bare-shinned workers with their tunics bundled round their waists; labourers brought it up the hill by the slow cartload. They were paid 2 sous 6 deniers a day, with women at half-rate, against 4 sous 8 deniers for the masters and stonecutters who chipped the rocks into shape.

Quicklime for the mortar came from a furnace by the river run by a redoubtable widow, Dona Guizas. Into her courtyard came the peasants from the high plateaux, fathers with sons, brothers together, their carts piled high with dry springing bundles of broom that went to feed the furnace. These bundles were often all the crop their poor fields could produce. Once the lime was burned, ox-carts took it slowly up to town, where it was stored in the basement kitchen of the consuls' old meeting house.

Meanwhile, up on the edges of town, stone was set laboriously on stone in the foundation ditches, the mortar spread (it was the quicklime that hurt the builders' hands, rubbing them raw), wooden scaffolding put up for the high work. Sometimes the start of a wall was attended with grand ceremonial, drinks all round and tips for the builders, as the consuls got their robes muddy laying the first stone; sometimes it was all rushed, grim and businesslike, because the English were expected. Once the walls were the right height, carpenters were hired to build walkways and watch chambers over the towers and to put wooden floors inside them. And all the time the work was interrupted by the need to deal with suppliers, bickering and thirsty, sweat soaking their hair (the drinks they had to be given were factored into the wall accounts), and by the consuls, whose chief prerogative was to keep changing their minds.

At least there was no shortage of labour. In the mornings del Cayro would arrive to find the workers waiting: fourteen or fifteen regulars from town and, hanging back slightly, countrymen who had walked for miles, or refugees, with bowls and bundled blankets, driven by the mercenaries. In the evenings he would see the pay handed out, sometimes in coin, sometimes in pieces of bacon, to these still nameless folk, while the paymaster flapped and panicked. ('Paid to Master Guilhem Vigorous, 10 sous, which he gave to the people who worked on the ditch at Bullieyra; which 10 sous are not accounted for, because he got mixed up and didn't know who he had paid them to.')

Such people were a headache to officialdom. If they could not be named, they could not be taxed; they were a burden on the purse, and no use. 'Let's see who all the foreigners are and write their names down,' suggested one treasurer; 'then we'll be able to see who we can throw out.' Some of these 'foreigners', in time of peace, would have bypassed Rodez to find piece-work on warmer farms farther south, making their bed in hedges and hay-barns rather than on the hard street. But in time of war Rodez, on its hill, was safer. So they stayed, finding a corner to creep into or a counter to creep under, from which they would eventually be winkled by the estimator of taxes, who missed nobody: 'But they're worth nothing, because nobody knows who they are.'

Sometimes these refugees were taken in and helped in spite of official disapproval. The fact that so many were listed in the one survey that was taken fifteen years later, in

the 1385 arrears book, suggests that many of the good folk
of Rodez were giving them a roof, if little more. Their pitiful
condition must have touched people's hearts. But outright
foreigners were generally less welcome, especially those who
came from beyond the two-league limit outside town. Rodez
instinctively set its back to these folk, expecting the worst.
Foreigners cheated with their faces (which, being unknown,
could be given false names and histories); with their money,
of dubious worth and weight; with their dialects, which
endowed them with a secret language. And Rodez, it must
be said, was not above cheating back.

In the last years of the fourteenth century, the most exotic
strangers were no longer there. There had been Jews in
Rodez for a while, most of them moneylenders, closeted
with other Jews because they were forbidden to live or eat
with Christians or to teach Christian children. They wore
discs on their chests to distinguish them (though the men,
with their hats and flowing beards, scarcely needed them),
and on the days of Christ's Passion they kept out of sight,
shadows into shadows.

Jews appeared in the court records when a man called
Astruc was attacked by another Jew, Bonhome ('Goodman'),
as he sat robed on his prayer bench to recite the Mystery
'according to the Law'. Bonhome spat out some remark
about unleavened bread, pulled Astruc's beard and upset
the prayer bench; Astruc punched him in the teeth and
struck him in the face with his hat. It was a quarrel in a
tiny, enclosed world: the only witnesses were Jews, too. But
their internal bickering paled beside the fog of hatred in
which they lived, blamed for crop failures and pestilence
as well as usurious practice. By 1370 all had long been
driven out of town, and out of most of Languedoc, unless
they had converted. The very old of Rodez remembered
them, dimly, with their separate cemetery and their separate
ways.

The strangeness of the Jews was not exceptional. Foreigners never shed their foreignness, even if they lived in town. They would still be 'lo Lemozi' (from the Limousin), 'the baker from Espalion', 'the tailor from Olemps'. After a while, most 'foreign people', such as Peyrinet lo Frances, who mended the public clocks, were given the courtesy of a Christian name. All were known by their origins, which seemed blazoned on them. Richard Ardit ('L'Engles'), the town's only true Englishman, was beaten within an inch of his life in 1355; ironically, he was on watch duty against those other English. Within a few years, he moved away. In 1356, 'Germans' turned up to work on the walls; and were as soon gone again, vanishing over the moors, back to wherever they had really come from.

Thus far, there was nothing to distinguish Huc del Cayro from hundreds of town masons all over France. And yet, in one respect, his life was quite different. Other towns were building up their external walls; the enemy was outside. In Rodez, del Cayro and his colleagues were also building and repairing walls that ran through the middle of town, severing one half from the other. This may have been a settlement of 5,000 people on the top of a precipitous hill, beaten by winds, but it was also a partitioned town. It was divided into the City, ruled by the bishop, and the Bourg, ruled by the count: two communities shackled like Siamese twins, back-to-back. The City was the half in which del Cayro lived; the Bourg was the half from which Manha and Segui had toiled up the hill to find him.

Between Bourg and City ran ditches and the remains of thirteenth-century walls on which a new wall had now been erected, complete with lockable gates. In effect, this made two towns. Each had two main focus points, a larger-than-usual square and a larger-than-usual church, and round

these points, hugger-mugger, each led a more or less dis-
crete life. As we shall see, the border had porous qualities;
people, jobs, trade and ideas moved across it. Del Cayro
himself, in 1385, decided to move across too, since so much
of his work was coming from the Bourg. It was foolish not
to. Yet, as we know from more modern examples, a wall is
still a wall. It creates antagonism, bluster and ignorance:
especially when that wall, as in Rodez, was kept in careful
and voluntary repair by the consuls of both sides, and not
simply imposed by some arbitrary power from far away. At
one time, the two lords had insisted on it. By 1370, they
cared occasionally. The wall and ditches were mostly kept
in repair because they were a useful device by which to
calculate who owed what taxes to which side.

None the less, the lines of division meant that, quite
naturally, the two halves of Rodez looked away from each
other. In each half-town the instinctive groupings were little
cells of activity looking inwards on a courtyard, a square or
a big house, not necessarily connected by a street. Lavatories
drained down common walls, leaving a pale pungent slime;
buckets were slopped in other people's gardens; houses were
higgledy-piggledy with other people's sheds and yards and
staircases. On occasion, neighbours had to climb through
windows in order to visit each other.

Within each little cell, places and buildings might have
nicknames that only locals knew. This increased the sense
of self-absorption and probably, in the end, the sense of
partition. In the Bourg's main square there was a place
called La Cadena, 'The Chain'. Teenagers hung out here,
and it was here that a party of boisterous young men were
accosted by women (as they insisted) on their way home
from dinner. One witness in an inquiry twenty years earlier
remembered an accident at La Cadena: a child had lost his
foot when a jousting fence fell on him. No witness ever

bothered to say what La Cadena was — it was probably a drinking house — but it did not matter; the people who lived there knew. This minute sense of topography was seldom extended to the other half of town.

Other towns were divided into City and Bourg, but this usually marked a distinction between the more spiritual and more commercial districts of a single place. In Rodez, the City was undoubtedly uphill and spiritual (it contained the cathedral and, as del Cayro was now reminded, almost all the masons, that most elevated calling); the Bourg was downhill and commercial. But the two sides also had different governments, different lords, different laws, different weights and measures, different taxes, and a vigorously competitive attitude to everything under the sun. This arrangement was both rare in Languedoc and, at times, peculiarly awkward.

Back-to-back as they were, the two halves even fought the war in opposite ways. After the Treaty of Brétigny in 1360, which suspended hostilities in England's favour, the City (which was technically a free place, not owing homage to anyone) paid homage to the English Crown in the person of the Black Prince. The Bourg (which was technically part of the County of Armagnac, a fief of the Kingdom of France) refused to. Both were ordered to do so; both wavered for two or three years over the right course of action; but the Bourg, in the end, was clearer in its vassalage and braver in its defiance. Its lord, Jean I of Armagnac, had paid homage in person to the English prince, but this never held him back; he was one of the prince's most powerful local enemies, and his own vassals knew exactly where they stood.

So the City complied, and the Bourg did not. The City in 1365 made sure the English arms were up on all the gates, 'the consuls being afraid to incur the displeasure of our lord the prince'. And, meekly, it paid its English taxes. When the first request came in 1364 from the English regional seneschal, Thomas de Wetenhale, the City promptly forked out its 69 gold *guianes*; the receipt came back swiftly from the Black Prince's treasurer at Villefranche, with the standard remark 'and we are well pleased with it'. Johan Manha, as a City consul, went twice to Villefranche to pay in 1365, and the treasurer was equally pleased with him.

The Bourg, on the other hand, refused every English demand, whether for homage or for taxes. Sometimes, when its courage failed, it would hide behind its lord. In 1364, five days after Christmas, two Bourg consuls trailed Johan *cadet* d'Armagnac, who was riding into Gascony, as far as Villefranche 'to remind him to recommend this county to the prince's seneschal, please, and ask him to shut up about the hearth tax'. But sometimes, boldly, the Bourg stepped out on its own. The record of that same hearth tax began, after the invocation 'Ave Maria', with the words 'the consuls went on the defensive'. On their first visit to the Bourg, a week before the feast of St Andrew at the end of November (which was usually fair week), the Black Prince's tax commissioners were refused entry on the advice of the count's council. The consuls were summoned to Villefranche for default of payment; they sent delegates who managed to postpone the tax, if only for fifteen days.

This was the pattern for the rest of the English occupation. The City continued to pay its English imposts, even contributing a specially reduced sum to the hearth tax of January 1368 which re-opened the war between England and France. The Bourg consuls, on the other hand, kept up a courteous and desperate refusal, sending de Wetenhale wine and green ginger 'because otherwise they could never escape his aggravation because he summons them and molests them all the time, and besides he wants to force all the inhabitants of the Bourg to go to Villefranche . . . he scolds them and menaces them all the time because they won't agree to the hearth tax and he says that he'll make them go there and back every day'.

This sounds principled and patriotic, and there was clearly some element of bravery in it. But hyperbole too crept into the accounts, both in the threats and in the defiance; and besides, the Bourg mostly resisted English demands because it hated taxes. It resisted French taxation equally. Throughout the negotiations of the 1360s the Bourg paid a fitting deference to 'Moss. lo Prince', including a gift of 20 florins to messengers in 1366 who announced the birth of his son, the future Richard II. In 1368 the Bourg consuls wrote to deputy seneschal David Cradoc (or 'noble e poyssan senhor Moss. Davit Tredoc', as they addressed him) explaining why they could not pay taxes, 'excusing themselves with all possible reverence, humility and goodwill, because the Bourg and its people are and always have been free from paying hearth taxes'. It was a dislike not so much of obedience, as of coughing up. None the less, the City was still the place where 'because we are simple men' the Black Prince's arms went up on the gates, and the Bourg was not.

At the time del Cayro was called away from his work by the overburdened Manha, the City of Rodez had just turned French again. In 1369 a letter had come from the Duke of Anjou, Charles V's lieutenant in Languedoc, demanding that the town should break with the English and recognise the King of France as sovereign. The City consuls dithered for a while, merely sending the letter on to Millau, the next town of size. Then on February 27th two wooden shields painted with the fleur-de-lys, the arms of France, went up where men could not avoid seeing them: on the City meeting house — Manha's second home — and on the shed that housed the public weights.

The shields went up, according to the account books, *am nostra voluntat*, 'because we want them to'; and the City was, in fact, the first town in the kingdom officially to throw off the English yoke. Rodez was, and indeed still is, pretty proud of that. But at the time there was not much enthusiasm in it. When Manha and Natas went on their subsequent trek to Paris to get the town's privileges confirmed (Manha going for the City and Natas for the Bourg), and brought back letters sealed with green wax and their accompanying copies sealed with white wax, their efforts were taken to mean that Rodez was 'excused from all royal things' for the next ten years. And when it came to active authority, neither Manha nor Natas nor del Cayro would have wanted the King of France to exercise it anywhere too close to them, unless their own local lord became impossible to deal with.

Sovereignty was, in any case, a fairly vague matter. When they were asked about kingship, del Cayro possibly, and Manha probably, would have paid the usual lip service to the king *nostre senhor*, as was expected; but it might not mean much. In 1352, eighteen years before, there had been an inquiry about the extent of royal power in the town — surveillance of duels, cognisance of forgery, declarations of war. The townsmen had to explain themselves because they had allowed a duel to be held illegally, despite letters from the king's seneschal ordering them not to, between two town sergeants, one of whom was said to have schemed to sell Rodez to the English for 200 gold ecus. They answered the questions with an air of innocent surprise. 'I've never seen any other lords in Rodez except the count and the bishop.' 'I've heard that the seneschal sent letters mentioning a duel, but I don't know what sort of letters or what was in them. In any case, the count and bishop have all jurisdiction here.' 'I never heard the king's seneschal forbidding anything.' 'When the king's people come here, they can't do a thing.'

Power therefore belonged to the lords close at hand, count or bishop; it meant something only if men could see that power displayed or exercised. The word *sobeyra* itself (from which 'sovereign' came) was used to mean simply 'he who is in control', as when Peyre Redon admitted that since he was on foot and Guilhem Camboulas was on horseback (*desobre me*), he could not 'give him what for with his sword.' And there was often not much more philosophy in it than that.

Pragmatists like these were disinclined to attribute lordship to a king they seldom, if ever, saw, and even signs of him were scarce. Manha's trip to Paris had been highly unusual; for all practical purposes the consuls corresponded with the king's lieutenant in Languedoc, his brother the Duke of Anjou, who was fighting the war for him. His regional officers, the seneschal and the judge of Rouergue, visited occasionally to discuss loans, lodging in hastily cleaned rooms and eating off borrowed pewter; they were always sent presents of wine, soft cheese and spices at Christmas, but mostly because form required it. These men also supervised the king's *gabelle*, the tax of one-thirteenth or one-fourteenth on most goods sold wholesale (especially wine and salt) that was imposed by Anjou throughout Languedoc; and this, passed on in the price of a quick jar of red or a slice of bacon, may be as close as royal power came to the del Cayros of this world.

Lesser royal officers actually lived in Rodez, usually posted there as a formal garrison of sergeants to enforce payment of taxes. They met with rather limited success. Those we know of seemed solitary characters, ostracised from normal life. When they tried to push into town politics they were often rebuffed again. One of them, around 1350, had made sterling efforts to stop the illegal duel between the sergeants, delivering the seneschal's letters and reading the prohibitions out aloud in public as instructed; but, having failed, the king's representative was next seen hanging over the duelling fence, urging the contenders on as loudly as the next man.

Royal bureaucracy, moreover, did its bit to force the communities even further apart. For purposes of war organisation and taxes, Rouergue (of which Rodez was then, and is now, the capital) was divided into three Estates; the Bassa Marcha, the Alta Marcha and the County of Rodez. The Bourg, naturally, was in the county, which extended to the north-east of town. The City was at the edge of the Alta Marcha, which centred around Millau, 40 miles south-east. Both City and Bourg took something of an organising rôle in their official areas, but this forced them into strange ways: not only to look in different directions, but to consider any number of distant towns more intimately tied to them, and more friendly, than the community they happened to adjoin. Hence the sour mutter from the Bourg in 1378: 'We want to pay according to our capacity, like the City and other royal places do.' A few yards away, on the other side of the ditch-and-wall, the Bourg felt isolated and left out.

The only war ventures that were organised jointly were the sending of spies (safety in numbers); the building of one border barbican, the *Tor Grossa*, which could hardly be done otherwise; and occasionally — to give each other moral support — resistance to tax. As on the trip to Paris, two people always went; a joint representative was unheard of. Bourg and City also kept a joint watch outside the walls at moments of extreme danger; but the guards were paid separately, and the site of the watches was always at either end of the dividing ditch. Each watchman still stood on his own turf because he did not quite know — or trust — the man at his own shoulder.

The lack of trust was justified; for, when it came down to it, the two sides did not even see the enemy in the same light. By the 1360s, the Bourg was already trafficking with the English wholesale. When the City chucked out its visiting *routiers* in 1375, the Bourg hesitated; these gangsters (who were being put up in Bourg hotels and even recruited for watch duty) had their uses. And in later years the division of opinion continued. In the City residents were fined for making sales to the English, as also for failing to inflict on them, day and night, 'all the war and damage you can'. The same reminder was read out publicly in the Bourg, but *burgenses* were let off the fines. In fact, the Bourg consuls had already decreed *am trompa*, with sharp blasts of the trumpet, 'that anyone should sell and can sell anything at all from this time on to Ramonet de Sortz [a notorious brigand] and his companions'. The count had given them permission, and money for the licence was busily being raised by 'three good men of the Bourg who, up till now, have had nothing whatever to do with the English'.

The Bourg, essentially the commercial half of town, kept its eye on the main chance. It knew that the *routiers* needed food, drink, comfortable beds, equipment, horses and grain, and could usually pay for them either with the curious assortment of loose change they carried in their saddlebags (Merigot Marches's 'fresh money every day'), or with stolen cattle, or with promises of good behaviour. The City, with individual exceptions, tried to keep to the rules. When the *routiers* began to camp not far from town, squatting round watch fires that glowed orange in the woods, the Bourg sent emissaries promptly to make sure the campers launched no attacks on its food supplies. The City, which did not think of negotiating until much later, suffered alone until, slowly, it worked out why. Thus the two halves of Rodez, like separate boats swept along on a river, constantly tried to keep to independent courses, when every current of warfare should have driven them together.

The men of Rodez understood this was not normal. The more lettered ones acknowledged that in Carcassonne or Toulouse there was only one town and only one lord. Del Cayro himself knew that, in the ideal town, amenities were there to be shared rather than fought over. But the thought was somewhat abstract. He was asked in court what the *res publica* was (a concept that was presumably put into Occitan for him), and answered, cautiously: 'I'm not absolutely sure, but I think the Res Publica is something that's of use to all the people who live in one place.'

Rodez did not correspond to that picture; but then, for del Cayro, the City was one *polis* and the Bourg was another. To all the other outsiders in his life — the peasants with their broom-loads, the refugees clamouring for work, that odd man from another town in a shop down the street, the ravaging unseen English — were added folk who lived and worked a hundred yards away.

This was the background against which our characters lived and against which our story is told. It was full of stresses, obstacles and opportunities which were unusual in medieval France; but to some of us, at the end of the twentieth century, they are not as unfamiliar as all that.

When del Cayro, that day, saw Manha and Segui running his way, he may have felt flattered. Bourg and City hardly ever acted in concert like this; some extraordinary emergency was clearly afoot. And as it happened, both men were desperate; they were making for the only person who seemed able to help. The foundations of the Segui cloth shop in the Bourg, which was managed by Deodat's widowed mother, were flooded. Mother and son had found the trouble, a blocked drain under the floor, and were trying to clean it out; but the blockage was under the shop of their neighbour, Peyre Marques. Could del Cayro please come with his tools and take a look?

Del Cayro left what he was doing, crossed through the border gate, and went down the hill into the Bourg. A crowd of people had gathered by the Segui shop; he pushed through them. The shop was a basement, down a few steps, dimly lit through two barred windows at street level. At the back was a workroom where men and women usually laboured over their benches by candlelight, bending close to check on a straight cut or a line of stitching. These niches were empty now, the workers out milling in the street. In front, at the bottom of the steps, were two tables usually set with bolts of cloth, but now cleared and moved aside. The floor was damp, even wet, with puddles of greasy water backed up from the drain.

Del Cayro stepped in, still feeling the press of the onlookers at his back. As it happened, he had been to this shop before. In fact, with his colleague, Stefe Cayrosa, he had helped build it; that, presumably, was why he had been called back. But neither he nor Cayrosa had had a hand in building the drain or had even looked at it before. This was something new. He inspected it now, crouching in the semi-dark, prodding at accretions of mud and stones with the tools he had brought with him.

His expert eye noticed a pipe laid in stone sections that carried water to the main Bourg drain. He had never, he said, seen a pipe quite like that anywhere else. The main drain, he knew 'by report', ran north-south, from the higher part of the Bourg down past the Marques shop, though he did not know where it went after that; most of the Bourg was still foreign to him. The pipe in the shop ran east-west, 'and there was, I think, a lavatory over it'. In short, the place stank. He spent a while slopping about in the water with a lighted candle; Cayrosa, who was now a City building inspector, waded in too with his advice. When del Cayro emerged, it was with a grim message: 'Well, I can't open that up or do a thing there until Peyre Marques gives me permission.'

The scene that followed was baffling. Marques came out, with his wife and grown-up children, to face his disgruntled neighbours. They were crowding round and shouting by now, Manha and Segui at the forefront, trying to get something done. But Marques, an elderly man and somewhat hard of hearing, could not decide. He stood by the blocked drain, confused, with the slightly querulous look of a deaf man bludgeoned by noise. Beside him were his wife and his son-in-law, arguing with the practised impatience of people who pushed him habitually. Around him were the exasperated, the great and the good.

Del Cayro noticed that the family seemed rich enough, for they wore good clothes and decent shoes. He did not know them, but he understood that Peyre's father had been wealthy and assumed that the wealth had been passed on. He also observed how hesitant Marques was, even allowing for his evident deafness. He needed guiding and prodding: in the end, it was not only Marques who made the decision, but his wife and his son-in-law as well. Del Cayro's observation that the other two took charge was to have its importance later.

At last Marques spoke: yes, he would let them open up the drain. At this point, del Cayro passed the buck. He told Segui that he would need to get a different builder in to do the job. He had done his bit; he had located the problem; but he already had work to do, a prestige job on the other side of town. These Bourg people, he implied, would have to sort themselves out.

It was a decision which, in time, he may have come to regret.

2

Johan Gasc
and the pride of partition

THE BUILDERS were hired. Three turned up: Johan Gasc from the City, Marti Barbier from the Bourg, and Marot de Namaria, from out in the country somewhere. Gasc would not have come cheap. He was an accomplished mason, with 'master' before his name (unlike del Cayro) to indicate that he had paid his entry fee into the craft of builders. He owned more than one house in Sant Stefe, the richest part of the City; and in court later he acquitted himself rather better than del Cayro on the *res publica* question, as if he was a deeper or more careful thinker.

I know that churches, squares, fairgrounds, drinking fountains and streets are *res publicae*, and are called that because whoever wants to can go and pray in churches, whether they're strangers or not — as long as the churches are open, that is — and they can draw and drink water from fountains, and stand and walk about in squares and streets and fairgrounds, and it's a perfectly free activity for whoever wants to do it.

His colleagues did less well. Barbier had no idea what the lawyer was talking about. Marot, who seems to have been something of a wiseacre, burst out: 'Oh yes, I know: churches, streets, squares, fairgrounds and roads. Otherwise, I've no idea.' Marot did not stay long; in the manner of cowboy workers everywhere, he soon got a better job out towards Missas farm, near Valady, on business for the cathedral chapter. For the moment, however, the three men set to.

They spent a sweaty afternoon under Marques's shop floor in the Plassa de l'Olmet, Little Elm Tree Square, off the main square of the Bourg. Hectic commerce was going on all round them. Stalls and traders covered almost every inch of ground: butchers, cloth-sellers, cheesemongers, pastry-cooks. Flies buzzed on the dripping quarters of meat, on the hard round rye-loaves stacked in tiers, on the glistening scales of river-fish laid on reed mats. Jugglers and dice-players squatted under the small, battered elm tree that shaded the centre of the square. The clamour was tremendous. Women wandered about: some with trays of vegetables from those steep little plots on the hillside, others, showing an ankle or a shoulder, with better kinds of fruit to sell. Marot and Barbier, perhaps half-naked as they worked, might have shouted some encouragement. But Gasc was middle-aged, with a reputation to sustain; and besides, as a City man, he knew that the low-life on show in the Bourg square was one of the main reasons why the City was nobler, and why he was lucky to live there.

This business of nobility was endlessly debated and keenly felt. The City too had squares; but as the bishop's lawyers had argued in court years earlier, in the 1320s, the City's open spaces were bigger and better than the Bourg's, and were crowded only with desirable people. The City had grand approaches and entrances, proper bridges, broad roads: coming from another town, you automatically entered Rodez by its best and most open side. The Bourg, by contrast, was squashed, crooked and swarming; once in, you were lucky to crawl out. The City had silversmiths, painters, gilders, scabbard-makers; the Bourg had leather-workers and cheesemongers. The Bourg had butchers; the City also had *triparias*, doing up the local speciality, bleached stinking honeycombs of cows' stomachs, for the visiting trade. The Bourg had bakers; the City had *pasticieras* or *fogassieyras*, specialists in sweet luxury wheaten stuff sprinkled with sugar and angelica.

'Better people come to the City, don't they?' the bishop's lawyers had asked, all those years ago. 'They come either for ordination, or for jobs in the court, or to attend the fairs, or to take up canonries, or to attend the councils that the lawyers hold there, or to study.' The witnesses, citizens themselves, wondered about that. Nobody had heard of the lawyers' symposiums. As for the school, back then it had taken in about sixty or seventy boys a year, some from quite far away, and kitted them out in robes with hoods, like small monks, and taught them singing and grammar; but by 1370 the schoolmaster needed help with his rent, because there were so few pupils. In short, the crowd in the City, though dotted more with priests and lawyers and the odd grubby schoolboy, was not evidently different from the one across the border.

Yet there was, everyone agreed, a pervasive difference of atmosphere and culture. In the end, the greater nobility of the City seemed indeed to boil down to its architecture, its churches and squares, in a way that masons like Gasc or del Cayro could appreciate. The City was nobler, one episcopal witness argued, because it had the cathedral and the canons (like himself), but also simply because there was more space. 'The Bourg has more people, though,' he admitted. Another said that bourgs were always less important than cities, 'at least when they're owned by the same lord, but not necessarily otherwise'. Yet another made the old, uncontestable observation that the City was built on much higher ground. No-one could miss the connotations of 'much higher'.

The Bourg, according to a royal ordinance of 1335, also had wide local fame as a place where both consuls and people sold things for more than they were worth and changed money at too high a rate. But the most damaging remark, made by City witnesses again and again, had to do with the main Bourg square, just yards away from where Gasc was working. This 'used to be a cemetery, and is consecrated ground, and everybody knows it'. All the usual activities of trading, therefore, the dealing and undercutting and dismembering and evisceration, the haggling and swearing, took place on ground that was meant to be holy. It was not unusual, in those days, for graveyards to be gathering places or even places of trade; but once the City had got hold of this argument, it would never let go.

The status of the square was not much in doubt. It was close to the main Bourg church of St Amans, though not directly beside it; and it was also close to the Peace Hospital, the largest in town, which had no graveyard of its own. In plague years, the Peace Hospital had a duty to take in all paupers who dropped dead in the street, wrap them in shrouds and bury them. (The idea of contagion was not well understood; plague was assumed to drift in the air, rather than to spread from its victims; and there was an obligation of pity and decency in death, even to people who, like the plague bacillus itself, were drifters and strangers in the town.)

When witnesses had been called to discuss the Bourg square in 1350, several of them had seen men from the hospital being buried there. The chaplain of St Amans officiated, in his stole, with brief prayers; indeed the whole affair seems to have been hasty, the grave left unmarked, as if it was a token rite rather than a serious one. But the rite was still performed. There were also signs of older burials. When people dug down a little way, as Gasc was digging, bones turned up, and stone tomb-covers could be spotted here and there: in front of the butchers' quarter with its standing pools of blood, by the corn-stone with its great wooden balance where grain was bought and sold, and by the count's minting house.

All around these tombs, and over them, unhallowed things went on. Johan Sedassier, a Bourg merchant of about fifty, had seen men playing a game called 'At the Races' and a version of *boule*, for money. Johan Monmato, who was about the same age, reported bawds and prostitutes and dishonest people playing at dice 'and blaspheming against God and the saints and Blessed Mary, saying "I'll deny God!" and things like that'. He had also, he confessed, seen honest men and women going about their business, especially in the mornings, but he had noticed more prostitutes there than in other places. Women also came to sell bread and cabbages and leeks from their gardens, and he could not tell whether they were honest or not.

Both men had also heard of murders in the square. So many butchers and traders needed to use knives longer than one palm (about eight inches) that the Bourg had given up trying to regulate them, though bartenders were supposed to ask their customers to put them down. (One favoured weapon, a bit flash, illegally long and with a squared-off blade, was called a *misericordia*, since mercy was what you gasped for when it was laid against your throat.) As Monmato remembered, someone called Galabru had killed someone called Boyo in the corner of the square by the Peace Hospital, and Monmato had pressed into the square afterwards among the crowd, but had seen no blood. Sedassier, caught up in the same crowd, saw blood all right: 'lots of it, and Boyo dead'. Both he and Monmato had also heard of knifings, some of which Monmato had missed because he had been busy in his workshop on the downhill side of the square. One he witnessed from a long way off, saw the flash of the sword-blade, heard the scream and presumed the blood: but, prudently, 'I didn't go near them'.

Here then was the central square of the Bourg — the very heart of the *polis*, the grand civic ideal of open public space — and when burgenses gathered there, this was all they seemed good for. As it happened, other witnesses produced sightings — and some, more boldly, recalled incidents they had been a part of — that capped even Monmato's. One had discovered a man on top of a woman as he was crossing the square one night, going through the butchers' quarter. 'I don't know who they were', he said, 'but I think they were committing adultery.'

Peyre Massabuou, too, remembered being part of a merry drinking party, with Guilhem Gaffuer and Johan Ebrart the apothecary, who bantered with a girl called Guilberta and her friend at La Cadena, in the square, after supper on the Thursday after Christmas. It cannot have been loitering weather, up in those cold hills, and Peyre's opening gambit was direct: 'Shall we do it with you or will you do it with us?' 'You can't, we're cousins,' Guilberta told him. Peyre then seized her and, according to Gaffuer, 'hugged' her on top of one of the work benches, 'but I didn't see whether he did anything else to her'. Guilberta certainly thought he had.

So much for warm, live bodies; but the square was also a cemetery, after all. Citizen Gasc, being from the other side of town, might not have heard the stories; but Marti Barbier, shovelling beside him, would certainly have been aware of the bodies and bones people found when they were digging. It happened all the time: when Peyre Duran extended his shop, and when Ramon Pages had built cellars under his house. They had turned up the bones openly, publicly, and without fuss. Peyre Robbert had dug up human remains, and the site had been made into a public tavern, and it seemed to be all above board; no-one knew what had happened to the bones. Some people thought they had been given a Christian burial, others that they had been thrown away. In the Bourg, such sacrilege seemed all too possible.

In the City, on the other hand, where bones of 'good people' had been disinterred in 1358 as the foundations were dug for the new walls, matters were handled differently. Possibly Gasc or del Cayro had been there as the tell-tale bones turned up: the foot-long shin-bones and coin-sized knuckle-bones, the grinning skulls. Earth, and the whiff of death, lay in the sockets of the eyes; abashed, the workmen laid down their spades. A Mass of the Dead was said for the remains, and they were decently wrapped in linen and taken into the church, the best place, to be buried. The consuls even paid the fee for the priest. But that was in Gasc's half, the better half, of town.

The Bourg bones were more contentious, because nobody was sure whose they were. Possibly they belonged to good Christian men; but possibly, too, they were Saracen. The Saracens had reached Rodez, and destroyed its first cathedral, in 725. They had soon left, chilled and demoralised so far out of the sun; but to townsmen in the fourteenth century their sojourn was much more vivid than that of the Romans, who had stayed longer.

Some said the town had been founded by Saracens, or had belonged to them, ages ago. It was not simply bones that turned up when you dug down, but pieces of tile and broken-down sections of wall. Johan Sedassier had a Saracen wall in the cellar of his house, and Huc Serras (so Sedassier said) had a yard of Saracen wall in his; Ramon Maurel had dug up slivers of glazed tile from a 'pavement' in his garden which, when turned over and held in the hand, had looked to be Saracen all right. The cathedral chapter rented out a garden at a place it called the Saracen Wall, just below the windmill; so even the canons gave credence to the story.

For his part, Sedassier thought Saracens were buried all over the town. There were also rocks and caves and defiles that were called 'Saracen', sometimes the same as those, usually lowering or precipitous, that were being given the name of 'English' in the year when our story is set. New demons, old devils; some safely underground, some, as we have seen, haunting the woods and erupting on to the roads.

As Gasc and Barbier laboured on, however, they found neither bones nor Saracen pots, nor anything worth mentioning. At sunset they were ready to go; the border gates between Bourg and City were about to be locked for the night, and Gasc had to get home. Barbier was watching Gasc straddling the drain, still digging, when the shovel hit something hard. It was, Gasc remembered, 'a pewter wine-jug, about a quart capacity, without a lid, stopped up with a stone. It fell over and gold coins came out . . . it was almost full of gold.' In the murk of the shop, in the twilight, the coins shone. Perhaps Gasc and Barbier would always have been honest; or perhaps it was their bad luck that Gerald Canac, Marques's son-in-law, came down the steps with his wife at just this crucial moment. Gasc told him what they had found; Canac immediately, imperiously, told them not to mention the jug and took charge of it.

At another time, that might have seemed odd to Gasc. But he did not have time to contest it. The light was fading; the border gates were closing. He needed to pack up his tools and go.

He climbed up the hill to the City. It was not steep, but he must have been weary, and damp with sweat. His limbs ached; his tools were heavy. It was hard to forget the scene in the basement of Marques's shop: how the spade had jarred in his hand, how the heavy jug had fallen on its side, how the bright coins had spilled out. Gold coins were rare in Rodez. The town's usual money was the count's home-made variety, minted of the poorest silver on premises just off the Bourg square. If you were given a piece of gold, you bit it or weighed it to make sure it was true; you did not trust it on its face. Even rich men handed such coins to their servants to do their assaying for them.

Gasc could have put a coin or two in his pocket, but he had not done so. On the other hand, there had been no reason so readily to give the jug to Canac. He was not his servant, or not directly. He was not even under contract to him; in fact, it was Deodat Segui and his mother who had employed him. Besides, it was not Canac's shop, though he seemed to boss his father-in-law about and was full of self-importance. If it was not his shop, the chances were that it was not his money. Either way, it seemed a poor reward for honesty to be sent home empty-handed.

The Bourg gate at Pas was still open. *Pas* meant peace, but the gate had been given this harmonious name only because the Peace Hospital (properly speaking, the Hospital of the Poor of Our Lady of Peace) stood beside it. Gasc had to pass through the Gate of Peace, cross a neutral space, and possibly go through another gate on the City side, in order to get home. There was no sentry, but at nightfall the man who lived next door would come and shut the gate, lock it, and put a metal bar across. Sometimes the gate would look closed, but would actually be jammed part-open and part-shut with rubbish and mud; for the authorities organised cleaning only intermittently, when they felt like it, when matters got out of hand, or when the lord was about to visit. If the gate was stuck shut, you could sometimes squeeze through it. If it was locked shut, the only hope was to appeal to the gatekeeper. Occasionally every ploy failed, and you were trapped.

It had happened most famously to Peyre Jalenca and
Berengar Seyrac two decades earlier, in 1347. That was a
plague year in Europe and a plague year in Rodez, though
the infection was not nearly so bad as the one that was to
strike in 1375, carrying off three consuls in office and leaving in the tax books a devastating litany of deleted names:
mort es, mort es, mort es. Still, the 1347 outbreak was the worst
that had been known so far; gravediggers were on a bonus,
and were told to dig the graves deep for fear of corruption.
Jalenca and Seyrac, both with sick children, had been trying
to do Gasc's journey in reverse: come out of the City by the
Sant Stefe Gate, cross the neutral space, and go back
through the Gate of Peace into the Bourg. But everything
went wrong. Seyrac told the story.

I was in the City on the Feast of the Nativity of St
John the Baptist [June 24th] this year, quite late, after
vespers. I was in Berengar de Segur's house — he's a
doctor of law — and Peyre Jalenca and Huc Domergue
of the Bourg came in . . .

It was daylight, even if late; a deceptive time of year. Business
was going on as usual; as it happened, Jalenca was trying to
sort out a loan for his daughter's dowry, a transaction that
had been going on for months. There was a little bantering
about the money, and then

It was getting very late, so Peyre (with the money)
and myself and Huc Domergue, together with Master
Bernard Bandeli, Peyre Regandi, his brother Bernard,
Fontanier de Mauro, and one of Berengar's servants to
carry the light for us, left Berengar's house to go home
to bed. [After the curfew had sounded, the light was
obligatory.] Jalenca, Domergue and myself were
especially eager to get home because we lived in the

Bourg, and I wanted to hurry because I had a son sick at home and I was afraid he would die. So we went along with our two wax torches to the City gate at Sant Stefe, just by Johan Gabriac's workshop and Guilhem Fabre's house. We thought the gate would be open, but when we got there it was shut, bolted and locked. We started shouting for either Gabriac or Peyre Ginesta, who lives in that street and has a set of keys apparently, and one of them woke up and came to the window in his shirt.

This was Gabriac. The Gabriacs, Johan and Ramon, were big property-owners in Sant Stefe, with several houses and an orchard. Gasc, had he been there, would have known the fellow in the nightshirt as a neighbour; but Seyrac and Jalenca, coming from the Bourg, did not recognise him. A flickering oil lamp, on a bracket above the gate, lit up the apparition. He told them that the gate was not locked, only bolted, and that they could open it.

Here the accounts of the City prosecutors and the defendants began to diverge a bit. Seyrac said someone, he did not know who, picked up a stone and chipped at the bolt to shift it, for it was new and stiff; Jalenca and Domergue said it was Seyrac, and that he had to hammer quite hard; the prosecutors claimed that the whole party broke the gate open with stones and swords and sticks.

However it happened, they got through and crossed the Plassa Sant Stefe to the Gate of Peace beside the hospital. The hospital was full then with the plague's most pitiful victims; payment had already been entered in the Bourg accounts 'for picking up the poor men lying in the streets and taking them to the hospital'; but no sense of horror kept the party away. 'We thought we could get into the Bourg from there', said Seyrac, 'but the gate was shut . . . so we went back to the gate at Sant Stefe . . .'

The Gate of Peace was probably not locked, just jammed up; but the party retraced its steps. At the Sant Stefe Gate Gabriac was still blearily waiting, perhaps feeling qualms of conscience for having let them through and for not having locked up in the first place, as he was meant to.

> We found the man who'd told us the gate wasn't locked, the one we'd made get up, and we told him to stay by the gate while we went back into the City and tried all the other gates and barbicans to see if any were open, because we wanted to get out and go home.

To get out this way meant going through the old perimeter wall of the town itself (it was three years before the order came to build new walls) and round in a great circle, from the north to the south, through all those slippery cluttered little allotments on the side of the hill, in hope of finding an open gate on the Bourg side. The party seemed prepared to chance it.

> Eventually we came to the houses of Peyre Veziac and Gui de Pessolis, who are citizens and apparently have keys to the other gates. We shouted and banged on the doors and asked whether they had the keys, and one of them said he wasn't going to open up and we couldn't get out. So myself and the others, with our torches, went to one of the City gates called Le Perthus.

They were now at the northern edge of the town. The ground was beginning to fall away steeply to the river. A scent of hayfields filled the night air and, creaking slightly, the City windmill with its great drooping sails loomed like a ship in the darkness. Sections of broken wall lay ahead of them: the Saracen Wall, built long before men could remember, the same that cropped up in Berengar's brother's cellar. The prosecutors called this stretch 'a high public wall', but it did not seem that way to the malefactors.

> We hoped the gate might be open. It was shut, but we saw a fence beside it, by the windmill. It wasn't very high . . . we thought it was the enclosure round Peyre Moysset's meadow, not the City wall. Myself and Peyre and Huc and Master Bertrand [sic] and Fontanier climbed over it and got into the meadow and went home from there. We left Master Peyre Regandi and his brother in the City, where they slept.

The wall, according to the City lawyers, was five feet high on the City side, with an eight-foot drop to the meadow: in the dark, the fugitives must have landed hard. No-one hurt himself, but someone — we do not know who — reported them. Unluckily for the trespassers, some sleepless soul in that other, foreign side of town had known who they were; they were neither as invisible nor as anonymous as they might have hoped.

At this point, or perhaps at several points on their long tramp round the border, Seyrac and his colleagues might have remembered St Amans, the town patron, and his cunning way with walls. On one occasion two beggars, guests in the saint's house, had stolen the linen and ornaments from his altar at night. God then 'arranged' that they should wander round the houses of the town walls until daybreak, when, still befuddled and lost in a sort of magical fog, they were picked up for loitering down by the Auterne bridge. On another occasion, a man broke into St Amans's garden at night to steal cabbages; when he tried to get out again he found the garden — enclosed by a little hedge, as he had thought — suddenly surrounded by towering walls.

High walls or not, little hedge or not, the City prosecutor bore down heavily on Seyrac at the hearing. Wasn't he ashamed of what he had done? Hadn't he caused immense damage to the City and the *res publica*? (That phrase again, always a good way to invest inanimate objects with particular power!) There were regulations in force against climbing on the walls, especially at late and suspicious hours, at times of war or danger, and when people were asleep; and the party had done so secretly and violently, bringing down a lot of stones with them. Seyrac remained defiant. 'I didn't do it to set a bad example. I don't think you can blame me. It was a case of necessity. I was frightened for my sick son, and all of us wanted to go home to the Bourg and go to bed.'

Jalenca had an even more heart-wrenching story which, given the year, may perhaps have been true. 'I did it because my wife and son were lying sick unto death in my house in the Bourg and there was no-one in the house that night to look after them. My son died of his sickness. I have no other male child, and that was why I was so desperate to leave the City and go to my son in my house in the Bourg.'

Different members of the party added their own embellishments, but the basic facts remained. Here was a party of people bent on quite ordinary business, not criminally inclined, who ended the evening by breaking the law. No-one seemed more surprised than Huc Domergue, who had meant to spend the comfortable after-supper hours of midsummer sitting out in the street to watch the world go by. He had no reason at all to go into the City, except to take a stroll with a friend. 'It was quite late, after compline,' he told the court. (He said compline, Seyrac said vespers; either someone was lying or, more likely, these laymen did not have much idea which bells meant what.) 'I'd had dinner with my wife and family. Peyre Jalenca came past and hailed me and asked me to go with him to Berengar Seyrac's house and I said Yes, all right. There could be nothing more natural than that.

But this was a partitioned town; there was nothing natural about it. Division made unnatural rules, and one of them was that people could not walk around where they pleased. Almost a century before our story, one of Gerald Canac's forebears was in court giving evidence on that count. He and a group of friends had accosted a City man at twilight in the Bourg and asked him what he was doing there. In fact, the City man was not quite sure what he was doing, or why he had gone into the Bourg at all; but one or two of his City friends, in training for the priesthood, had already slipped off ('God's stomach, I'm going in there!') through the doors of various brothels. So he answered, 'I'm walking down the street like anybody else.' The Bourg men had chased him out, screaming that they would kill him.

These were the horror stories men remembered. Yet here was Gasc, believing — as he said with some eloquence — that the streets and squares of a town were places where a man, even a stranger, could walk freely. This was not always true in Rodez, in practice. But it was still an ideal on paper. As Gasc passed through the Gate of Peace he found himself in the Plassa Sant Stefe, St Stephen's Square, the neutral space between City and Bourg. The ditch-building and wall-building had been going on in Rodez, intermittently, since 1161, when the count and the bishop, who were then brothers, had decided that physical barriers were the only way to clear up their dispute about their inheritance. But the feuding brothers had decided to make an exception of the centre of town. Building in Sant Stefe had been discouraged by a compromise drafted in 1195, and a treaty of 1278 forbade the construction there of any walls, defences or works, civilian or military. It was intended as an open space between Bourg and City, a breathing space which people were free to cross as they liked. In fact, every object in the Plassa Sant Stefe (grandly so-called, since it was more of a wedge-shape hemmed in by houses) was charged with political and partisan feeling.

Gasc crossed it now, in the dusk. The Gate of Peace was at his back. To his right was the hospital, a warren of houses and gardens hidden by a wall, within which were enclosed the murmur of nunnish prayers and the cries of the sick. To his left was the common courthouse, barricaded at night with a lead chain. Both buildings spoke of shared interests and common jurisdiction between the Bourg and the City. The count and the bishop were joint patrons of the hospital, and notaries worked for them jointly in the common courthouse. Shared government had been meant to prevail ever since a serious riot, which we shall come to later, in 1315. At that point, a measure of co-operation, known as a Pariage, had been ordered by a royal commissioner. But royal commissioners, we know, had trouble getting their orders obeyed or their airs taken seriously in Rodez. By 1370 official cross-border co-operation was still fragile, and still mostly a lie.

Gasc could prove that simply by looking about him. The hospital and the courthouse both stood in the old ditch of 1161, which was now full of houses, gardens, trees, rubbish, nettles, and bits of old walls; but the count, as lord of the Bourg, still claimed it aggressively. He also claimed some of the butchers' benches where Gasc went to buy his meat. Indeed, customers might sometimes be standing there, haggling over the mutton and the hens, when City officers would come up with measuring strings, dangling them from the roofs of the stalls or taking them round the back, shouting numbers to each other, to prove that the benches were on their territory and not on that of the count. The stone supporting pillar of one of these stalls, and the little fence beside it, had actually been placed under royal protection to keep the count out; they were hung with wooden fleur-de-lys shields, a rare enough sight in Rodez. But the count was not deterred. Johan Canac (another Canac — they were like weeds) had his pastry stall unceremoniously tipped over in 1380 because it stood in the ditch 'in contempt' of the lord who claimed to own it.

Some people seemed to get away with their contempt. The Ebrarts did. The count wanted to keep the ditch clear; they believed in filling it. Johan Ebrart bought his first garden in the shallower part of the dividing ditch, and a little later bought another farther towards the centre; his brother Ramon had a garden so far into the ditch that it was actually in the City. All were improved in the same way. First a few vegetables were planted, or fruit trees, or even vines, just under the old dividing wall, where people might overlook them and where they were sheltered from the frost; then the ground would need terracing to keep them in; then a little wall would be needed to keep strays out; and then the most permanent fixtures could be installed, as, in the Ebrarts' case, stone troughs to wash the cloth they sold. The ditch was still a slightly disreputable place to be, as the Ebrarts' cloth-washing girl discovered when a man tried to rape her there, and steal the cloths, 'and did other things against her will' among the obscuring walnut trees. It remained a no-man's land, neither City nor Bourg, one place or the other.

Sant Stefe, where Gasc now walked, was the same. Nothing there was unpolitical. The border, even if invisible, made its presence felt. It ran circles round trees, dipped into basements and courtyards, climbed the pillars of the market stalls. Since every object had to declare its loyalty, every object had to have an owner. Even a pit in Gasc's garden was given its own listing in the City tax book in 1364, with the appellation 'Hole, outsider-owned.'

A City drain ran at Gasc's feet. That day, he must have had enough of drains; but this one always gave trouble. The water that ran in it, obedient to geography, flowed downhill towards the Bourg. It was meant to flow neutrally, to neither place. A pear tree hung over the hospital wall. In spring its frail white blossoms fell to the ground, in autumn its yellowing fruit; they dropped in both jurisdictions. A boundary commission was to recommend later that the tree should be 'cut down and entirely got rid of'. It committed no offence as far as ordinary men like Gasc were concerned.

At the centre of Sant Stefe stood a flat circular stone. From this stone the community criers made their announcements, often of identical content, with the City crier shouting north and the Bourg man shouting south, as if the air formed a high and trembling screen between them. The City claimed that the Bourg crier, with his brass trumpet, sometimes dared to stand inside the City to do so; undoubtedly the City crier sometimes trespassed too, with his feet a few inches the wrong side of the centre of the stone. From his house, with the door open, Gasc could probably hear either equally well.

Sant Stefe was considered a fine and exclusive place; Johan Manha lived there too. The two- and three-storey houses were expensive, and their owners paid high taxes. But some had a nightmarish life, at odds with two bureaucracies. Estol Aribert was a case in point. He was a citizen; his house, like that of the Maurels next door, who were Bourg men ('burgenses'), precisely straddled the border. Each year the count claimed a high rent of 7 sous 6 deniers on this property; and, because the basement had once been a smithy, an extra yearly rent of 24 nails and four horseshoes which was sometimes commuted for cash.

Before Aribert moved there, citizens and burgenses had sometimes lived together in the house, and the governments of both sides had taxed them. Aribert's predecessors, the Bonifaci brothers Guilhem and Duran, had met both sets of obligations for a while (though they were a bit lax about the rent); they had even, nobly, done their watch duty for both sides. But after a time inspiration struck, and they began to divide their tax liability, and their loyalties, between them. Guilhem paid the Bourg hearth tax, contributed more to Bourg loans, and in 1345 became a Bourg consul; Duran appeared alone in the City tax list, and his neighbours thought he was a 'real' citizen (*veran cieutada*, as the phrase was). How he gave that impression is difficult to say: there seemed to be some mark, as obvious as red hair or a beard or a limp, that distinguished baker from baker and tax-evader from tax-evader all through the town. But people sometimes gave up with the Bonifacis, so that when they appeared in the bishop's court in 1331 for non-payment of rent they were just 'from Rodez', when everyone else recorded was from one side or the other.

With Aribert in the house, there was no doubt. He was a citizen of renown, as Gasc, his neighbour, would have known: consul several times, top bidder in the year of our story for the farm of the royal wine tax. He and his wife Chiragua lived in fine comfort on the top floor, where it was possible to open the windows without smelling the sweet rot of the butchers' quarter; and the whole of the rest of the house was occupied by citizens, too.

Aribert's neighbours on the ground floor were the Palhol brothers, Huc and Ramon, lawyers, who kept an office here and slept in a room adjoining. Beneath them, in the base-ment, the Peyra family kept a cloth shop spanned with stone pillars, one of which was presumed to mark the border. Yet these citizens still paid a county rent; Ramon Palhol was to buy his part of the house at a Bourg auction held on his own doorstep; and the Ariberts did homage to the count, who was not their lord, for all of it. Aribert also helped raise subsidies for the count, and made him war loans, as if in some respects he was as neutral as the soil of the square itself; as perhaps he was.

Officials from both sides jostled continuously over the divided house. Gasc had no doubt seen the sergeants from both City and Bourg banging on the doors for non-payment of tax, and taking furniture out. It was a constant farce. Huc Palhol, 'bachelor in law', living on the ground floor among his writs and *mandamenta*, at last became so angry that he excommunicated both sets of consuls for failing to pay back the tax they had wrongly taken from him. ('He sentenced us three times', reads the hurt entry in the Bourg accounts, 'and the absolutions cost six sous.') As for the Peyras, each time they crossed the shop floor — carrying their work to the light, searching for the cutting scissors, going for a snack — they also crossed the border, for what it was worth.

The same strange twists occurred next door in the house where the Maurels lived. These were Bourg men (at least that was not in dispute) and merchants (some of the family being in cloth, some in wine, and some butchers), with a house and a market-stall just at the gateway to the common courthouse. Most of this property was in the Bourg and liable to taxes there; but one small piece, the gateway and entrance to the courtyard (recently ornamented with a wooden watch-shed), was listed in the City tax book. This ludicrous little part of a building — *l'intrada*, or sometimes 'the bit that's in the City' — was valued at 25 livres in 1355, when the whole house was valued at 400; but it was never omitted from the City lists. And, equally, Maurel never paid what he owed for it. The City consuls came through his famous gate several times a year, buying wine and spices and sweets for other consuls, or for those finicky French-speaking royal officials, or for the papal collector; what sign was there, as they came and went, that they were crossing a frontier? There was none, so the point was made, at least as far as Maurel was concerned.

These confusions arose because, in the middle of Sant Stefe, the border itself went unmarked. Elsewhere in the town it was mapped out with boundary stones: two-foot pillars of red sandstone, carved with the symbol of the bishop (a mitre and cross) on one side, and the Bourg (three wheels) on the other. If there was not enough room for a marker, a small sandstone escutcheon, marked with the lord's arms, was put on the side of the first convenient object. As it happened, Gasc was considered something of an expert on these markers. As a mason, and a man who lived in Sant Stefe, he was assumed to know and care where they went, enough to help the City lawyers draw up their arguments against the count's incursions. His name appears among the witnesses who spent days in court, some time towards the end of the century, rehearsing where the markers stood, or ought to have stood, all along the border. The butchers on those contentious meat-stalls gave evidence alongside him.

In Sant Stefe there was one sandstone marker on the eastern side, hidden in among the pillars of the meat-stalls, and one on the west, in a smithy courtyard. In the dusk, they were hard to spot unless you knew they were there. But Gasc knew. His knowledge of the other border markers was probably less precise; but he may well have been out with the consuls, slipping about on the steep edges of the town, when they took their readings 'from properly built fences and well-set stone walls', to fashion the partition-propaganda he later lent his name to.

A enormous reverence attached to these border markers: a reverence that was much to blame for keeping the fact of partition alive. Ordinary folk naturally tried to cross the line, make gardens in the ditches and generally blur the distinctions; we can sense all the time, alongside the ritual official stand-offishness, that many citizens and burgenses were trying to extend hands to each other in a normal, neighbourly way. Official reaction to this was terse: 'They ought to know better.' For the boundary stones marked out, as clear as day, where one side could tax and the other could not. They mapped out a line in the dirt that was almost sacred.

In the writs and tax books of both sides, therefore, the markers were heavily dramatised. They were given charac ters, endowed with feelings. If they were vandalised, they had stood *ses injuria de neguna persona*, without hurting anyone. If they were moved (and some did disappear, especially one that was set into the wall just in front of the house of the Franciscans, on the western edge of town), this was done 'disrespectfully' and 'forgetting the fear of God'. When the Franciscans were left with nothing but a square hole in their garden wall, this was done sadly and unduly, *dolosamen e endegudamen*, as if people wept over these things. Another marker, which one side claimed it could not see, was described in furious terms by the other: 'This marker looks big, is big and has stood there as long as anyone can re- member.' In truth, they always looked larger to the side to which they belonged.

Running east towards the river the border grew even more confused. There were old vineyards here, long abandoned, the vines growing in grass. Children would come scrumping as soon as the small, poor grapes began to blacken, cram- ming their stained mouths; and Johan Riols and his Agassa came out here on a Saturday evening 'at the first bell of vespers, or round then', to walk about, as she put it, or to hunt for rabbits, as he put it, on either side of the invisible line.

Narrow roads led down to the river at Dona Guizas's lime-furnace, right on the border, and at a place called La Gascaria — possibly connected to the Gascs long ago, but now no longer theirs. The ground was muddy, the river close-packed with fulling and corn mills; and the mill at La Gascaria was hotly disputed. The City's arms were on the mill wheels (every so often, the consuls made the steep trek down to check they were still there, and not disrespectfully chipped off) and the bishop's seal was on the flour-dusted buckets and bins; but the count's fish nets were trailed across the water, almost into the race itself.

The property rights here, as everywhere else, were written down on paper and doubtless kept by the City consuls in some box; we shall see later that this filing system, which went for most things, had its disadvantages. But for the boundary inquiry they produced a piece of paper, 'written in the year 1338', in which they had ordered someone to mend the road at La Gascaria, which seemed to prove they owned it. For their part, the count's men produced a whole bundle of writs, including 'various inquiries against a person who stole salt meat on the road . . . between the Elms and the Auterne bridge; proving that these territories are within the count's jurisdiction. Catalogued under K'.

Officers patrolled the border by the river sporadically but fiercely, once even scaring away a passel of boys who were out to get magpies' nests ('they wanted to take our caps and our belts, but we raced off'); and the general public was usually at sea. Ramon Serroy had a meadow here for which he paid 10 sous rent a year, 'but, on my oath, I've no idea whether it's in the City or in the Bourg'. Deodat Fornols had met his little boys here in 1280, crying and being cuffed by a court officer who had also taken their fishing nets away; he never worked out the nature of the trespass, and indeed it was almost impossible to do so.

Gasc, too, went down to the river at the point where it met the border, because he had an allotment that he rented from the chapter at Ort de la Conqua, round the sides of the great shallow pit where part of the idol Ruth had plummeted to earth. And he would probably go too to fish with his net, sitting upstream of the count's drag lines but below the mill-race, where the water swirled under the towering trees. Men went there in parties sometimes, often taking advantage of the Saturday afternoon holiday before feast days, working broad nets that went right across the river; for fishing 'from Gascaria to the Malapeyra road' was reserved for townsmen, unless other landowners objected. At the end of the day they, like Gasc, would wend their way back, their catch on reeds round their necks, dampening their shirts; a party of chatting men weaving in and out of the border, hoping not to encounter the patrols who sometimes overtook them and swept their hats away.

Uphill from the mill, back towards town, a road was supposed to mark the boundary between indistinguishable fields. These were sometimes fenced or walled, sometimes open; cattle, churning up the muddy grass, did not observe the border, and often men did not. In 1395 a row of wooden stakes was to appear here, painted with the City's insignia of red shields. They were planted with great ceremony on a June evening, with an official dinner to follow, and 'checked up on' with another official procession, with fur-trimmed robes and hats, on a July day of sweltering heat: 'and when we'd finished we went off and had a drink'. In the 1370s, however, there was nothing particular there to mark out one place from another.

Yet the bishops' lawyers thought there was. When they had him in court, they asked Gasc about the removal of yet another boundary stone, in Guilhem Bastier's meadow near Gascaria. A man called Gui Pontier had moved it: a man said to have been prompted by the devil or some other wicked spirit, for otherwise the awful deed was impossible to explain. Pontier was arrested, thrown into prison, excommunicated and ordered to replace the stone, but before he could do so 'death choked him off, and he couldn't': *la mort lo estrangolet e non puoc*. He was buried in unconsecrated ground, a criminal.

The prosecutors asked Gasc to confirm that the story was true. He could hardly have answered no, or equivocated:

impossible to argue with a case as strong as that. The whole spiritual and moral weight of the City clearly lay behind it. Yet the marker in Bastier's meadow was no longer there, and may never have been there at all: another big obvious object changed to insignificant mist.

This then was the border. Gasc lived with it, as everyone did. But it made his life complicated. The walls and buildings at the centre of town were often old and dilapidated, constantly needing his attention. Yet he might not be trusted to do the work. It was too sensitive. The consuls made sure they kept authority over every inch of the dividing wall, ready to seize control in an emergency. Repairs tended to be farmed out to neutral builders, including, at one point, a roving Frenchman. Foreignness had its uses. To fix up border towers, a border watch-shed, even a border fish-stall, was politically explosive. To build a border latrine needed elaborate permissions, beside which the Marques drain looked almost straightforward. Everything, as we have seen, was too close together anyway; and through this jumble of habitation a border had to be driven plainly and officially. So beams could be driven only three feet into the dividing wall; sheds could be built, but with stipulated lengths and widths of timber; windows, if made on the wall side, had to be blocked up again. The official guideline was that a man could do what he liked with the wall, as far as the middle. Beyond the middle was another country.

We cannot trace Gasc's journey right to his door; we do not know whether he lived on the neutral ground of the Plassa Sant Stefe, or just on the other side of the Sant Stefe Gate. At any rate, come evening and the curfew, the gate would close. The little chapel beside it, dedicated to the saint, would already have its door shut. Bernard del Cros, sometime cloth-seller, sometime gatekeeper, would have taken his awning in, an awning once condemned as prejudicial to the City because it flapped over the border; he would have struggled from his workshop with the great iron bar, and locked up. Over the gate was the window where Gabriac had appeared, ghostlike, to Seyrac and Jalenca in those days when death had stalked every corner of the town; and yet death had not been sufficient excuse to let them through.

This was the town Gasc lived in. A town where, if you did huge favours for people on the other side, they did not necessarily thank you for it, but behaved as if you were still a stranger who could not entirely be trusted.

He went into his house and shut the door.

3

Gerald Canac
and the lord's demands

A T DAWN the next day, the workmen assembled again in Marques's basement. To Gasc's surprise, Canac, the son-in-law, was there before them. The basement was dark, with the only light showing through the low arched doorway at the top of the steps. Gasc could just make out the reddish stone of the central pillar and the mounds of earth from their work of the day before; the air was still damp and rank from the drain. And there stood Canac, waiting.

He was in his thirties, well-dressed by comparison with them, but with the sinewy arms of a man used to handling bales and shifting barrels. Canac dealt in both cloth and wine; he was rich, respected and sure of himself. This, after all, was the man who had singlehandedly taken hold of Marques's finances and turned them round, getting his property out of mortgage as soon as he had married his daughter. Yet, at that moment, in the damp shadows, there was something nervous and uncertain about him.

He greeted the workmen warmly. Then, drawing them aside, he said: 'You haven't told anyone?'

They told him no.

Canac then addressed them one by one, Marot de Namaria first. 'Marot,' he said, 'I beseech you, please, by all that's dear, don't mention this to my sister, because she's such a prattler [*tant lengosa es*], she'll spread it round immediately, and it will hurt me because they'll put me down for more tax.'

'Sure, I'll take good care not to tell her,' Marot replied.

To Gasc, Canac was more explicit. 'Be really secret, because if my sister gets to know, she'll talk about it, and with all these excessive taxes they keep imposing, we'll be knocked flat.'

They all agreed to be sworn to secrecy: a proper oath this time, not just an admonition. Then Canac, plunging his hand into his purse, gave Gasc four gold francs, the equivalent of about a week's wages. Gasc was thunderstruck. 'I didn't see what he gave the other two,' he said later. 'I didn't try to interfere, I was too pleased.'

Canac left; and Marot de Namaria seems to have gone at this point, too, while his luck was in. Gasc and Barbier went happily to work. The drain was not yet clear. But they had scarcely started when Alumbors, Peyre Marques's wife, burst into the shop.

'Why didn't you tell me?' she cried, beside herself. 'Why didn't you give the pot to me?'

Gasc, who had had a good morning so far, made a brave reply: 'I would have done, if you'd come first.'

This was a cavalier answer. Gasc had no idea who the money belonged to; and something Canac had said, together with remarks that were made in court afterwards, suggested that it might not belong to any of the people gathered in that damp basement. Whose ground, after all, did the drain run through? It did not belong to Marques. It belonged to his lord, the lord of the Bourg, Count Jean I of Rodez and Armagnac. Whether Marques paid rent directly to him or did him homage did not matter. All the earth of the Bourg was the count's territory: and, as property deeds often pointed out, the air above it, too. It was not mere chance that the Marques case ended up among the papers of the counts of Armagnac.

The lord's power was ubiquitous, but it was not personal. It was possible to live one's whole life in Rodez and see neither count nor bishop. (When Gasc knocked over that jug of coins in Marques's drain, the count's most recent visit to 'his own ground' had been for three weeks or so in February and March of 1369; the accounts for those short, dark days were inflated with tallow for his candles and wood for his fires.) The count's wars against the English or against the Count of Foix, his great rival, took him away, and the bishops had largely absented themselves since 1309, when the popes had begun their exile in Avignon. There were always better places to be, better things to do, than to linger in the wind-battered hills round Rodez.

To keep after these wandering lords was a great expense and, in wartime, dangerous, but both communities did it, endlessly struggling over the mountain roads to seek advice or approval. Any request from France or its representatives had to go to the lord first, 'wherever he is', in case it could be reduced, ignored or deflected; and the king, through his agents, was asking for money for his wars several times a year. So the lord, though a nuisance, was also continually cast in the role of saviour and protector. Disillusioned though the people of Rodez might be about lordship, they needed it; and besides, it was all they knew. As the Bourg consuls signed themselves at the end of their letters to the count, they were indeed *los tot vostres*, 'all yours'.

The lords were reverenced at their installations and mourned, with a certain cool formality, at their funerals.

The count's installation took place in the cathedral, half-built as it was. He was escorted into the church by the bishop, made an offering at the high altar, said prayers, and let the bishop seat him in the stone chair beside the episcopal throne. There he made a 'pronouncement of homage' to this man, whose pretensions he loathed and to whom he would not speak again if he could help it: standing, raising his hands, and being careful all the while to stare at the statue of Our Lady on her altar and not into the bishop's eyes. Had this been a true act of homage, like Jean I's equally reluctant homage to the Black Prince in Agen in 1364, he would have knelt at the bishop's feet, placed his joined hands between the hands of the other and allowed him to kiss him on the mouth. But there was never any question of that.

When the homage was done the bishop embraced the count, blessed him, put on his head the iron crown of Rodez — typically utilitarian and heavy and plain — and announced that he was surrendering to him all the towers of the town. The keys to these towers and to the bishop's palace were then presented to the count in a dish of silver; his officers, keys jangling, raced up the tower steps and hoisted the count's standard on each turret; and for three days they remained there, as if only the count ruled in Rodez.

When a new bishop made his formal first entry, the ceremony was only a little less provocative. He would wait outside the Amavergua Gate, on the north side of the City; two squires, wearing stiff new boots with silver spurs, swords at their sides and garlands of flowers round their necks, would take the reins on either side of him and lead him through. He would ride as far as the City weighing house, which was almost on the border, and then dismount, out of reverence for the relics being carried in procession. His attendant squires then claimed his horse as theirs, jumped on its back in turns and whipped it on southwards, through most streets of the Bourg and through the main square, changing over at each crossroads, trying not to stop and to get back to the City unmolested, while crowds of burgenses watched them.

In these joint ceremonies Rodez played for a day at being one place, but the games were elaborately careful: for the power was real and the territories mapped out. The ditches and walls, especially in the Bourg, were understood to be the lord's, standing on his ground, and there was an aggressive undertow to that. The lord's honour was invested in them, however tumbledown they seemed; and anything good found in or under them, by whatever effort or stroke of luck, belonged to him.

The counts talked of *burgus noster,* our town, closely and possessively, though they hardly ever set foot there. Permits were given to build against 'our wall', a deed of purchase was drafted in 'our street', repairs were made in 1367 'to Moss. the count's watch-tower' beside the Peace Hospital. Burgenses spoke of 'Moss. the count's road', and the count's wall. Houses commandeered by the Bourg consuls were for the use of the count or his staff if he wished, and only after that for the community; Johan Manha, a City tenant in one of these, had been summarily evicted in 1366 to make room for the count's doctor.

Besides all this, the count drew rent from properties all over the Bourg: live hens held squawking by their legs, white crumbling blocks of salt, purses of cash, not forgetting the four horseshoes and twenty-four horseshoe-nails from that contentious partitioned house in Sant Stefe. The Seguis, Marques's neighbours, owed the count 25 sous a year for their sprawling main house, payable on the feast of St Andrew; a measure of oats for an upper chamber and work-shop, with adjacent pigsty, near the count's ditch, payable on the feast of St Julia; and a hen for another large house in the next street. Marques, next door, may have paid a county rent too, unless he owned his house outright; but the notion of pure possession — without the lord claiming some corner of an interest — was relatively rare.

The count kept no high officers in Rodez and no permanent staff, except that doctor; and, when war taxes required someone to twist arms on the spot, his treasurer, Peyre Valeta. Valeta eventually took charge of the minting house, but for years he had worked in the very shop where Gasc and his colleagues now laboured. He had bought the use of it for nine years from Marques for the lowish lump rent of 80 florins; and Canac, as one of his first actions after his marriage to Marques's daughter, had tried to restore his father-in-law's fortunes by buying the shop back. We do not know what deal he and Valeta struck; but when Valeta handled a City loan in 1374 (part of a massive troop loan of 18,000 francs to the count from the three estates of Rouergue), he squeezed from the consuls a 'supplement' of 88 livres 16 sous 3 deniers. He provided a signed and sealed letter of receipt for this, labelled 'Special credit in the count's treasury'; but he paid back only 80 livres the next year, cavalierly pocketing the difference.

For Canac, therefore, the count's authority could be summed up graphically in the cash and receipts that piled up in his father-in-law's shop while Valeta was there; and it could be summed up, too, in the *sala comtal*, the original palace of the counts in the Bourg. The workmen in Marques's shop could see it across the Plassa de l'Olmet, through the dipping branches of the tree: a building with colonnades and new crenellations beside a round watchtower, just north of the church of St Amans. In 1370 builders were in mending the fireplace, and more men were crouched on the roof, like flies, re-laying tiles, because the building had been damaged by rainstorms. Three years before, a wall had fallen down. Huc Farcel, a neighbour and friend of Marques, had been engaged to rebuild this wall and shore up another for the bargain price of 25 florins 'all in', *tot sarrat*. Small wonder that only a handful of documents called this place *la palissa*, even relatively speaking.

The count's mansion backed on to gardens and allotments, most of them the size of pocket handkerchiefs, and a smaller house where minting was done. The mint, with two forges and an armed guard, was highly esteemed, although by the last decades of the century the shoemaker who rented part of the building seemed rather more productive. At least one adjoining house had a pigsty whose smell and muck trickled underfoot, for animals and men lived in close familiarity, even in the grandest places. The mansion watch tower was the Bourg prison, known as the Castle; this had just been converted, by Farcel again, into two cells and a room for interrogations, with a big lock on each door and a cistern for storing the water that was slopped out for prisoners. But there was little permanent furniture anywhere in the mansion. On the rare occasions when counts wished to stay there, the sheets, blankets, beds, bowls, plates and cups were 'borrowed' from burgenses.

Burgenses, indeed, came in and out of the building all the time. The great hall was also a courtroom and a council-chamber. The consuls made their yearly accounting in the *sala*, humping the leather-bound books in their arms. Criminals had their cases heard, pushed in from the Castle with their wrists still manacled together. And shopkeepers collected their vessels — such as Marques's quart jug of pewter, or the half-quarts and pints of copper that Canac used to measure out wine from his barrels — all stamped with the count's seal. The originals, also made of copper, were kept there too, so that men could check against a standard if they thought their measures were deficient. Notaries had their desks in the *sala*, sealing all contracts with the count's 'vigorous authenticating seal', and indeed they were not allowed to do their work anywhere else. What the mansion may have lacked in furniture, it obviously recouped in bureaucrats.

Canac had other reasons to come in and out, for this large bare room contained the great table where cloth was measured. As a cloth merchant, Canac could buy the local weave only in this hall; the bishop's cloth hall, in the City, would not have counted for him. The standards in the two halls were meant to be the same, but they were not expressed in the same way. On both sides, the ell-measure (about 27 inches) and the canne-measure (about 6 feet) were equal: but the ell in the City was to be *fortis, non flexibilis*, and in the Bourg *ben fortz, que noys puescant flechir.* In the count's hall they were kept locked in a chest in the corner, and they were not valid if the lord's stamp, the lion and three wheels (*rodes*, in the local tongue, meant wheels) was not on them.

Rodez cloth was rough burrel stuff, good only for the cheap end of the market. It was used for sheets and shirts for the poor and tunics for the border patrol, whose work involved much scrambling. Some of the cloth was blanched white with myrtle, which was sold in huge bundles in the Bourg square, the roots still clotted with mud and stones; some was woven into a check design, favoured for overcoats and labourers' cloaks. The local cloth was meant to be woven to a standard width of 34 threads, 'of good sheep's wool, with no goats' hair or dogs' hair or hair of cows and horses, or any other sort'. If it was up to quality — a quality Canac could feel as he handled it, and see as the bolt was shaken out over the long table — the count's seal was put on it and the inspector's thread was stitched in. The very cloth Canac sold, therefore, was shot through with the honour of the count.

In the City, the bishop tried to claim the same sort of lordship. His insignia, the mitre and cross, was on the ell-measure, the canne-measure and all the weights, and these had to be registered at his palace; but it was apparent straight away that he did not show the same possessiveness of the buildings or the ground. His palace, built in stone, was backed by gardens and raised private walkways and, again, largely empty of furniture: beds, towels and sheets all had to be borrowed when he deigned to call. The house was flanked by a round tower and a barbican bearing the bishop's arms; and, like the *sala comtal,* it did duty as a court-room and accounting chamber. The bishop also owned seven fortified houses 'with strong towers and turrets'; and most of Terralh, the street that ran between the cathedral and the palace, which was full of painters, incense-makers, priests and, at least in the 1390s, the schoolmaster and the bishop's baker. About two hundred citizens, including Gasc, owed rent to him for their houses; but outside these areas the ground and the buildings carried no shadow of him. Since he was hardly ever in the town (and sometimes, like the count, preferred to stay with the fine-living Franciscans when he was), the bishop left an officer called the Official as his deputy and factotum.

Had the jug of gold been found in the City — if Gasc had been digging in his own basement — would anyone have thought to say that the money belonged to the bishop? It seemed unlikely. But the bishop could occasionally take a stand, and Jean de Cardaillac was doing so even as Gasc laboured. Cardaillac was not technically the bishop; he was the church's perpetual administrator while Bishop Faydit d'Agrefolio was away, hanging round the retinue of the Pope in Avignon, nibbling on melons and lettuces in the warm south. But he became bishop shortly thereafter; and he took particular offence that the City consuls in 1367 had hired builders, perhaps including Gasc, to put up a barbican called the St Martial Gate between the bishop's garden and his palace. Bishop Faydit had tolerated this gate and kept its keys; but the consuls were now cementing and fortifying it, and de Cardaillac, who had a doctorate in law from Toulouse, complained that this was being done secretly, at night, deliberately to annoy him.

There was not much substance to this complaint; the consuls might well have ignored it. But lords, even when acting by proxy, even when grumbling for no good reason, had to be accommodated. So the consuls tried to mollify him; they gave him a set of keys too, even though, as they pointed out, 'in Cahors and Aurillac, where the bishop is temporal lord, the consuls keep the keys'. This brought a sharp rejoinder. The City, snapped de Cardaillac in his best legalese, was 'the bishop's manse, and the bishop is the true lord of the said City and its suburbs in *spiritualia* and in *temporalia*'. Gasc might have pointed out that the bishop (and even his 'perpetual' administrator) was seldom in the palace, night or day, to notice the loaded baskets creaking up and down or the masons, in protective gloves, slapping on their mortar. The palace windows looked out blankly. Inside, too, the rooms were bare, save for the writs and rent receipts that piled up in the corners like autumn leaves.

Gasc was asked, later, whether he knew that the counts had a claim to treasure trove found in Bourg drains 'after a year and a day, if it has no obvious owner'. He answered: 'I don't know about that.' It was a question almost nobody could answer, on either side of the border. The whole issue of lords' rights and subjects' rights was a vexed one. Both City and Bourg had charters of privileges in which the community's rights to raise taxes, or appoint officers, or stay free from oppression, were written down; when lords first entered Rodez, they were supposed to confirm them. Gasc

may well have been there when the City consuls asked
Bishop Ramon d'Agrefolio (Faydit's uncle) to do so in
August 1350, just by the Amavergua Gate, in a street
specially swept and draped with billowing linen for the
occasion, in the middle of a great crush of people. D'Agrefolio agreed, 'placing his right hand on his heart as a sign
of his oath, in the manner of prelates'. The consuls thought
this good, as they always did; but they also, just to be on the
safe side, asked for confirmation in writing.

On the count's side, liberties were usually granted to the
Bourg in the cloister of St Amans in front of a crowd of
notables, with the count's hand firmly on the Gospels and a
promise to act *per bona fe e ces engan*, in good faith and
without deceit. This was the same formula, to the word, that
the town also applied in its food regulations to taverners
and fish-sellers. Trust in the count appeared to go so far and
no further, and that was fair enough; for the liberties were
not exactly granted with an open hand. The counts routinely
kept restrictive clauses in them; as, indeed, did the bishops,
especially about bell-ringing. And the freedoms had a price.
In exchange for the whole set, the Bourg paid the count
each year a tax of 100 livres, a pair of white gloves, a lance
of white steel and a pair of gold spurs. In the City the
consuls presented the bishop with twelve silver cups on his
first entry, thereafter holding their privileges freely. These
gifts were not strictly a quid pro quo; the freedoms, once
granted, were understood to continue whether or not
anyone remembered to pay for them. In 1362 the Bourg
consuls paid out 17 florins for the lances, spurs and gloves
owing for seventeen years.

All these rights were recorded in multiple versions, and
very carefully sealed and stored in leather pouches inside
boxes; long journeys were made, as far as Avignon and
Bordeaux, when anything came up that brought them into
question. By the end of the century the City's book of

privileges was properly chained up in the 'archive room' (grandly so called) in the meeting house. Yet the subjects' rights were specific, and thus limited; the lords' were often vague and all-embracing *Imperium, auctoritas, executio, jurisdictio* could cover a multitude of grabbing and grasping.

One way and another, the count was continuously on the take. He was already overlord of all the stalls in the main square and along the façade of his mansion, and could order these stalls put up, taken down or decorated during the fairs. He kept a pillory there, and the criminals who stood in it, groggy with their beatings at the hands of his officers, or with their heads a sticky mess of blood from severed ears or tongues, had paid him cash fines for their misdemeanours.

The Bourg's covered corn-stone, right beside the pillory, was repaired by the count's men and brought him rents of one-third of the grain weighed. He took in fees of around 200 livres a year at the big weighing station for livestock, and about 40 livres from the smaller weighing house for oil, cheese and salt. His Treasurer of Provisions requisitioned small herds of sheep that were driven from the limestone moors right into the Bourg square, careering and bleating among the stalls. His officers even claimed the splattered *merda* off the streets when cattle herds came through, going up for the summer, as they still go up, to the bare hills of the Aubrac; and they claimed a charge on all goods brought into the Bourg (and salt, salt meat, cheese, oil, leather and live pigs brought into the City) by foreigners for sale.

This food tax, called *leuda*, was especially controversial because it crossed the border. In the City, hoteliers were meant to demand it from their out-of-town visitors and pay it over to the count's officers — which was why Guilhem Salustre found himself in court for sometimes failing to ask for it, and for tending to put it in his own pocket when he remembered. In the Bourg, the same tax was sometimes raised ferociously. Thus Ramon Bastier, travelling down 'the count's road' towards the river with three pack-horses laden with salt, suddenly found himself pursued by *leudarius* Guilhem Camboulas, red-faced and roaring, with his sword drawn. '*Arlot!*' hollered Camboulas, waving his sword in the air: 'You're getting away with the lord's rights!' 'No, I'm not,' Bastier retorted, shaken but dignified (by his own account); 'I don't owe anything except a measure of salt, and I've paid that.' The next thing he knew he was seized by the hair, yanked back, and almost pulled off his horse, while amazed bystanders tried to waylay Camboulas and calm him down. 'Lord's rights!' *Drechura del senhor!* that gentleman continued to gasp, spittle flecking his mouth.

The count also policed and organised the town's joint fairs, held every year at the end of November and the end of June. Each shop in the Bourg, Canac's included, was decorated then with canvas awnings and reed matting on the count's orders. Crowds filled the streets, the houses and the hotels; their curious hands were all over Canac's stock, their odd money piled on his table. The fairground itself was in the border meadows west of town, where the grass in June was cut raggedly short with sickles; visiting merchants camped like gypsies for two or three days, cloths spread out, horses round them, livestock tethered nearby or put into makeshift pens, from which they eagerly escaped into the vegetable gardens of Rodez.

At the edge of the fairground the meadow was left uncut, full of ox-eye daisies and feathery seeding grass that ran into the old abandoned vines. Respectable merchants like Canac avoided this part, for this was where the prostitutes set up shop. Every so often the count's officers would drag them out, confiscating their veils and the pouches, hoods, belts and knives of their customers; sometimes the officers would go after pickpockets, or charlatans playing 'country games' to cheat fairgoers of their money. Robbers were whipped

on the spot. Once, tragedy struck: the limp body of a boy
was pulled from a vineyard where Peyre Saur, the owner,
had beaten him to death for stealing grapes. County officers
arrested Saur. At twilight, as honest men went home, gangs
of young men with swords went swaggering through to hunt
for whores in the rustling grass.

The bishop always said there was no honour in these fairs.
It was the count's men who kept order at them, corralling
sulking girls or sheep that turned in stupid, bumping circles;
the count's men who separated drunks, broke up fights and
handed in lost purses full of money. The rules were strict,
but the nature of the fairs shone through them. 'No man
or woman to sell bread, wine or meat at more than the usual
price just because of the fair.' 'No man to carry offensive
weapons.' 'Hoteliers to take all weapons from their guests
and put them in their rooms, and to report anything suspicious.' 'No man to take low women or gamblers into his
room, nor to lend money for gambling.' At night the count's
officers would tramp through on hotel inspections, torches
blazing, while the landlords ran upstairs to rummage for
weapons in the beds.

Some of the fairground police, in fact, were bishop's men,
though so few people noticed them that it was sometimes
supposed they did the night watch, when honest folk were
asleep. But the fairs were so low and bawdy, in any case, that
the bishop may have preferred to keep his distance from
them, as from most sorts of commerce. An ordinance of
1279 had also forbidden him or any citizen to erect a corn-
market in the City or to devise any other new method of
weighing corn, as if he would try. By 1370 there was certainly
a corn-stone in the City; the bishop's arms were on it, as on
the weights themselves. It charged one obol (a halfpenny)
per sestier of grain, against the penny charged in the Bourg.
But this was not really a competitive venture; for the bishop,

unlike the count, seems not to have cared what grubby trading brought him. The City competed for lawyer-business, often successfully; and that was all.

When, in 1316, the two partitioned halves of town were ordered to try to be co-operative, everyone worried most about how the lords would behave. And they had cause. In effect, the count and bishop never agreed to co-operate. The count considered he was bringing far too large a share of trade and taxes to the agreement. Such a gift would not be fair. The bishop, for his part, thought co-operation might endanger the Church. What worried their subjects, however, was something else: whether a different lord could love them as much as their own. For they assumed their own lord did love them, whatever the appearance. As one citizen put it in 1326, if the two lords got involved in each other's patches, 'the count could hurt us more than he did before; but possibly, too, he could love us more.'

Possibly: for the two emotions, hurt and love, were obviously close. The count expected burgenses, like members of his family, to serve in his wars (though, as we have seen, they usually wriggled out of that), and to contribute to the marriage costs which he could not afford. He called them his *fieusals*, vassals, a word that was both paternal and spiked with menace. These overtones were nicely caught in a note that our consul Johan Manha sent, by a servant, from Toulouse in January 1370: 'Moss. d'Armagnac doesn't want us to ask the king for those various things [tax exemptions] that are so necessary for the town, because he wants us to write to *him* about them.' The mixture of protectiveness and fury was unmistakable and not, on any account, to be resisted, even though Manha was not the count's man. So the count's secretary wrote the letters to the count on best parchment, and Manha slipped him some money for his trouble; and a diplomatic pause ensued, before Manha and Natas went to Paris anyway.

Keeping the lord sweet did not matter so much in the City; but in the Bourg, as Canac had implied to Gasc, it mattered terribly. He had complained about *talhas excessivas que totjorn se fan*, huge taxes that somehow imposed themselves, and could knock him flat. He had talked about 'them' putting him down for more of the same. And there was nothing he could do about it.

These nameless oppressors, at one level, were the Bourg consuls, the six men chosen every year to govern and raise taxes. It was the consuls who had to find the money for the new walls, as well as for roads, bridges, sergeants' wages, and whatever else town government got up to. They kept a book called a *cadastre* in which every property was listed, with a careful account of its exact position, outhouses, useful amenities (a kiln, an oven, a stone enclosure for livestock), and its gardens, rents and furniture; and this was the basis on which each adult was taxed. As Canac knew, sudden wealth would be noted in the book too; and the value of movable goods was pre-emptively assessed at half the value of the property to allow a wide margin for fraud, such as hiding away money suddenly discovered in drains.

But all this was only part of the liability he faced. In Rodez, as in most towns in Languedoc in 1370, the consuls were also waging a constant struggle to meet the demands of the local lord. Whatever the consuls routinely asked for was easily overshadowed, in the Bourg, by the count's importunings for money for the war. The City, whose lord did not fight, had a much lighter fiscal burden; which was why Canac had to remind Gasc, the citizen, that careless talk could empty money-chests.

That year, when the count stayed in town, using up all that firewood and all those tallow candles, the Bourg consuls paid two florins to the Dominicans 'that they might sing to the Holy Spirit and pray to Our Lord that He might give us good advice and good management of the things that Sir asked of us.' What Sir asked of them, from the 1360s onwards, was thousands of francs a year in extraordinary taxation, besides unlimited supplies of wheat, oats, wine and pack-horses and unlimited loans of household equipment. Since Peyre Valeta, as treasurer, was sometimes in charge of those, the shop he leased from Canac's father-in-law also filled up from time to time with blankets, bowls and pans, all airily borrowed without receipts.

Burgenses were meant to be free of these arbitrary *presas*, but most of them probably did not know that. The consuls were said to have a guarantee in writing somewhere, with the count's seal on it, 'that everything we have caused to be taken, we will give back'. But if you lent the count pots or pans they would come back with the bottoms blackened, or bent out of shape; if you lent him sheets, they came back filthy, needing three washes before they were clean, or ripped to shreds, as if his men had slept in their armour; if you lent him pack-horses, he probably kept them for good. Even the City was sometimes called on for these 'borrowings'; but because citizens were not the count's subjects, and did not accept his carelessness with a vassal's shrug of the shoulders, they actually went to the count's country seat to look for things that had not been returned.

Jean I of Armagnac, who was count in 1370, was not the most rapacious; but he had had to be ransomed out of jail, at great expense, in 1365, and his sudden conversion to the French cause in 1369 brought on a prodigious appetite for loans and borrowings for the war. In effect he and the Duke of Anjou, the king's lieutenant, joined forces and soaked the taxpayers of Rodez together. Even Gasc, in the City, had had to dip into his pocket for him, since Estol Aribert — he of the divided house — had contracted to raise a tax all over town the year before, 'to keep [the count] in his proper estate and to pay for the men-at-arms he is keeping to defend Rouergue'. Poor Aribert lost 35 florins on this tax, 'because people couldn't pay'.

To keep Jean I in his proper estate was a nicely open-ended phrase. He was, as it happens, something of a wine buff, preferring his wine nicely aged and ordering taverners not to sell consignments that had been shaken about too much. His butler was subsidised for a house and workshop at Marcillac, among the vineyards and the sunny consular *résidences sécondaires*; but the count could ensure supplies of tipple simply by commandeering it, if he was prepared to risk disappointment. Because grapes were picked early, before there was much sugar in them, they were often rotting and infected before they were pressed; and wine of this sort — *mosit e fustat o agre*, putrid, bitter and musty — quickly found its way out of the count's stocks again, and into the taverns of Rodez. Those same taverns also took, uncomplainingly, the vintage that was ruined when English raiders tore through the count's vineyards at Marcillac, ripping the vines from their supports and bursting the grapes in the rich red dust.

The count also helped himself to a whole assortment of smaller luxuries, sometimes paid for, sometimes seized almost whimsically. In 1370 a fragrant bundle of spices, cloves and assorted nuts, all luxury items, was 'found' in Rodez. The bundle belonged to merchants who had 'left it behind' in the house of Peyre Segualar and Mauri d'Auzits, presumably to pay for something else. The count's seneschal promptly took half of it, 'besides the other portions that his officers took'. D'Auzits and Segualar seemed not to complain, although they were left with nothing to sell but a small bag of pepper. Similarly, Miquel del Verdier did not raise a murmur when 'he was touched for a donkey and two horses and a mule that they said would make good pack-animals for Sir, and Master Peyre de Mayres, Sir's secretary, said that Sir wanted them'.

The use of the phrases *fo tocat* (for the horses) and *foro trobadas* (for the nuts) was deliberate: everything in the Bourg was potentially for the count's use, spread out for him to rifle through. But even that was not enough, and for big occasions the Bourg bought exquisite and extra-ordinary gifts, the sort of things never otherwise seen in this hard-bitten town: sugared almonds, songbirds, meringues, fish plated with gold. Canac might well have been aghast at such fripperies, which could not even be guaranteed to have the desired effect. Attempts to mollify the count's successor, Jean II, came to an abrupt end in 1382 with a heartbreaking entry in the Bourg accounts: 'Item: about the present that was sent back from Gages [the count's country seat] when it turned out that he wouldn't accept it, and the jewels that we had taken there for a present, they've been sent back to where we got them from; and as for the future, we won't do a thing more.'

Because the counts were hardly ever in Rodez, but sent their requests for money from afar, they could not see the hardship their depredations caused. The Bourg consuls, struggling over the hills to Gages or beyond, petrified of attack 'by Englishmen, Frenchmen or anybody else', tried repeatedly to explain 'that at the moment we don't intend to pay anything more, and especially because the people haven't the wherewithal, and don't dare leave town to pursue their business'. They tried to explain too to the gatherings of principal taxpayers, in which Canac may have sat fretfully with the rest, how they were to cope with the latest request. 'They', as Canac put it, squirmed at the thought of asking for supplementary taxes, and found it hard to argue their case with much subtlety; one such tax was raised 'because the consuls need money'. But 'he', or

'Sir', was not to be refused. Agreements were made with the lord 'as best we can' or 'because we can't resist him', or because 'Sir the count has asked for that personally once, twice and many times, and we cannot say no to him.' When Jean II died in 1384, the Bourg consuls remarked that he had 'paid his debt to Nature'. He never paid it to them.

So could Gasc, the citizen, ever really grasp the financial agonies Canac was going through? Possibly not. The difference is certainly as clear as day in the tax registers, where the City's balance of payments was in the black continuously between 1350 and 1380, and the Bourg showed only two financial years (1359-60 and 1362-3) when it was not in the red. But very few people saw, and nobody would have had the chance to compare, these figures. Perhaps the worst that citizens knew of the count in 1370 was that 'his people' had unaccountably left a dead mule in the cathedral building office, bloated, stiff and staring, which cost 2 sous 6 deniers (or a workman's day's wages) to drag out and dispose of.

As for the bishops, these drove citizens mad in a different way. They were not avaricious; Gasc paid the bishop a fairly notional rent for his own houses. And they were not, as the counts could be, consistently careless or cruel; but they were even more consistently absent, and their heads were often in the clouds. Bishop Peyre de Plenacassanha had a library with 130 books in it, though after his death these were sold off, once the richest volumes had been picked out and sent to Avignon. Bishop Bernard d'Albi, in the 1330s, wrote poetry; he could turn out more than 300 lines in an hour, a feat which moved Petrarch (no less!) to tell him that if he carried on at that rate, he would certainly make progress.

In 1348, when the Black Death was devastating Rodez, a 'plague proclamation' came down from Bishop Guirbert de Cantobre. His idea of consolation was literary: 'This or a similar plague is mentioned in the book which is popularly called *Flores Sanctorum*, in "The Life of the Blessed Gregory", and possibly also in "The Life of Saint Sebastian", near the end.' Perhaps he sensed the blank reactions; for in the same year he left an order to his executors to buy 'a good, fine and correct version of the *Flores Sanctorum*, unless I buy it before I die.'

Beyond that, the worst that could be said of bishops in the 1370s was that, being physically as well as mentally distant, they were deeply frustrating to deal with. The bishop's lawyers, those doughty promoters of partisan feeling, liked to say that lords spiritual always loved their subjects more deeply than lords temporal. The men of the City had to take that on trust; they had little proof of it. One bishop, still fuming about the St Martial Gate some years later, remarked that 'it's a good City, but full of wicked and perverse people. It would be a better place if the people tended to good and not to evil.'

The following exchange, from about the same time, was also fairly typical. The City consuls had asked the bishop's representative to get a message to the bishop on a matter of urgency, an old man wrongfully held in prison. This is how the representative responded:

I'll consult the bishop's council, send someone to see the bishop, and have a reply next Wednesday.

[Next Wednesday]: I haven't been able to see the council, but I'll have a reply this evening, around vespers.

[Around vespers]: I haven't been able to start proceedings, but I've written to the bishop and I'll be in touch with the council tomorrow.

[Next day, at terce]: I haven't been able to discuss the matter, but the bishop will soon write; come back tomorrow at terce, and I'll have a reply.

At which point, as if exhausted, the record runs out.

The bishops also took their time — sometimes weeks — to sign letters granting the consuls permission to raise taxes, and other essential things; they allowed their secretaries to extort money ('he asked for five francs for sealing a letter; the consuls beat him down to two'); they enjoyed making messengers cool their heels in the stableyard at Palmas, the nearest episcopal retreat; and they believed in doubling up on delegations to Paris. Hence one annoyed entry in the City records: 'Gui Bonafos was paid 30 francs for going [to Paris] after Sen. Almaric Guitart had gone. [Another 68-day round trip, the threat of another bonanza of tips and tourist trinkets.] The bishop asked that he be paid 50 francs. We decided to pay him 30.' (Marginal note: 'We must try and get it back!')

The City consuls also agreed, in tones that would have been familiar in the Bourg, to pay a contingent of carpenters going to the siege of Turia the excessively high wages recommended by the bishop, 'for the need we have of Moss. of Rodez; and because it was the first thing he had asked for, the council did not think we should say no to him.'

Both lords, then, had their buildings, their stables, their walls, their towers, their arms on the weights, their 'justice of every kind, high and low', their fees for the use of seals, their rent-sacks of rye, or oats, or horseshoe nails; both men threw malefactors into dingy lock-ups called the Castle, and put their authority behind the selling of fish and the weaving of cloth; but the substance of their authority, their natural claims on their subjects, were as different as could be. Gasc's (and del Cayro's) lord was otherworldly, a distant nuisance;

Canac's was importuning, grasping, oppressive as a hot breath in the face. This man, whom he may never have seen, could still 'knock him flat'.

But that was Canac's problem. Gasc went on digging, the four francs jingling in his pocket.

4

Helias Porret
and the weight of the law

BY THE TIME Alumbors Marques arrived in the basement, Canac had already gone. He did not want to be
seen hanging round his father-in-law's house. He wanted
secrecy, and Alumbors's furious entry was the sign that he
was not likely to get it. For Alumbors knew about the jug of
gold; somehow, she had found out.

Who could have told her? Canac himself had seen the
workmen off at sunset, and he had been waiting for them,
alone, at dawn. He had tracked their movements as best he
could. At least it could not have been Gasc who had told
her; a strong set of gates had kept him away from Alumbors
that night. But what about Barbier, who lived in the Bourg?
Or Marot, now off on a different job entirely? Had Alumbors
somehow overheard something the evening before, and
crept after one or the other, and asked him? At that point,
Canac might well have berated himself for not giving the
workmen their money before he had asked them to keep
quiet.

He had the jug now, locked up safe in his house. Canac

was careful with money. He had been trained that way by his first employer, the much-travelled Manha, who had turned up the day before to fuss about the drain. Manha, trained as a weaver, had taught Canac all he knew about cloth: how to name the different weaves, how to test for quality, how to keep trade secrets and work to the advantage of his master. And because he was away such a lot, he used to send Canac to Duran de Monferrier, one of the richest men in town, chief stockist of fine cloth for the discerning, to borrow money for his trips. Monferrier testified later, talking of Canac, that 'I knew he was a good man, and trustworthy, so I'd give him the key to my strong-box and tell him how many coins he should take out of it . . . as many as he wanted . . . and he would do it even when I was away on Johan Manha's behalf'.

Careful with other people's money, careful with his own. That was how, steadily, Canac had become a success in the cloth trade. People said it was only his arrival in Marques's family, as a hard-working son-in-law, that had temporarily stopped the rot in the business. Canac had not only bought back the use of his father-in-law's shop, but had also satisfied some of the creditors. Yet Marques was simply too old to take these lessons in good management, and possibly too stupid.

Canac knew that the money in the jug was not his. No-one ever suggested it was. But he was its steward, the one who had it in safe keeping. It could not have been left there, with builders about. Canac knew his status: he was the real head of the family, the man in charge, the one — as witnesses testified — who had rescued them all by marrying Guilhema. He had undoubtedly heard Marques's endless stories about his hidden money, because everyone had heard them: 'It was all my money, and I put it in one big jug and one little jug and in other containers, and I put it underground in two or three places in my shop, and I can't remember where.' But that did not mean the stories were true; no-one ever said for sure that the money found in the drain belonged to Marques, either. He had put it underground, so he often said, because he was afraid of the English. Now the English were all round the town, holed up in the woods as Manha and his colleagues imagined them, bartering for grain and cattle-hides, riding the roads to shipwreck the unwary; but Marques seemed to have panicked before anyone in Rodez had even set eyes on an Englishman.

Yet the fact remained that the hidden money was now unhidden. And now that Alumbors knew what Canac had done, he had two courses of action. He could hang on to the jug, and go to law to defend himself; or he could get an apprentice to take the jug to the parish priest of St Amans, as people were meant to do when they found items of value, and ask him to announce the find from the pulpit. People did this rather reluctantly, since if no-one claimed objects they went to the poor; but if you did not go through the motions, you were fairly soon denounced as a thief.

When one well-known rogue, Bernat Camboulas (brother of the red-faced *leudarius* we have already met), wished to prove that he had acted honourably in the matter of some silver chains that had been stolen from Ramon Bergonho, he told this tale:

I remember the time well. It was about two years ago, when the fair was on, though I've no idea which day it was. There were crowds of people in my house, and a boy found those chains you're talking about in my house beside the well. When he'd found them, another boy who was living with me came to tell me: 'Sir, a boy's found some silver chains by your well. You make him come here.' I sent the boy off to fetch him, and took the chains off him, and afterwards took them to the chaplain of St Amans in case he could help or knew whose they were.

A bit later the chaplain and Johan Bergonho came to my house. Johan said the chains were his brother's, and I gave them back to him in front of the chaplain.

Q. When did the boy find these chains?

A. During Lent some time.

Q. And how long did you keep them after he'd found them?

A. About a fortnight.

Q. When did you take them to the chaplain?

A. At once.

Q. What do you mean, at once? You said you kept them a fortnight.

A. Well, I can't really remember whether it was at once, or within two to five days.

Q. Where did you find the chaplain?

A. I don't really remember — in the cloister, or the church.

That figured. Camboulas's tale of honest recourse to the chaplain was shown up later both by the boy, who denied every particular of it, and by Bergonho himself, who said the bishop's Official had charged all chaplains to tell their parishioners that if anyone had stolen those two silver chains they were to give them back on pain of excommunication: 'And when the time was well and truly up, Bernat gave them back.'

If Canac did not hand the jug in, Marques might do what Bergonho had done, and turn up at Canac's house with the

priest beside him; and there would be a public scandal if
Canac resisted. If he handed it in, he might lose it anyway.
Either he clung to it and got some legal reinforcement, or
he admitted it was not his.

But was he a thief like Camboulas, or was he not? To steal
was to take something that obviously belonged to someone
else: it was a clear crime and a clear sin. In the legends of
St Amans a criminal who had stolen an old woman's purse
with a few coins in it was suddenly confronted with the devil,
cloven-hooved and bristling, in the middle of a wine-shop;
he wept in repentance. On another occasion, three horsemen had robbed two small boys of the fish they had pulled
from the Aveyron; but the fish, when put in the pan, simply
grew fresher and fresher, pink-gilled and flopping, until the
horsemen confessed to St Amans, 'who whipped them
round their heads a bit with the hem of his cloak'. There
was a tale, too, of a man who stole honey from the hives in
the saint's garden and hid it in his house, only to find it
turned to tar. A stolen object brought no benefit to the
thief, but stickiness and trouble.

On the other hand, if a man took something he knew was
not his but that seemed to belong to no-one in particular
— a cap, say, lying in the street — this was not quite the
same as stealing. As Johan Capelier once said of taking a
spade left in a sand quarry down by the river, 'I knew it
wasn't mine, but I'd lost mine and I took this one home
because I didn't know whose it was.' Capelier was still fined
by the court; the authorities had found out who owned it.
But what if nobody had?

Other actions, which looked like stealing, might turn out
on closer inspection to be virtual acts of charity. This was
the case with Marques's next-door neighbour Bernard
Gasto, who had gone round to the house of his business
partner, Johan Andreas, to clear out his cupboards after his
death. Andreas was a City man, and he believed in saving;

he carried his money (from making shoes) back over the border every night, just as Gasc did when he was working on the Marques drain. By his death, he had amassed a tidy sum of money, 'over 60 gold pennies [ecus, florins and *agnos*], other gold coins and silver coins worth more than 50 livres', according to his lawyer, and had hidden them, Marques-style, in various cupboards and boxes in different parts of his house. Gasto called round, as he described it later,

on the day that Andreas died . . . and while I was there his widow gave me the key to one of the cupboards . . . where she said the money was. I opened the cupboard with her full permission and found a quantity of gold pennies and other smaller coins, black and white [that is, debased money with very little pure metal in it, and good money]. I don't remember how much money was there exactly. I took the money out of the cupboard to hand it to Favia so that she could take charge of it for the children, but she was in bed and didn't want to take it. She asked me to take it to my house in the Bourg and look after it . . . So I took the money and counted it out in the presence of several respectable men, though I can't remember at the moment how much there was. I put the money in a sack and had it sealed by Guilhem Castanhier, a merchant of the City; then, with the widow's permission, I took it to my house in the Bourg. Later . . . I took it back and entered it in an inventory of the property.

He added: '[Andreas] wasn't as rich as the charges make out.'

Gasto had been a shoemaker, and a good one. But the court got him all the same; he was accused of 'carrying the money under his cloak, furtively, like a robber'. He had the widow's permission two or three times over. He had had the money placed under seal, and made a record of it. There could be no better example of an incompetent and sick person being gently relieved of the burden of coping with money, relieved of it before she even had time to fret. Yet, as if none of this mattered, Gasto was arrested, and tried, and punished.

As Canac knew, the punishment that thieves received depended on what they had done. Smaller thefts carried only a fine, based very carefully on the value of the thing stolen: 2 sous for the candle-maker's coat, but 2 livres 13 sous 4 deniers for the mill-stone and the six-foot axle that Huc Paget somehow staggered away with from Molinau, down by the river. Sometimes lesser thefts called for more imaginative humiliations, as when a man and his son were punished for stealing grapes from one of those grassy, scrubby vineyards near Gascaria at night: the man was put in the count's pillory and his son tied on beside him, with a basket of grapes on his head and the purple juice dribbling down his face.

Yet some thefts carried the worst penalty of all. And every time Canac went to the fair with his cloth samples, or when he went on a business trip (for the western route through the fairground was the only easy way out of town), he would pass the place where this punishment occurred. Three trees had once grown not far from the fairground. By 1370 they were gone, replaced by a newish road, but the place was still named after them and retained something of their shadows. These had been old elms, creaking, busy with crows, and busy too with lawyers; everything about them had been contentious, from the ground they stood on (which was the City's) to the ownership of the branches that fell from them with every gust of wind (disputed between the chapter and the count, whose officers occasionally fiddled around marking every last twig with the count's insignia). The land right

up to these trees, and underneath them, was called Mas
de las Forcas, Gallows Farm, and was rented by Ramon de
Fontencha for three sestiers of oats, 20 sous, a quarter of
his grain crop and a hen, paid each year to the City consuls.

Just here, at the side of the road, a shepherd from the
wild high country had been burned for heresy; the flames
had claimed him as a conniver with the devil. And the
count had hanged people there, on the trees. It had not
happened often; most people, when asked, could remember
only two or three occasions. It hardly mattered. The point
was that the gallows had been 'near, indeed within sight of,
the bishop's and the canons' houses': thrust in their faces,
so to speak. ('But I don't think you can smell it from the
bishop's house,' said one count's man, cruelly.) Men had
been led out of the count's prison, across the Bourg square
and along this road, weighed down with chains or with the
thick rope already round their necks, with an officer striding
in front to shout a warning: 'See what justice is.' Sometimes
he made it plainer: 'If this is what you do, this is what you
get.'

By 1370 executions had moved a little farther outside
town, 'so that people can enjoy this place and not be disturbed by the bodies of the dead'; but mention of the Elms
would still have been enough to bring the subject to mind.
On the newer gallows, which were conifers — specially
planted to grow suitable branches, 15 feet from the ground,
in the shortest possible time — a woman called Galhardeta
had been strung up for killing one of her children, and a
man had been hanged for stealing chalices from the church
of the Franciscans. Everyone remembered Galhardeta:
dragged to the gallows at the tail of a horse, bumping down
the flagstones of Santa Martra with her long hair tangl-
ing behind her, and strung up like a man. The bodies of
the miscreants had stayed there, gradually falling into tat-
ters, and stinking when the wind blew. 'You could certainly

smell them from the fair', one witness said, 'if you got close enough.'

Generally, though, stealing was not a hanging offence, unless it was horse-stealing, or the theft of cloths left out drying overnight, or of cattle: the theft of a livelihood, in other words. In 1370 most such stealing was done by mercenaries — *coredors*, men who galloped through — who evaded capture under cover of darkness. But others sometimes tried. A man once robbed Dona Cambola's house at night, and fled town; a court officer and a sergeant chased him as far as Millau, forty miles to the south-east, and he was hanged for evasion and exhaustion of officers as much as anything else.

Yet the chalice-stealer had been hanged. There were special circumstances, of course, to that. He had broken into the church to take the cups, and they were evidently precious — and holy, because they had held Christ's blood. If only a little of that blood remained, he would have been stealing Christ. No crime was more enormous than that. Priests even had to get on their knees and lick the ground if they spilled a drop as they drank, because God was spilled there. Nothing could compare that theft with the theft of shoes, or money, or a coat; let alone, in Canac's view, with the careful stewardship of a jar of gold coins.

So court was the option that Canac decided, in the end, to take. He would go to law to defend his claim and would argue, with as many witnesses as he could muster, that he was the only competent custodian of the pewter jug of gold.

Going to law was fraught with risks, only one of which was the expense. Once lawyers got into a case, they milked it for all it was worth. It was little wonder that the consuls sometimes begged for matters to be settled out of court *sine strepitu judicorum*, without judges' prattle. Self-importance was the creed of the profession, and their appetite for words, paper and parchment was as keen as the count's for the hard-earned money of his subjects.

It is possible that Canac himself came from a family of lawyers; two Canacs, who were notaries, were living in the City in mid-century. That apart, the lawyer the family knew best — indeed, had known for fourteen years, according to his own estimate — was Helias Porret, one of whose handles was 'notary ordinary of the court of the Pariage', or the common court of Rodez. Porret seemed to have a weakness for titles, the more pedantic the better. He insisted, for example, on his 'Master', as not all notaries did; and even with his nickname he was still 'Master Heli', no-one daring to drop it.

Porret also liked obscure historical stories and little-known facts, and he and Marques, he said later, would exchange these by the dozen as they did their watch duty at night. Together they would clamber up the steep spiral stairs to patrol the blustery battlements or to huddle in the wooden *gachils* above the towers, watching their wax torches burn down: two most unlikely friends among the dozen men on the watch rota, the one meticulously organised, the other unable to get his life together.

The partition of Rodez did not bother men like Porret; it was bread in their mouths and money on the counter. When Porret sat in the common courthouse, in the count's ditch right on the border, he worked for either the Bourg or the City as the business came in, hunched amid his piles and bags and bundles of papers, drawing up deeds for the sale of leases on properties mortgaged for tax debts. As we have seen, the common court, with its officers, was almost the only step the town had made in the direction of power-sharing; and, even then, Rodez did not take to it whole-heartedly. The bishops and counts still kept all criminal justice for themselves separately, while the common court was left with the much less lucrative civil work and the tax cases; and Canac had got to know Porret fairly well over the years as the various bits of his father-in-law's property had been mortgaged, then redeemed, then mortgaged again.

Porret, it seemed, was seldom short of work. The court-house was always full of people waiting, in various degrees of irritation, to acknowledge debts or buy back pledges or complain about the actions of sergeants; while the sergeants themselves wandered in and out, swinging their official sticks, and the notaries laboriously scratched their pieces of paper. When the usufructs (or rights of use) of properties were sold, as Marques's were, Porret had to attend the auction and produce a full report, though 'without superfluous writings', for which he was paid 5 sous and no more, unless the parties requested a copy. For debt quittances (or for extensions, which ran for no more than a fortnight), Porret would take 6 deniers a time; and there were many, many times as far as Marques was concerned.

Yet all that was merely part of Porret's brief. He worked in the count's mansion, too, next door to the priory of St Amans; and then he was obliged to write his notes and keep his desk in the hall all day, 'from the end of the monks' Mass to the hour of communal lunch, and from after lunch until the time when court cases are heard'. The rhythm of his working day followed the sounds through the wall: the bells, the closing bars of plainchant, the scrape of benches across the floor, the clatter of horn spoons. And as he worked there, buffeted too by the shopkeepers coming to and fro and by the hammering of tilers on the roof, he liked to style himself 'notary for the inhabitants of the Bourg of Rodez by the authority of the count'. He may have made this title up; nobody else ever laid claim to it. And, not least, it took up room. Each parchment page (26 lines to the page, 84 letters to the line) was charged at 6 deniers, 'allowing for titles and reasonable abbreviations'. And Porret filled his pages; there was not a notary in Rodez who could be accused of leaving too much space.

It was Porret who had engrossed the instrument of repurchase of Marques's shop, at Canac's request, after Canac had married Guilhema. From this he had formed the opinion, like so many others, that the arrival of Canac had caused a sudden and radical improvement in Marques's fortunes. As Canac handled the cloth at the measuring table he would be able to see Porret labouring away, amassing those heaps of notes which he was forbidden to show to anyone except on his boss's orders, working in the thick sharp scent of candle grease and sealing wax; and between the two men there would have been a certain understanding, that they were managing the affairs of a man who was declining.

How much Porret made, Canac could not easily imagine. Certainly it was enough for him to farm the Chancery of the Count's Seal (that is, to collect the revenues for a fee) for two years, in 1378 and 1379, for 72 livres on each occasion. He lived with his wife Sebienda virtually next door to Marques, on the corner of the Plassa de l'Olmet next to St Amans, right by the apse of the church. This house, according to the county deed that Porret might have drafted himself, had a shop, workroom, upper chambers, living rooms, and (a sure sign of luxury) a courtyard with an entrance passage. It was a warren of a place; indeed, the Seguis were the original owners, and it was considered grand enough for the chaplain-major of St Amans when his own house fell down. Yet Porret did not even deal in trials and inquiries, which would require county lawyers of a still rarer and grander sort: men such as Huc Palhol, from the partitioned house, who could put *jurisperitus* or *discretus vir* (how Porret would have loved that!) after their names.

It was not merely expense, but time too, that seemed to

stretch out infinitely in the presence of lawyers. Rodez was a town which, because of its strange partitioned character, had spent more than fifty years engrossed in one lawsuit. Granted, it was not about a jug of gold in a drain, but about arson and murder; indeed, the case had been described as 'the worst and most execrable crime in the county of Toulouse and the province of Bordeaux since men can remember'. This was the case that had precipitated the royal commission, the Pariage and the common courthouse: the Great Riot at the fairground in June 1315. Few people remembered the year exactly; remembering years exactly was for men like Porret. But had you asked Canac, or even Marques, they could have answered 'about fifty years ago'; for it was the biggest thing that had happened in Rodez, and still the most contentious.

For reasons to do with pure territorial arrogance, the bishop's and the count's men had started fighting. People had been killed, and a house had been burned down. The riot, short enough in itself, had led to inquiries and the questioning of witnesses not merely over weeks, but over years. As memories faded, the testimony became more confused and more easily led by the opposing teams of lawyers; stories, invented in passing, took on a life of their own. To the extent that Rodez was still riven by mutual suspicions, each half still living back-to-back with its gates shut to the other side, it was largely the result of this endless litigation. The matter had not even been resolved by 1370; the parties were merely tired. But had Johan Gasc, from the City, been asked to give his version of the events of 1315, he would have done so with vehemence; and it would not have been the same as Canac's, from the Bourg. The wound was still fresh because it had been kept fresh by the lawyers who lived on it.

Porret and Canac knew the site of the fighting. Who did not? It was a street on the border called Santa Martra, at the western edge of town: undistinguished houses running down to the fairground, a dowdy little church, a monumental cross raised on three steps beside a pit where both sides dumped their rubbish, occasionally burying one of those 'large' markers that were meant to show where the border was. Marques had a garden here, a sad little plot which, true to form, he neglected completely. By 1370 it was lost under nettles and weeds. A fruit tree or two might poke out of it, bent by the wind, and a goat or two might be turned loose in it, browsing beard-deep; for it was fairly usual, in Santa Martra, for gardens and livestock to get mixed up. To Canac, passing by, the garden was yet another example of his father-in-law's simplicity, his laziness, his miserable goat-like bleating about his gold and silver. 'I lost my money, it was all the money I had, I put it under the ground, I don't remember where, I was young then . . . '

Not so far from the hummocky site of the hanging-trees, not so far from Marques's garden, a house stood at the start of the paved road that led into town. It was in ruins, with the charred rafters still poking into the sky. This was the house that had been burned in the riot of 1315 and still stood, barely, waiting for the lawyers to finish their arguments. Its history still screamed from it: the story everyone in Rodez knew, but few people knew in the same way; the story that kept the town divided. It was a cautionary tale for anyone about to get caught up with the law.

The house had been solid and large. It was also fairly new, for witnesses could remember another house on the spot, where the count's officers had once nailed a man's ear and hand to the door. There was space enough in the new house for three families, the Randaynes, the Contets and the Montes, although they did not live in style. 'Simple country folk' was how the court records described them, and may have been how they described themselves. The house was not theirs; they rented it from the cathedral chapter. The Randaynes menfolk (a bit richer than the rest, since they paid 40 sous a year for their part of the house) were butchers. By day they worked in the City *mazel*, the butchers' quarter; each evening they arrived home with their bloody aprons. In 1315 they were to witness blood of a different sort.

The house stood by the fairground. The fairs, of course, were mostly the count's show, but both count and bishop policed them. The families in this house, therefore, were used to seeing officers about, and they obeyed them all — for a quiet life – without discrimination. Duran Montes explained that he had grown used to patrols in the street, which were sometimes from the City and sometimes from the Bourg. He recognised the sergeants by their faces and did not need to check the armorial bearings on their staves. Either patrol had a right to tell him what to do.

As it happened, the bishop's men usually called in on the eve of the fairs to tell Montes not to obey the count's officers 'in respect of anything concerning the house while the fairs are on'. They would go down the street with the same message, banging on all the doors. When the fairs began, Montes said, he obeyed the count's officers if he met them in the street; the street was within their jurisdiction. But the house was not. The count's officers had turned up at his door once, with a bleating herd of sheep and goats they had rounded up at the fair and wanted to put in a safe place for a bit; Montes, obedient to his orders, would not let them in.

For several years, this diplomatic approach worked perfectly. Then, on the feast of Saints Peter and Paul in 1315 — a Sunday that year as well as a fair day, with most people off work — a group of episcopal officers holed up in the house, apparently expecting trouble. It started that afternoon, and the opening incident was later described by Duran Montes's small daughter, Helis, who happened to be watching from the window.

> I saw a Gascon called Perri and another called lo Roch ['Red'], coming to the fair with a lot of other armed men, mounted and on foot. They came down Santa Martra, looking round and up and down all the time, until they reached the house, the one that was burned afterwards. I was in the house, living there with Duran Montes who is my father. A little while after that Perri came to the door and shouted 'Open up! Open up!' I went to the window and told him I hadn't got the keys, and then he said in Gascon, 'Open up, because if you don't you'll see some nasty things happen to your little house here.' And soon afterwards, when I had asked the other people in the house whether I should open the door, I saw that Perri and lo Roch had come in, and I was frightened and ran away and hid in a well inside the house.

What was going on? Here was a group of strangers in a town where men from outside did not cast off their foreignness for years: a band of 'Gascons', a word which carried the same connotations in the early years of the century as 'English' carried in Porret's time, murderers and marauders; yet a small girl at a window knew their names and understood what they said to her, 'in Gascon'. Was there any truth to her story, or had the lawyers just produced Helis for her pathos, the child who hadn't got the keys, running away?

The answer was a mixture of both. Helis's 'Gascons' seemed to be a small contingent of the real article, raised by the Count of Armagnac to fight the king's wars in Flanders. They appeared to be under the temporary command of Guilhem de Moncado, a county officer; and they joined up quite naturally with the count's routine fairground patrol, including Perri and lo Roch, who, despite their mercenary-gangster names, were ordinary Bourg sergeants.

Somehow, the bishop's men had got wind of this curious alliance. They decided to place a small force of sergeants somewhere near the fairground to defend the bishop's rights, if it came to that. As it happened, they chose to put themselves upstairs in Duran Montes's house. When the motley crew of armed troops passed along Santa Martra, just inside the bishop's jurisdiction, the episcopal sergeants in Montes's house appeared to panic and began to stone the troops. The soldiers replied by attacking and eventually firing the house.

About fourteen people were said to have died; most of them innocent fairgoers who, caught in the crowded street, simply got in the way. The death-toll, though much disputed, transformed the incident into a political crisis. Two months later, in August, royal commissioners were sent to sort out Rodez and to propose a most radical solution to the fighting and killing. There was to be a 'pariage', a fashionable idea which, in 1370, was still struggling to unsatisfactory life: without unifying the town, the lords were to pool and share their power in the interests of peace.

But this was not the question that obsessed the lords of Rodez or their lawyers. Peace was boilerplate, something everyone naturally supported. The lawyers wanted to know which side had started the fighting and who was to blame. Whoever was innocent ought to profit by power-sharing; whoever was guilty ought to lose. So the count's men played down the rioting, or attributed it to the bishop's stow-away officers, plotting and conniving; the bishop's men sought to inflate the incident into tragedy, massacre and conspiracy. Caught between the two, most of the witnesses ended up merely embroidering one official version or the other.

Official reports by the bishop's lawyers presumed that every member of the fairground patrol, which they did not distinguish from the troops passing through, had a mind to do wrong that day. They had ridden into town under the count's snapping banners, hollering 'Armagnac, Armagnac!' and had profaned the monumental cross, 'built in honour of Christ Crucified and of Our Blessed Lady his mother'. They had driven animals into the cramped Santa Martra gardens, where grain and vegetables were growing, ruining the crops and distressing the tenants; and had burned down the Montes house, disregarding private property. They had attacked the 'simple, peaceful men of good reputation' who lived in the house. And lastly (the lawyers really working here) they had gone back that evening to ride their horses over the wounded in the street and to loot the bodies of the dead until neighbours, out of compassion, had carried them away.

Such heartbreaking stuff was a far cry from the arguments of the count's lawyers, all wide-eyed innocence and mystification. 'Is it normal for the count's men to guard the fairs with mounted and foot soldiers? Do they normally start fires? Was anyone really robbed and, if so, what was taken? Did anyone from the City try to stop it?'

This barrage of conflicting propaganda was not all the witnesses had to contend with. The story was already set, had become news. It was hard to sort out what people heard later from what they discerned at the time. Thus Helis Montes called Perri and lo Roch 'Gascons' even though they were Bourg sergeants, and she knew them, as her father did; and thus, she maintained, they must have been speaking Gascon, since Gascons was what they were. Helis 'knew' they were Gascon because, when she gave her testimony several weeks after the event, that was how the story went. The lawyers did not question the breathless circularity of this little girl's logic; they let her talk, the talk of a child excited by monsters and scraps of grown-up conversation, and left it at that.

Two months, in fact, had gone by. The royal commission, as is the nature of commissions, had been slow to get going. Memories had faded; myths had taken their place; apocryphal conversations had become real. The riot was hard to pin down in any case. It had flared up without warning as people went about their business, and nobody had quite seen the start of it. Indeed, at that distance from the events, few people could give proofs of guilt in any conclusive way. Most gave their evidence in terms of odd things, half-noticed at the time, which assumed a rational shape only under the prodding of the lawyers.

The earliest signs of trouble were reported by Catorna Randaynes and Berengar Contet, residents of the house in Santa Martra. In the middle of the night of June 28th Catorna saw armed episcopal sergeants in the building, who made her swear to keep 'a number of matters' quiet. This seemed odd to her, as it did to her husband Johan. 'I never saw armed men shut up in the house except once,' he said, his son Peyre nodding in agreement; 'there's no other house near the fairground where you could attack the men guarding the fairs like that.' Contet remembered that the armed men had made a hole in one of the inside walls of the house, on the vicar's orders, so they said. Bernard del Cros, who had been inside the house, had opened the door to them, but he had not seen anyone leave. The rest of the household seem to have settled uneasily to sleep, with the bishop's men squatting amidships.

To these witnesses there was a plot brewing, and its source was in the City. Their evidence was confirmed by another citizen, Father Berengar Charay, whose living was the little church of Santa Martra among the rubbish heaps. 'On the day of the riot', he remembered, 'at about the hour of prime [that is, very early in the morning], Bec de Limayrac warned me secretly that that Sunday, which was the day the riot happened, I ought to close the building so that no-one could get into it and take refuge there. It's always my custom to keep the church open for anyone who wants to come in during the fairs, as at other times. So I did what he asked, and kept it closed. And it appears from that that the attack was premeditated.'

Certainly all the clues pointed that way. But what if the episcopal forces had been trying to defend the City, because the premeditated attack had come from the other side? Most of the bishop's witnesses claimed to have sensed, as soon as the count's soldiers entered town, an aggressive jostling and hustling that made them uneasy. Huc Sandral described the men coming along Santa Martra 'armed with lances and steel helmets ... with blaring trumpets going before them, and a jester beating on a drum.' The Bourg sergeants seemed to have picked up armour too: lo Roch had a crossbow with bolts, while Perri had his bottom half hung with pieces of plate; and though they were a thin force for an army, 'up to 13 men on horseback and 15 on foot', they were altogether too many for a routine fairground patrol. Other witnesses noticed merely that the men were armed, which was threat enough; and we have heard Helis Montes mention how they swivelled their heads and raised their eyes towards the house, as though they had marked it out already and went there with a purpose.

Several witnesses remembered Perri and lo Roch approaching the house, lo Roch with his crossbow levelled; Perri seized the latch and shook the door, shouting that they wanted to come in. (Nobody related any answer: Helis's little voice did not carry far.) Within seconds, however, the fighting was so fierce that few could put any order in it. Most of the missiles were squarish big cobblestones torn out of the *carrieyra* Santa Martra, one of the town's few paved streets. The allocation of blame hinged on the throwing of those stones, whether up to a window or down into the road. Huc Sandral, 'Witness 14', had to admit that his careful recollection of events gave out there: 'I saw a stone come down next to Perri as he was shouting, and I think it came from above him, but I didn't see it.' He added, diplomatically, 'I didn't see which side started it.'

But who started it, of course, was crucial. Here the Bourg produced a star witness, Guilhem Caissac, whose sense of the train of events was perfect. Caissac had first seen Moncado and his men asking to be shown the boundaries of the fair, 'saying that he didn't wish to occupy any part of the bishop's jurisdiction'. Moncado's exemplary behaviour went on from there:

> He also made some people come down from the steps of the cross, the one near the fair, saying they were acting in prejudice of the bishop. Before I saw any fighting I heard the cathedral bell striking, the big bell, and the people who were shut up in the house attacked others and threw stones and cobbles at them ... they wounded one of the horses belonging to Moncado's men, and Moncado shouted many times to the men in the house that they should stop throwing stones and disturbing the fair; and that they should come down, because he would take them to the bishop in safety and protect them from harm. Then they threw stones all the harder, before the others threw any and before the house was entered or attacked ...
>
> The people in the house started the trouble. I know this because they started throwing stones, and if they hadn't done this nothing would have happened. Everyone in the Bourg says they were to blame.

And everyone did. Caissac spoke with such authority that the string of Bourg witnesses behind him were content to say they agreed with him, and leave it at that. Presented with this damning evidence, the City lawyers were reduced to scratching fierce remarks in the margins when the record was written up later. At the point where Caissac said he agreed with a number of assertions laid out by the count's lawyer, the marginalium appeared: 'Well, I'd be surprised if he agreed with what the other side says.'

Whoever started the trouble, the house was quickly on fire. Sandral once again didn't quite see how: he heard two of the Gascons shouting 'Fire!', *A fuoc!*, then the house roaring up, 'but not because any fire was sent in there'. At that point, he ran away. Indeed, in the terror and confusion most witnesses thought simply of saving their own skins. To add to the panic, bells began to ring in the City. Everyone remembered this: the deep note of the bell that citizens called 'Marsal', but that to burgenses like Caissac was just the cathedral's big bell, tolling above the racket. Marsal's note was distinctive, at least to City ears, because it was rung 'to make the earth fruitful' after the Ave Maria between May and September; and also, by a strange reversal of thought, to give warning of fire or invasion.

Like the precise throwing of stones, it mattered terribly when the bell had sounded. And probably few could remember, exactly; but they tried to be obliging to the lawyers for their side. Sandral, the citizen, had heard Marsal ringing just before he ran away, and thought it was because of the fighting. Caissac said he had heard the bell as a signal before the stones were thrown from the house, and again everyone lined up behind him. Astruc de Monmato made the point with both weight and topographical inexactitude: 'Before the house was entered the great bell chimed in the monastery of Our Lady.' There was no monastery in the City; but on the other side of the divide, as on the moon, people did / not know that.

Peyre de Veyrac, the principal witness to the 'killing', had counted ten or eleven men killed in Santa Martra. Guilhem Robert saw two people killed there and one, whom he recognised, cut down at the door of the besieged house. These were all assumed to be bishop's men, largely because they had happened to be in a City street. The highest estimate from the bishop's lawyers was 'fourteen or sixteen, besides those killed in the fire'. But no list of the dead was ever produced; none, apart from 'B. Johan's nephew', was ever named; and the 'great murder' seemed a curiously bloodless affair, more vivid in the minds of the lawyers than to those who were supposed to have seen it. Nobody on the Bourg side (almost needless to say) saw anyone killed at all. At most, Monmato saw 'many Gascons' wounded, but Gascons, being half-mythical, did not count.

By the time of the testimonies, some dramatic and pitiful embroideries had been invented. Some were possibly true, but few have that feel about them; they were growing in the telling. Huc Viguier remembered seeing a soldier of the count's party, on a white horse, cutting down one of the bishop's men; having come out of the Bourg to do so, the soldier and his colleagues retreated there like cowards when they were done, and the next day ventured out again in their armour. Guilhem Deodat, from the Bourg, knew where they had stayed that night. He had seen them in Guiral de Scoralha's house, which was lit up as if for callous merry-making, the windows yellow and flickering with a blaze of candles; and in Guilhem Massabuou's hotel, where he heard one of the Gascons promising to pay as he left.

Deodat Sampso of the City, who could not have seen or heard any of those things, took the testimony further; after the 'murders' the Gascons had gone into the Bourg, showing their bloodstained lances and boasting of what they had done, in the presence of the count's officers. That story in turn was capped by Guilhema Bozesa, a nursing sister from the Peace Hospital. She had heard 'one of the criminals . . .

boasting that he had hit seven of the bishop's men with his bloody lances'. She added: 'And I heard D. Rossinhol [a prominent burgensis, not previously implicated] saying to someone walking with him, "And you know, we could have got half the City before anyone would have recognised us."'

The fact that the Gascons had stayed in the Bourg after the rioting — and hotelier Massabuou admitted it candidly to the bishop's lawyers, speaking of them as of any ordinary customers, calling their crimes 'alleged' — brought the whole Bourg under suspicion. These people, the bishop's lawyers concluded, were walking around openly and were not arrested, even though everyone knew what they had done. Worse, some burgenses took them in, let them share bread and meat at their tables, and listened as they described, 'gesturing with their hands and eyes and faces', how many bishop's men they had killed. Some of them wore the count's livery, and seemed to enjoy his favour even after the event: men such as Guilhem de Moncado, the apparent ringleader of the troublemakers, who was seen by one witness 'eating and drinking in the count's house in the count's presence'.

So the Bourg tolerated criminals, and made them welcome; and that bad reputation was harped on as the iniquities multiplied. Neither side had much belief in the theory of a *callida mellaya*, a hot brawl, for which no party could ultimately be blamed. Indeed, the Bourg lawyer admitted that the count had apologised to the bishop; and noted, hurt, 'that the other side says this doesn't imply forgiveness.' ('Well said!' came a smug marginalium from the bishop's lawyer: 'There's no forgiveness because it can't be forgiven.')

In any case, something deeper was involved here. Plottings, flaws of character, bad habits established over time added up to that amorphous thing called *fama*: a reputation everyone gossiped about and agreed on and which could not be thrown off. '*Es fama*', was what the folk of Rodez said whenever they were asked how they knew something to be true: 'it's obvious', 'everyone says it', 'everyone knows that'. And everyone in the City knew about the sins of the worse side of town. The very heart of the Bourg, with its jugglers and hucksters and low women — the place where Porret and Canac lived — showed its true nature. By 1370 the Bourg had still not shed that reputation for callous bad behaviour: a reputation earned in a night, like thieving.

Now Canac's reputation too was in the balance. A lawsuit would lay him open to much the same lapses of memory, embroideries and calumnies that had coloured the riot inquiry. Of course, in his case there would be no partisan politics or lordly honour simmering behind it; but there would still be petty jealousies, commercial rivalries, pieces of unsubstantiated gossip. By the time his neighbours and colleagues had finished their rummaging through the details of his life, they might even make a thoroughgoing criminal of him.

But Canac may also have grasped something else, a point underlined by the ruins of that burnt-out house in Santa Martra. The house was meant to have been rebuilt, and the victims rehoused in it, once blame for the fire was established. Chaplaincies were going to be set up to pray for the souls of the dead. The tenants were going to get compensation; Johan Randaynes reckoned he had lost 60 livres' worth of goods, 'besides half the house, which is rented, and I don't know how to estimate that'. But the Bourg never admitted responsibility and never accepted the City's charges. By 1370 the use of the Randaynes properties in Santa Martra — a jumble of houses, yards and gardens right beside the burned house — had been sold to cover Peyre Randaynes's debts; and Peyre himself, in a strange twist of fate, was said to have attempted an act of arson against the house of a neighbour.

It was a familiar story. Once a case was put in the hands of lawyers, there were no quick winners. The litigation might easily drag on for years. There might be no way of proving the truth one way or the other. But the money in the jug, meanwhile, would be spent by the man who had first shown the enterprise to grab it, as Canac all his working life had shown such enterprise; and to Marques would go, if he insisted, the empty vessel, like the burnt-out house, as the sign of an argument that had already been won.

5

Peyre Marques
and the will to succeed

BACK AT THE SHOP, Gasc and Barbier were still working. The drain was cleared out, but there was no going home; they were now excavating the floor. All through the morning, fretfully, obsessively, Marques and his wife came in and urged them on. 'Fellows,' he said, '*companhos*, when you're clearing that drain out, and doing all the other things, be really careful, because there must be a lot of other gold money round here in two or three places, that's to say, in a little copper bowl in one place, and in a pewter pot somewhere else, and in other containers... by your faith, fellows, be terribly careful and look hard, because I promise you you'll be really well rewarded if you find anything.'

The *companhos* was a bit overdone, and Alumbors went further. Standing at the top of the shop steps, pleading with them 'for the love of God' to look really hard, she called them 'senhors': the title for consuls and gentlemen of quality, applied to two workmen covered with mud and sweat and filth, delvers in darkness.

Both husband and wife seem scarcely to have left the scene, transfixed by the thought that more money might turn up. 'We trust you, Johan Gasc', they told him again and again. 'We really do, much more than anyone else who's here; please give us your word that you'll look really carefully.' They called him *tu*, in a familiar way; but then they also used his full name, because they did not know him. That rang a bit false; and besides, there were no more crocks of gold.

Marques could not understand it. He knew he had hidden at least two pots of money. Perhaps there had even been more than that. He remembered exactly what the vessels looked like, the copper sheen of one, the dull pewter of the other; he remembered scraping the earth away, and how deep the hole had been to hide them. His memory might be fading in some ways, but in others it was sharp enough, as his tenants said. He had had gold to save, and hide, in the old days. What had happened in his life since then to make him so confused, so hesitant and so unlucky?

He had not always cut such a sad figure. His family had been a good one, harness-makers and cloth-merchants in a town that made a living by cloth and livestock-trading. His father had died rich and honoured, called 'En Marques', or 'the worthy', even in the City, and Marques had inherited his house in Bal, the smartest part of the Bourg, which was rated at a high 12 deniers for tax in 1351.

As a teenager, Peyre was apprenticed to his uncle Bartelemi to learn the rules of the cloth trade. He lived in his house with him, ate at his table, was given clothes, shoes and a small wage, and was worked as hard as he could stand. Business was good. *Ton-ton* Marques dealt not only in the poor burrels and flecked weaves that Rodez produced, but in cloth from as far as Flanders, brought down by pack-horse for the few in the town who could afford it. His own house in Bal was rated at 18 deniers for tax in 1361, when Jorda Segui's was rated at 2 deniers. He had twice been consul; when he married off his daughter to Johan Balsac, in 1347, the Bourg consuls sent a present of twelve hens and wine. The next year, Balsac was a consul himself.

Yet the story was not one of seamless success. Those who believed that Marques's business sense was fashioned by his uncle, for good or bad, could point to ups and downs in Bartelemi's fortunes too. For much of the 1340s his taxes were in arrears. He had bought a ground rent from Bernard del Cros (of the burnt-out house in Santa Martra), for which he seemed disinclined to pay: 'Show him the deed and prove he's bought it,' the treasurer snapped. In 1346 he was one of only two Bourg defaulters. But the next year he lent the consuls 72 sous, and was plainly restored to favour with them. The lesson, if there was one there for Peyre, was rather inconclusive.

After his apprenticeship Peyre continued to do well, but bad luck began to show itself. His uncle died, and he was left the care of three sickly cousins whose taxes he had to pay. The eldest, luckily, was sent off to become a monk in a place a relative called 'Dorssans', in England. The two who remained, Guilhem and Helena, were dead by 1363; but until then Peyre was paying large amounts on their behalf (26 sous 3 deniers for a town loan in 1351, 11 florins 8 gros for the loan of 1362, and all the routine taxes in between). He got no thanks for this: Guilhem and Helena left their goods to Ramon de Carlat, 'a wise and most industrious man' who was minting money from building the Bourg walls, and not to Marques.

Marques, not yet as lackadaisical as he later became, contested the will and got Helena's share. He moved shortly afterwards to his uncle's old house in the Plassa de l'Olmet and bought lands outside town. He had already married

Alumbors Rostanh, from a prosperous City family. His neighbours remembered these fat times; they saw wheat and wine
barrels stacked in his house, the rents from his country
properties in the wooded hills round Sévérac and Salles-
Comtaux. His friend Alamanda Fromenta (who said in court
that she had known him for twenty-eight years) remembered
huge quantities of oats there. Marques was in the right trade,
in the right street, married to the right (if shrewish) woman;
he had begun to prosper.

Yet others were always doing better; and among those
others were his next-door neighbours. The Seguis, whose
basement he had now flooded, were doing particularly well.
They were rich, influential and politically active. Their house
contained numbers of workshops and upper rooms, and a
courtyard with a covered passage opening on to the Plassa
de l'Olmet. At least six of the menfolk had been consuls by
the time of the drain incident, and Duran Segui, husband
of Dona Seguina who currently ran the shop, had sat on the
innermost advisory board to the consuls, the secret council.

For a short time, around the late 1350s when his affairs
were going well, Marques too seemed to take some interest
in politics. His name appears on a list of 118 people
(including Johan Sedassier, our reporter on the vivid low
life in the square) who gathered to regulate the election of
Bourg consuls in 1358. But this was a particularly large
meeting, its sheer size suggesting that people had been
summoned off the street. Most town business was conducted
in general council meetings, smaller gatherings of the committed or chronically disaffected, at which the Seguis
starred.

The subject of these meetings was usually tax rates; the
verb *sen rancurar*, to complain (with a hint of aggrieved
muttering up the sleeve), encapsulated most of the action.
At one such meeting, Deodat Segui and two neighbours
spoke out so forcefully against a particular tax, in which

individuals were supposed publicly to assess themselves for
what they could manage, that one of the three was asked to
make a public apology for *paraulas odiozas* to the consuls.
But at least the Seguis said their piece, and tried to deter-
mine how the town spent their money; at least they did
not pose, like Marques and even Canac, as victims of their
government.

As consuls, the Seguis were the town's élite. These were
the oligarchs, the men who really governed; as indeed, consuls administered most larger towns in Languedoc in those
days. The City had four consuls, the Bourg between four
and six, depending on how many could prove themselves
fit for the post; both sets were elected annually in November.
Over the century, the consulate shifted among ninety-three
Bourg families and ninety-six City ones. The Bourg secret
council, with an average of six members advising the consuls, was staffed by twenty-five families over twenty-three
years.

A man was thought fit for the consulate when his house
was rated for tax at more than 4 deniers, where each denier
represented 50 livres' worth of property. Houses worth 200
livres or more were to be found only at the centre of town,
not down the slope or among the allotments; so the consuls
came, in the Bourg, from Bal and Pas near the main square,
and in the City from Sant Stefe and Carrieyra Nova, the new
grand (paved) street. Marques's house, with its old tax-rating
of 18 deniers, was exactly in consular territory; but the
title of consul, unlike the property tax or assessments for
the corn charity, did not go with the building. It went with
the man.

One consul from each set, City and Bourg, was supposed
to be a knight. No more were necessary, and often none
was found. Most consuls were grocers, cloth-merchants or
lawyers; some were the higher sort of artisan. Two men who
fell just short of the standard in 1355 — they were made

deputies, but not consuls — show where the subtle class distinctions lay. Both were rich, capable and in the food trade. But Peyre Bru was a tavern-keeper just outside town, where he entertained such rowdy customers as 'the cow-herds of Faet' at a safe distance, while Huc Ferrand provided meals for the men who worked on the new walls. Both were slightly grubby.

The consuls of both sides of town agreed on one thing: they knew their standing, and made sure others would. Their title was *honorables, savis et discretz senhors*, honourable, wise and discreet. The virtue of the community was heavy upon them, together with the parti-coloured robes of *mesclat de Melines*, trimmed with fur, and the fur-trimmed doublets, and the hats they were obliged to wear at meetings. Many of these robes cost as much as a house in the poorer parts of town, and the old-boy network of clothier-consuls kept their successors supplied with bolts of the newest stuff from Flanders, lovingly fingered and inspected. Johan Manha was one of these clothier-consuls, robed and distinguished (as del Cayro remembered him), even to look at a drain. As for the Seguis, they served officials from both sides in their shop, and this trade drew other, grander customers, including the counts. (Jorda Segui in the 1360s even extended his range of stock to account ledgers, sealing wax and, as a special order, a set of Gospels.) For the Marques family, any dispute with these well-known, competent people was an embarrassment; a blocked drain was humiliation.

In each community the consuls had a meeting house, the *mayo cominal*, which functioned as a combination club, town hall and lumber room. The Bourg house had once belonged to a priest of means; it stood just beside the cemetery of St Amans, with a new bell-tower especially erected to call the élite to discussions. In this house the consuls met every Thursday evening, after dinner, to discuss business. They were enjoined, once again, to wear their hats, as was required for all public business and on all public occasions. If privacy were needed, the windows were hung with linen curtains provided by one of Marques's neighbours, Peyre Bolas, who also made winding-sheets for the dead.

There was a certain mystique about the meeting house, and a sense of deserved luxury. During sessions to allocate taxation visitors were given spiced wine, precious as fine brandy now; it came from a well-stocked cellar, and the Bourg's arms were painted on the kegs. Often, as they drank, the consuls would have a semi-official exchange of gifts: yet more wine, or spices to spike it with, or packages of nougat-like sweets. The City house, which in 1370 was newly acquired and grand, had an arcade of ground-floor shops rented out to favoured people and, at the back, a paved courtyard and garden, with seats set out under fruit trees. The dining-room table was so huge that it had to be cut in half when the consuls moved to their new quarters. Straw was ordered by the ass-load (at 12 deniers a time) to keep mud off the floors and to warm the consular feet during long winter sessions. Stems of that straw found their way into the registers, together with feathers and flies.

The meeting house was also the stage-set for lockings-in of tax assessors, who had to check all the accounts each year most carefully on oath, and who were not allowed out until they had finished. This was not the purgatory it sounded. Paper and candles were laid in in quantity, and food and drink were brought across the courtyard from the kitchen: bread, wine, veal, pork, chicken, tripes, pâté, eggs, codfish, cabbages, leeks, rice, fruit and nuts, with the bread hot, because it had been baked on site. Aromas of sauces and crusts and roasting meat must have drifted into many a deliberation, setting the taste-buds watering.

Those on the outside looking in, as Marques did, viewed these goings-on with some disgruntlement. We can see, from the records of those general council meetings which Deodat

Segui attended and Marques did not, that democratic con-
sultation was a nebulous idea in the minds of the men of
Rodez. Those ringing phrases, *voluntat del poble* and *auctoritat
del comu*, were based on some pretty thin numbers. In the
Bourg, between 1370 and 1400, an average of thirty-seven
householders (out of a possible 500-600) attended each
council meeting. In the City in 1376, a meeting to discuss
the Duke of Anjou's 12-denier food tax was open to all
heads of households; fifty-seven turned up, of whom thirty-
four had either held office or had helped in some other
way, with money or materials, towards the war effort. In the
Bourg, at the end of the century, two meetings had to be
reconvened for lack of interest.

As the City consuls noticed at one point, the same men
who disliked coming to meetings also tended not to show
up for watch and sentry duty; but we know, at least, that
Marques pulled his weight in that department. And it may
be significant, given the failings of his character, that he was
given no chance to debate that; his name was down on a
list, and he had no choice.

Just occasionally, the unrepresented and inattentive spoke
their minds. From the 1350s onwards the Bourg wanted to
build a new meeting house in the square, and a selection
of people, Marques's and Segui's neighbours, none of them
anything in government, were asked what they thought of
the idea. They were unexcited. 'I want the house to be built
if it's going to be useful to the community and to everyone,
and otherwise not.' 'I don't care much either way.' 'I don't
expect the building to do me much good personally, and
I'm a bit doubtful about it altogether.' One voice makes us
sit up, the voice of a man against the grain of partition: 'I
think the house would be useful in the Bourg, and it would
be equally useful in the City.' But the typical respondent
did not think so far. 'If it isn't built it won't do me much
harm, and if it is built it won't do me much good.' The

scepticism about big projects, the suspicion of privilege, the tight-fistedness, the bluntness of tone, were typical. So too was the fatalism, which had come to wash over Marques like a river.

The signs of his decline appeared quickly. He began to lease his house extensively, then his shop, to meet his taxes. The shop stayed let for nine years to Peyre Valeta, the count's treasurer, who ran the mint-house and dealt daily — almost carelessly — with quantities of the small, light coin that Marques found it so hard to hang on to. In the rest of the house, some of the tenants never left.

For a while Marques's fortunes improved a little, or so the neighbours thought, with Canac's marriage to Guilhema. But in the late 1360s taxes soared in the Bourg, until they were soaking up as much as three-quarters of a man's wages. Marques borrowed to pay them, and then could not pay the debts back, at which his creditors would ask the parish priest to excommunicate him. This was a fairly routine rebuke (one neighbour was excommunicated over a shipment of faulty nails), but it was damaging, nonetheless. And the borrowing was not enough; in the end, Marques began to sell his landed estates. In the process, carelessly, he 'sold' some he had never owned. This was the last straw. A City priest, Ramon Griffe, was appointed to manage his property for him and obviously, in some sense (as notary Porret put it), to keep an eye on the man as well. Such was Marques's situation when the case of the coins came up.

By now, Marques was established as a bad manager. This reputation placed him as far as possible from the élite circles of the town. Although the consuls could seem spendthrift, they were picked precisely for their skill at handling money, as illustrated in their own businesses; and they were expected to run the town with the same responsibility and frugality. Frugality, as Marques had learned, was a virtue much admired. People in government checked on things, especially the spending of money; they made lists; they threw nothing away. In 1355, for example, someone went round the City meeting house and made an inventory of stock:

—4 cupboards with keys, in which the town archives are kept
—6 chests, as many large as small
—another small chest, in which are some of the charters.
—one table [covered with cloth, and sporting a large inkwell and a pen-sharpener on a chain]
—three benches
—one bench studded with nails, behind the table.
—one metal arm from the big scales
—4 brass bucklers
—one metal helmet
—20 good crossbows, one broken (that happened when the sergeants were sent to Villefranche), some with a wheel-lock, and one with a reverse lock.
—And there are some damaged ones too, which are not mentioned in the account because they aren't worth anything.

The inventory ran on and on. Seals, pikes, breastplates, crossbow bolts, odd bits of armour, all kinds of weights and measures, 10,000 pike handles 'bought by the consuls this year', metal cones for lighting torches, 'a piece of lead which someone found', and 150 hemp slings provided by Sen. Duran Ayceli. 'And', the stock-taker concluded, 'this doesn't include the weapons that were lent out to people at the time of the scare: that's all written down in the tax book.' It was small wonder that, from the equally untidy house in the Bourg, a furious note appeared: 'Item, we couldn't find the keys of the box in which we had the documents about what the town had to pay [in royal taxes]. Paid, for three keys for the box, and for getting the locks taken off, and for making locks that were different, and other irritations.'

In the way of petty officials everywhere, there was always someone whose life's purpose seemed to be to keep an eye on these things. An entry in the City accounts for December 14th 1368 mentioned a payment of 6 sous 6 deniers to Master Johan Tomas for four spades for the work on the ditches. Treasurer Huc Bocart added a curt marginalium: 'Where are they?' The next July, Ramon Palhargues was put down for 18 sous for an arquebus. 'Where is it?' asked the treasurer's sharp, inquiring pen. When the accounts noted that Huc de Peyrasmortas was owed '4 florins 6 gros for wood and stones since the time of the worthy P. Vigorous and W. Carbonel', Bocart snapped 'Prove it!' Digging round in the glorious junk-room that was the meeting house, he also found important documents being badly treated. 'Gentlemen,' read his final comment, 'remember to cover the charter about the meeting house!' A comment dated five years later followed up, a touch sheepishly: '1st Sept. 1374. I paid for everything, and the charter about the house was bound, and I paid $3\frac{1}{2}$ florins. R. Boysonnada, treasurer.'

When Boysonnada said he had paid, he did not mean from some stock of money kept in one of those six chests, 'as many large as small'; he meant from his own pocket. The idea of personal responsibility and, if necessary, personal spending for the common good was strongly impressed. Officers were made to feel that their conduct mattered, that misconduct hurt, and that their own substance and the community's were bound together as if by ties of blood. This deep investment provided another reason, if affection for the lord was lacking, to keep partisan spirit alive and burning.

In 1358 Johan Marques, probably Peyre's brother, made

a bid for the farm of the Bourg weights; he was told to administer them as if the revenue were his own, *se era sieu lo emolumen*. Forty years later the City's estimator, Daurde Cabiscol, was given six quires of paper stitched with red thread to make a tax survey, with the warning that he would pay all taxes owing if he left anything out or failed to register anyone. Perhaps the most poignant statement of this sort was made in 1375 by Peyre Payra, a man who had seen three consuls die in office the previous year from the plague; and a man who, as a baker, was possibly a little under-qualified for the treasurer's job. 'I tell you all, honourable consuls . . . that if I've made any mistake, or forgotten to write anything, out of negligence, in receipts or outgoings, I'll correct it and set it right and clarify it, and make the amounts smaller or bigger, and I'll do it once, or twice, or many times, as right and truth direct.'

Fiscal probity was complicated by the fact that the consuls found themselves dealing with every kind of money. Livres, sous and deniers of Rodez; livres, sous and deniers *tournois* (of better metal and more reliable); francs, florins, ecus, marks, *agnos, patatas, mealhas, paipalholas, volantes, bandegnos*, and 'pennies' (so called) from all over the place. Some were of good metal, some bad wartime issue; some were 'white', some 'black'; the king's effigy was sometimes a proof of sound money, sometimes of nothing at all. But once the alloy had passed muster the coin was usually accepted, and its rate of exchange against others was roughly worked out later. Indeed, even counterfeit money, seized in boxes from the forgers' tables, usually contained just enough good metal to be 'put to the use of the lords of Rodez and their treasurers'; and when kings or princes, English or French, offered to establish a strong coinage in return for more taxes, the men of Rodez usually decided that they could live without one.

None the less, money lost over currency transactions (as

when the City lost 1 livre 10 sous on the money it borrowed to buy the new meeting house in 1369) seems to have caused poor Bocart actual pain. 'Lesser-weight gold, chiselled off, false,' he howled in his accounts. His successor, Arnal Serras, as the war dragged on and the currency weakened, ended his opening invocation of the whole celestial court of Paradise with a note of the current (for that day) exchange rate: 'the franc being at 20 sous and the French florin at 16 sous'.

Money lost over presents was also especially galling. A note of pique still rings down the centuries from the Bourg account book of 1345: 'We bought a cup to give to Master Rufel [one of those stand-offish royal commissioners] and he wouldn't take it, and when we sold it again we lost 6 sous, because we'd had it polished up.' The consuls seldom failed to note that the cost of presents included packing; and when wine was sent at Christmas, sergeants were despatched soon afterwards to get the barrels back.

Official trips out of town along wartime roads occasionally made large holes in the budget. When Huc Boyer got in the way of the English assault on Clairvaux and was robbed of 1 florin 5 sous, besides being beaten up so badly that he needed five weeks in hospital, the poor fellow had to swear a solemn oath 'that he had lost all this in the cause of the town' before the consuls would pay. A long-winded errand, like Peyrasmortas's seventeen-day trip to Toulouse in 1369 to negotiate exemptions from tax, was simply not to be paid for in full. Bocart again in the margin of the tax book: 'It's too much.' And later, when Peyrasmortas was still owed money, 'He must not take a thing.'

Very occasionally, when something had happened that the consuls felt sorry for or, for some reason, bad about, a note of compassion crept into the account books. It happened in 1358, when Diau Miquel, one of the City *baniers* who patrolled the border, fell and hit his head in the butchers' quarter. The *baniers* were the lowliest of the town's servants, scrambling round on the steep limits of the town in their robes of rough Rodez cloth, and when Miquel was hurt — and he was hurt badly — he could pay for nothing he needed. So Peyre Bru the taverner, who, as we have seen, was not quite worthy enough to be a consul, took bread and wine to him as he lay dying, and someone else paid the eventual funeral fees, while the consuls paid for his shroud and picked up the other expenses. These acts of kindness are poignant not only because of their rarity, but because the strain on the balance of payments rises almost palpably from the pages of the register.

Where, in this eagle-eyed town, was a man who could not even remember where his money was? For Marques could not, and all his hopes rested on it. He remembered packing the coins and hiding them, but not where. Forgetting the details of the operation, as he complained once to Alamanda Fromenta, was 'a disaster ... that's got me completely rattled [*tot turbat*]'. But it was not so disastrous as depending on the lost hoard, Micawber-like, to see him out of trouble.

As the years passed, Marques's dependence on this dream grew ever stronger and less precise. He first mentioned 'a certain amount of money' which, he thought, would have lost its value with the stronger currency issues of a few subsequent years. This was still a businessman speaking. Later, neighbours were told of a 'large amount' of undepreciated silver. By the time Father Griffe took charge of his estates, the hoard was 'all my money', *ma pecunia tota*. It was now 'his', although he had told some people previously that it was his uncle's, and that he had been instructed as an apprentice to hide it from the English. If this was true — witnesses did not really know what to believe — then even the famous hoard, a sort of magical inheritance, was not money he had earned.

Was the loss of it merely bad luck? On one occasion at least Marques seemed to doubt it, and blamed himself. His confession came at the end of a wearying business trip of around a hundred miles to Toulouse with his colleagues, a trip that usually took three days each way. They were coming back on the usual winding road along the valley of the Tarn, the river loud on one side, overhanging rocks on the other, the pack-horses swaying under the weight of their loads. Perhaps the possibility of encountering English *routiers* had triggered the memory in Marques's mind, or perhaps the trading had gone badly. At any rate, Bernard Claustras described the scene:

Peyre was riding last in the party. At one point I turned round and noticed he was crying. I said 'What's up? Aren't you feeling well?' [*Que has? No vos sentes pas be?*] Then Peyre burst into tears and told me that he was a wretched man . . . he couldn't remember where he had hidden his money, because he was only young then.

When the court case opened, Canac's lawyers worked hard to wring out evidence like this. They listed the statements they 'knew' to be true — that Peyre was a pauper, not much good at providing for his family, careless with his property, excommunicated for years at a time — and asked the witnesses to refute or explain them. In other words, the lawyers wanted to find out whether Marques had ever been capable of managing his money, and to suggest that he had not. Father Griffe testified, in a way that seemed kindly, that he had noticed a rather sudden change in him. 'At one time', he said, 'Peyre worked harder, and had a better reputation, than he has now. It was quite a long time ago that I saw him keeping a good shop and a good house and stocking up fine wines there. Then it seemed to me that his memory got bad, and he lost some of his sense and rationality.' Matters then went downhill, 'and he squandered his substance in all sorts of ways'.

Perhaps he was ill, then. The lawyers had thought of that: they asked witnesses whether Peyre had had, since his youth, 'any illness which might have caused him to lose his reason or his memory'. But what precisely did 'illness' mean? A proper illness confined you to bed, like the paupers in the Peace Hospital, where you were bled and fed on broth until eventually, almost inevitably, you died. Medicines, decoctions of herbs, wine and gall, might be as bad as the disease; priests receiving any were excused from attending services 'for the day they receive the medicine and for two days afterwards'. An illness might mean fever, and that in turn was not far from madness, which the devil brought on with hissings and promptings. But it was also understood that illness might mean the loss of memory and reason in a sound body; or the sort of lassitude and melancholy that had caused Favia, the shoemaker's widow, to turn her head away from her husband's money as she lay hopelessly in the bed she had shared with him.

Asked about illness in Marques, then, several witnesses, including notary Porret, simply replied that they had never seen him ill at all. But others understood that any sort of physical or mental frailty might be included, as well as thoroughgoing sickness. So they did not hesitate to mention little things: though hesitantly, because they were not sure what they might be used to prove, or how useful they were to the arguments at hand.

The Marques they could see was not in the pink, and for years he had shown the small disabilities of age. Considerately, and rather tactfully, the neighbours pointed them out. 'He's getting on a bit, I think.' 'He's always been rather deaf, just as he is now.' 'I don't think his memory's as good as it was. He often leaves his shop open at night and he's always leaving his coat behind in places when he takes it off.' Several witnesses testified that his memory was failing, but as Johan Riol, who had bought a house from him, said, 'he had a good enough memory when I owed him anything.'

He was also renowned for having an old man's garrulousness. Notary Porret, as we have seen, remembered being told all kinds of old stories. His tenants, too, said they were often regaled with *gesta*, tales of the knights of old, at the kitchen table. Andreas Formis, another tenant who was evidently fond of him, made a fair point: 'He's a bit deaf, but that doesn't mean he hasn't got a good memory. I've heard him relate all kinds of really long and old things that I didn't remember.'

This was not the point, however. Old men (and women) were naturally full of tales; in other court cases, the older a witness was, the more difficult it often was to stop him talking. Canac's lawyers wished to prove something quite different about Marques: a basic lack of business sense. And his creditors were willing to oblige. They readily asserted that once out of his apprenticeship, out on his own, Marques got into trouble over money. Berengar Natas, who, besides being a rich man and one of Marques's creditors, was also the cousin of the wife of Marques's Uncle Bartelemi (and therefore a fund of knowledge about the family), put forward an odd but plausible theory. 'Before his uncle died, Marques was poor and didn't have much. But after his uncle died he was excommunicated a good deal more than he was before; I saw him denounced ever so many more times.' This seemed to imply that while Marques was an apprentice, or still had his uncle about to advise him, he at least stayed solvent; but once his uncle had gone, his confidence disappeared.

His creditors, in general, were not sympathetic. The exception was Natas, who evidently felt some blood-loyalty towards him. When Natas himself borrowed money, it was on official business and on a grand scale. On that famous trip to Paris with Johan Manha he had borrowed 310 francs, through a Montpellier merchant and a Lombard banker, in rather urgent circumstances. His expenses included the board and lodging of the servant who helped with his trunk (68 days at one gold *mouton* a day), that cloak 'made in Paris' (17 livres), and commission on the sum borrowed (8 livres 10 sous, including 7 livres 10 sous 'for services rendered' and one livre 'lost in the exchange'). But Paris was Paris.

When Natas was asked, as everyone was, whether Marques was 'a simple man, moderately competent and moderately businesslike', he replied, 'Yes, that's true; but he's a good man and does no harm to anyone.' From what he heard at Mass in St Amans, he said, there had certainly been a lot of excommunications for debts owing; but (with a slightly sardonic twist) 'Peyre's in a better and more prosperous state than at several other times in his life ... I mean the times when Johan Girma and I had him excommunicated because he didn't pay us what he owed us ... just at the moment he hasn't been excommunicated by anybody.'

Girma gave evidence of Marques's incompetence with even more warmth: 'Simple-minded and always was.' Here was another ex-consul, one of the few smiths in the Bourg, its chief provider of silverware for fine occasions and cloth for the consular robes. This was a man rich enough, in 1374, to bid 1,000 francs for the farm of the Bourg wine tax, and rich enough, five years later, to lose a silver cup from his house almost casually. Girma was not a man of resounding virtue: the records show that he later trafficked with the English, and was fined for it; but for the moment he was the very image of industriousness and sufficiency and success. And it was Girma's rents at Marcillac, the town's favourite wine-growing spot, that Marques had sold by mistake when he had sold his own.

Marques's disgrace did not end there, at least as far as his rich creditors were concerned. They also thought him hopeless because he had leased his shop to meet his expenses. It was commonplace to lease out a house and put people up in various cramped corners, including shops, which were usually in the basement; but it was serious to forfeit the use of a place, as opposed to rooms you could spare.

When Marques leased his shop he automatically suspended his trade and his profits, but with typical bad management he went on paying tax for it. He paid tax because he still kept some of his stock there. The authorities in Rodez, battered by demands for war money, could not afford to miss a trick; they watched where stock went, and tried to make sure the taxman followed. But it was difficult to track things from place to place, especially where a border intervened. The truly ingenious, therefore, moved their stock — barrels, hay bales, bolts of cloth — over the border to the other side: where, because they were not residents, the taxman was unsure how to treat their goods. The sensible rented workshops or barns apart from their houses and tried to store as much as possible there; and if they rented out space in their own houses to other people, they tried to erase their connection with both the renters and the place.

Marques might have taken a lesson from one of his in-laws, Ramon Rostanh, who leased with success a spare house he owned in Bullieyra, in the City. Ramon, we know, was a bit of a sharp customer; two years before our story, he had been in the count's court for selling a sword for more than it was worth. However that may be, he let out his house to a nameless 'foreign' man and the shop beneath to a nameless woman, who paid a little tax for it out of the profits they made. These profits also came back to Ramon as rent, but he paid no tax on the house or the shop because he had moved his stock away and ceased to go there. The taxman, at any rate, was taken in: 'He gets nothing, so he pays nothing' read Ramon's entry in the register.

Johan Manha got round the taxman in a similar way. He let out his hay barn to an outsider, a taverner (the hay went on the tavern floor to sop up spills), and the taverner paid the tax Manha owed on it. Manha also let out his workshop later to two women who could not be identified, quite possibly war refugees, so neither he nor they paid a penny of tax for that.

Marques might equally have taken a lesson from a few of his own tenants, poor as they were. They lived in discomfort in the place where they worked — adults and children, sometimes, squeezed in one small room, palliasses under the bench, work-tools stowed in a box — to avoid paying taxes on a house. They had some reason. By the 1370s, the need for public money was so great that the rate was no longer fixed by the year; it was set at so much, 'and more if we increase it'. But all these room-tenants paid were their rents to Marques. And, whether out of kindness or foolishness, he kept those rents at a reasonable rate, while taxes for the war and for 'loans' to the count went on inexorably rising.

Some people, even more cunning than the tenants, actually moved house regularly to escape the taxman. The Bourg consuls in the 1340s complained bitterly about one Duran Coderc, 'who sometimes makes his hearth in the City and sometimes in the Bourg, as he pleases, and especially when taxes are imposed in the Bourg, moves his hearth into the City.' Coderc (who, in the end, was buried in neither Bourg nor City, but in the church at Luc, in the tomb of his parents — his loyalties unresolved even in death) was issued with a warning to stay still, or pay two lots of back-taxes.

The making of fire in a hearth implied other things:

cooking, meals at a table, circles of friends, loyalty to a place.
Residents were taxed for their plate and their furniture,
precious belongings that they would want to keep close.
Outsiders were not, because it was assumed they kept
nothing of value in their houses. But in a divided town,
much as consuls and border-markers might try to pigeon-
hole people in one half, those people — and their goods,
and their working contacts — often cropped up in the other.
They were not 'outsiders' to quite the degree the authorities
presumed. Some of Marques's colleagues were so peripatetic
that it was hard to place them at all, and they doubtless
profited from it by confusing the taxman.

So the tax tricks were known; and Marques, once again,
had missed out. This mistake swayed the balance with Girma:
there was an unmistakable note of censure in his remark
that 'I also saw him buy back the bit of house where he lives
now and makes his fire.' Even the neighbours, generally
kinder, understood the disgrace involved. Alamanda Fromenta, the most loyal of his friends, who thought Marques
had been excommunicated for no reason at all, and said
stoutly that she would 'deny our Lord Jesus Christ if he ever
stayed excommunicated for as much as a whole year', tried
to minimise the troubles over the shop: 'It wasn't leased out
for long, in fact he bought it back out of pledge almost at
once.' But her very insistence on this kind lie made it clear
that the matter was grave.

Managing money was therefore not simply a case of
keeping property in hand: it was often a case of keeping
quiet. And there, as we have seen, the border helped considerably. The Gasto & Andreas shoemaking partnership
next-door, which got into something of a tangle when
Andreas died and his widow could not cope, had worked
well enough when he was alive. Andreas, the citizen, had
taken the money home every night and had barely spent
any of it; instead, he had hidden it. That way, no taxman

from either Bourg or City could touch him. The money was in his pouch, or in his cupboards; it did not appear as a new bed or extra shop space. And as long as it remained unspent, there was nothing to tax. Treasure was safe, unless, as Canac said, you kept talking about it. And hiding money under the floor was therefore not so foolish, unless you forgot where it was.

Other Marques failures could be listed, too. The garden at Santa Martra was an obvious one. Any man of even moderate standing in Rodez had a garden or a smallholding, often at some distance from where he lived, on which he could keep stock, grow hay or plant vegetables. And this, again, was often on the other side of the border, where it was a little further from the eye of the taxman. Marques had learned that lesson, but once again he had learned it only up to a point.

When his Uncle Bartelemi died, his Santa Martra garden was rated at $2^1/_2$ deniers for tax. Peyre improved it until it was worth 6 deniers; but then he let it go. Nettles and white-headed thistles took it over. Over twelve recorded years, he never once paid the tax the City demanded. His rating fell as the weeds grew, from 6 deniers to 2 deniers to nothing at all. Once overgrown it was a reminder, mute but public, of his mismanagement.

So too was the famous drain. Witnesses to the inquiry agreed that if you had a drain under your house, it was your responsibility to clean it out; 'and no-one else's', said a stern Stefe Cayrosa, who, as a building inspector, knew what he was talking about. Marques's reluctance to take charge, and his apparent hope that the Bourg consuls might do it for him, made a particularly bad impression. The consuls did not pay for things to be cleaned or mended except in public emergencies, which was why Manha's and Natas's presence in the case had attracted such attention. Men were supposed to take charge of matters that impinged on their own lives, unless these were politically difficult: such as cleaning streets near the border, an action which the public-spirited folk of Sant Stefe were actually rebuked for.

Official disclaimers of responsibility extended even to the mess and destruction caused to build the walls. Compensation was by no means automatic. It was up to the man who owned the property, the one who cared, to make a fuss and prove he needed paying for such freakish natural occurrences as the 'falling down' of his fences, or the 'carrying away' of all his trees; and this was in cases where the consuls were clearly responsible. Now if a man, by carelessness or negligence, had somehow allowed his own drain to get blocked up, why on earth should those tightly-laced public purses be loosened on his behalf?

It is possible, of course, that Marques did not pass the buck out of laziness. Perhaps he simply did not know what to do and, seeing a consul like Manha taking such a keen interest, simply hoped officialdom would help. He was already in the hands of his manager, Father Griffe, for difficult matters such as running estates. But Father Griffe's remit did not run to drains, though it seemed to extend even to paying the tax on Marques's little scraps of property outside town; and that brought its own humiliation. After his appointment a poignant entry appeared in the City tax register, the confusion over names suggesting that Marques was almost unmanned by his misfortunes: 'Father R. Griffe owes — for the fields of P. Rostanh, from the Bourg.'

If men did not prosper in one half of Rodez, there was an obvious alternative. They could try and attach themselves to the other half. The Natas family had done that, buying houses and workshops in Carrieyra Nova, New Street, in the City in the 1330s; and Girma's family had done it, until their City smithies in the 1350s were rated at 200 livres for tax. The Rostanhs had done it and, once they were established in the City, Marques himself had tapped into the cross-border wealth by marrying Alumbors. But the tactic did not necessarily work unless you reinforced it with hard work, as he was slowly to discover.

The same was true of moving house. Rodez afforded more chances than usual of turning over a new leaf by moving a street or so away; it was, in effect, like moving to another town with a different set of liabilities. But moving was no guarantee of success. Between 1360 and 1380, forty-four taxpayers moved in the City, thirty-five to other streets and nine to the Bourg. Twenty-four can be traced to their new addresses. Eight did better; eight did worse; eight stayed as they were. Nine were compulsive movers, changing houses as they changed hats; they came from many different trades, but in the end they did less well than fellow-workers. The successful technique was to stay still, to keep a house in one place, but always to be on call, like Gasc and del Cayro, to work over the border; and, in readiness for the chance of work, to keep up with the needs and deficiencies and different rules of the other side, like any businessman seeking a niche in a market.

Two famous City masons, Galhart Guisardo and Cayrosa (besides del Cayro, the mason of first resort), were called to give evidence in the Marques case because their knowledge of Bourg building regulations was second to none. The Bourg could have produced its own masons; but with men of this calibre straddling the divide, it had no need to.

Guisardo was something of a star, under more or less permanent contract to the Bourg consuls for huge numbers of buildings and works, *ganre de edificis e ganre de obras*, all through the 1370s. Although he had great difficulty getting paid, his private wealth was accumulating by leaps and bounds; the taxable value of his fixed property went up by 150 livres in that decade, and the value of his furniture by 750 livres. By the end, he had enough money to farm various taxes and to lend the count cash, in quantity, to bribe certain English captains to go away. There were times indeed when Guisardo, by virtue of the respect he enjoyed and the money he was amassing, seemed almost to be running the town.

From the beginning, the Guisardo brothers — Johan was a notary — had no clear affiliation to one community or the other. They looked for the main chance; and, as luck would have it, both masons and notaries were in great demand during the war years on both sides. So Galhart lived in the City, renting one of the select workshops in the meeting house itself, and becoming a consul in 1373; but he directed the wall-building for both City and Bourg. He had also taken over Dona Guizas's old quarry and quicklime furnace right on the border, down by the Auterne bridge. Johan lived in the Bourg, where he was eminent enough to oversee the engrossment of the privileges with silk cords and three colours of wax; but he also contributed timber to the City's fortifications.

Transborder contacts brought their problems. It is clear from both the tone and the detail of the Bourg's main contract with Guisardo in 1373, when Duran de Monferrier was a consul, that he was not altogether trusted. The walls went past sensitive points. There was, for example, a small wall and ditch to be built from the Franciscan church at the top of Santa Martra up to another existing wall, 'leaving out the road to Molinau which runs beside the church'. This was all border slopes and gardens, a treacherous spot. The wall had to run at the bottom of Guilhem Mata's garden and in front of Berengar Natas's; and Natas — consul, emissary, Marques's creditor — was not a man who could be handled carelessly.

From there, Guisardo had to run the wall up through several yards of grass, following the markers on the wall. In the road beside the Mata garden he had to make a 'good and adequate' drain, and take it up to an enclosure of wooden stakes round Guirbert Engles's garden. (Guirbert, a cobbler, was one of Marques's tenants; the fence suggests that he took better care of his garden than his landlord did.) That done, Guisardo had to make a plug for the drain, and since this was on the border there was no room for compromise: it had to be made 'just like the one in a drain which is in the City ditch near the Bullieyra Gate'. The job had to be finished 'by All Saints next coming' — or in one and a half months.

Every specification was laid down. If Guisardo dug more than he should, or where he was not asked, or made a mistake, some of his money was deducted. ('Incorrect measurements', or 'ditch not dug as specified' were the main reasons for deductions in his case, suggesting a bit too much speed on the job.) Finishing off, filling in holes and levelling the road where he had been were all to be done at his own expense. This was possibly standard for any contractor; but in Guisardo's case, 'before anyone pays him a penny', two men from the Bourg had to inspect the wall and confirm that it was built as required. Those two little words, *del borc*, would not have appeared if he had not been an outsider.

Yet Guisardo was a rare bird, with both sides in his pocket, and knew it. He was not above sharp practice, and did not miss a trick. In 1369 he claimed the City owed him 3 florins 6 gros for stone and rocks he had had to remove from the ditches, 'and he said that we had agreed with him that he could take [such stuff] out wherever he found it, and he did, and he puts that on the conscience of the consuls'. He eventually squeezed 2 florins out of them.

He gave his evidence to the Marques inquiry not as a neighbour or a colleague, but as a self-made man with firm, indeed vindicated, views about the management of money. Some of his remarks were blunt. For example, 'I know pretty much nothing about laws.' And 'If I had a drain in my shop I'd clean it out for my own good, and so would anyone, otherwise what's the use of it?'

Other remarks were surprising, as those of management gurus tend to be. Marques blamed much of his failure on his over-complicated attempts to hide the pots of money, but Guisardo said: 'I'd do that myself if I had money and wanted to hide it.' He remarked, too, that if he himself found on his own property 'anything good, whatever it was, I'd take it as mine and I'd make use of it as mine, no question – though I wouldn't do it if I absolutely knew it belonged to someone else. That seems quite obvious to me.'

That little word 'absolutely' (*expresse*, as the notary rendered it in Latin) was one Canac might have noted. How often, when you found things (or when someone else uncovered them just in front of you), did you 'absolutely' know who they belonged to? And if you had half an inkling, were you obliged to find out? It was unlikely that Guisardo did, not only because of that weasel word, but because of the straightforward clause that was written into his own building contracts: 'Whatever the said Master G.G. finds in his work, digging the said ditch . . . belongs to him.'

So the Guisardos of this world agreed with the Canacs of this world, whichever side of town they came from. Success lay in hard work, good management, participation, responsibility. Success lay in grasping, and not feeling guilty about it; it lay in taking chances, especially the sort that partition could provide. The man who could do none of these things would be left as Marques was left, watching the mounds of empty earth pile up around him, while his wife nagged and wept, and the workmen whistled.

Mas tornet pas monta,
Ne trobet pas lo bago.

Al' pon da Mirabel
Catarina plorabo.

6

Alumbors Marques
and the shame of debt

A T SOME POINT over the next few days, Peyre and Alumbors took a calculated risk. They had nothing left to
lose. The workmen had gone, leaving a hummocky floor
and the smell of sweat and sewage; yet Alumbors, especially,
could not bear to leave matters at that. They would bring
diviners in.

This was certain sin. Diviners were excommunicate as
surely as murderers and men who vandalised churches; to
believe in them was the sort of superstition that reigned in
the wild high moors, among the sheep and devils. Yet it
seemed innocent enough. The visit was short and incon-
sequential; it involved no fetishes, no bowls of water, no
incantations. Two women came: the Diviner of Serra, so-
called, and another, younger practitioner. They moved
round the shop floor, silently palping the air. For a moment
there was excitement: the Diviner of Serra paused near the
central pillar. 'You will see the money you've hidden by
the pillar,' she said. 'Look there if you will, because I can
sense something.' The end of the day probably brought

more furious arguments between husband and wife, when they scratched up the floor and found nothing.

By all accounts, Alumbors argued a lot. One neighbour mentioned the constant shouting that went on in the house, presumably because Marques was deaf as well as intractable. Gasc remembered vividly her outburst over the money, and also the way she had lingered on the steps, sharp-eyed, suspicious, blocking the light, and nagged at him. Alumbors had no alternative but to push her husband and show her shrewish nature. Marques himself had given up. As she complained once to Father Griffe, as she tried to arrange an absolution for him, 'He's so daft, he just doesn't bother.'

She had been rich when she married Peyre; the marriage had done her no favours in that sense. She owned her own land, and provided oats on her own account for the City consuls in 1358. Alumbors was, after all, a Rostanh. Her family were wealthy skin-dealers who had traded in the Bourg square for seventy years and kept huge houses on both sides of the border. The family had marriage or business connections with the Bergonhos, the Massabuous, the Malavilas, the Maurels, almost all those worthy resplendent names who also traded round the square. Her father's house, rented from the chapter and valued at 200 livres, contained two workshops, a stable, a strongroom, two rooms above, a hayloft, an upper chamber and a room above that: a house full of industry and accumulated profit, overlaid with the sweet breath of beasts.

Alumbors was not used to scraping and saving. To have too little money was humiliating. To be left to plead with creditors was worse. So she nagged, and fretted, and shouted. And because she had to organise everything, it was probably Alumbors who brought the diviners in: the last desperate throw to salvage her husband's reputation, and to bring him once again into the circle of the prosperous and respected.

*

The Diviner of Serra must have enjoyed wide fame. Serra was a tiny place that clung above the Aveyron gorges to the west of town, perhaps ten hard-walking miles away. Most oddities lived outside town, like the hermit whose rations of bread and coarse shirts, or seasonal Christmas present, would be taken into the woods and stuffed through a barred window; or like the prostitutes who lived under the hanging cliffs by the river, with their brood of snivelling children by different fathers, in penetrating damp and smoke.

The lepers, too, were out of town; the City's leper-house, tiny and isolated, lay in fields that Alumbors and Peyre would have ridden through on their way to Marcillac to look at their vineyards. A little graveyard stood beside it, with tilting dilapidated stones. In time of war the house was hardly secure; in July 1369 passing raiders smashed it up, perhaps because there was no-one there. Indeed, it was often empty. A decade earlier a woman called Biatris had run the house, sharing it with one sick woman, a pig, four bedsteads, two fire-dogs, two iron-bound barrels, a pick, a spade and a pruning-hook. Yet the town *baniers* had come to prune the trees in the lepers' meadow and to slaughter the pig, as if Biatris, a leper herself, could not manage it; they never entered the house, from which the women watched them through iron grilles. In the Bourg leper-house the animals were sometimes corralled with the sick, neither being allowed out 'for fear of disgracing the town'; and when the sheets of the City's lepers needed cleaning they were washed by the lepers of the Bourg, a poignant and necessary alliance of untouchables.

Lepers were suspected of contagion not merely through the skin. Some of them, like the Jews we have already encountered, were said to make a habit of poisoning fountains and wells, for evil magic as well as good could be spread by water. In this country of impermeable rocks, water ran over the ground and trickled down the face of cliffs:

difficult to catch, impossible to be sure of. When it was caught, in cupped hands or leather buckets or, at public fountains, in iron cups chained to the rock, it tasted of all the metals in the world, whether poisoned or not.

Diviners, too, were linked to wells and rivers; they were associated with spirits, storms and the old pagan ways. If these still existed in Rodez, they had somehow avoided the powerful disinfecting action of saints like Amans and Martial, the town's patron-bishops. The synodal statutes of 1270 condemned unequivocally people who danced naked in lightning, tearing themselves with thorns, or who stole the holy chrism to make witchcraft; but these dancers and pilferers also knew things that were not to be explained. Even Alumbors's brother Huc, a canon of the church, was as quick to talk of bad luck, *malastruc*, as Marques was, though its literal meaning was bad or unfavourable stars. And even he talked of *casech*, a tumble off the wheel of fortune, as if the mechanisms of the world were not entirely in God's hands.

Indeed, they did not seem to be; independently of how hard men prayed, they rose and fell. The Seguis in particular, whose shop Alumbors and Peyre had unwittingly flooded, had somehow overtaken them in wealth some time ago. Because Peyre's decline seems to have been gradual, the Marques family did not have to move away; they stayed in their good street, with their rich neighbours, but in a house that grew shabbier, poorer and more disorganised. And it was very easy, once matters started slipping, for neighbours' and even brothers' attitudes to harden.

A reputation was a delicate thing. It could be lost by foolish acts or bad behaviour; and there might even be something disreputable, it seemed, about merely standing still. Country women, for example, stood for hours in the Bourg square holding out small trays of what they had managed to grow or bake: leeks, apples, cabbages, fresh

loaves of bread. Alumbors, like any frugal housewife, probably bought from them. But they ran the gamut of people's
suspicions. 'I'm not sure whether they're honest or not,'
Johan Monmato had said once. After all, prostitutes
(*putanas*) lingered too, with their wares on display: skirts up
round their shins, showing their underskirts, and skimpy
veils perched on too much hair. Bernard Molenier told a
little story once about meeting such a woman loitering by
the cathedral building site late at night, where the dim piles
of stone and sand did not quite conceal her.

> She's married now, and lives at Le Monastère near
> Rodez. I asked her what she was doing, and whether I
> could escort her anywhere. She asked me to accompany
> her to a certain place where, as she put it, a gentleman
> friend was waiting for her to make satisfaction to him.
> I went with her as far as the hedge of Vivian Galvanh's
> garden, where she stopped. And yet [a sad coda] I
> believed in my soul that she was a good woman.

Poverty put people in that sort of circumstance: hanging
round the square, lingering in the dark in gentlemens'
gardens. It sometimes made men treat a woman contemptu-
ously, even when her dress was decent. Indeed, the register
of fines in the count's court for the 1360s and 1370s shows
a certain confusion about what decency in women was, and
who was to blame if it was violated. Rape was a serious crime,
carrying a fine of 5 francs (as did selling stone, corn or
weapons to the English). Taking prostitutes into your house
brought a fine of 2 francs, and at the fairs a sort of game
of tag went on between the meadow-whores and the
sergeants, who generally punished the men (by taking away
their belts, caps and knives) and let the girls off, sometimes
after rounding them up for fun. But when a girl called Viars
and her shoemaker-friend went all the way in the church of

St Amans, she was the one who had *participat carnalamen*, and she was the one who went into the pillory for it. In the same way, when Marguarida, a priest's servant, 'made Father Johan a baby', it was she who paid the fine — 10 sous — and bore all the disgrace. Possibly something similar had lain behind the case of Galhardeta, hanged on the stinking trees for the death of a child.

Earlier in the century Adhemar del Terralh had taken his suspicions of the country women to a logical conclusion, as one poor girl called Petronilla subsequently complained in court. She had walked from Clausa Vinha, several miles over rough tracks among the white rocks and the juniper bushes, to sell pears in the Bourg square. Probably she looked tired and, by town standards, down-at-heel as she held out the small wicker tray to prospective buyers. Dust lined the hem of her dress, and the pears had softened with travelling. She was asking 8 deniers for the lot: a fairly steep price, about a third of a working man's daily wages. Adhemar came up and made a pact with her: he would pay the money if he could taste the pears first, to see if they were good or not.

He led her away to the count's mansion, just across the square. As usual the lord was away, which was convenient. Then, quite suddenly (by Petronilla's account), he pushed her into a room and on to a bed, 'and wanted to lie with me, but I shouted "Help!" and ran away.' Adhemar's account differed in particulars: 'Petronilla took the pears to a room I rent in the count's house, and put them down. She said "You're cruel, you know. They weigh more than you're going to pay me for them, and I could have sold them to other people." So I said I would eat the pears with her, and caught hold of her arm to take them, and she pushed me and I fell on the bed; I didn't mean her any harm, and I didn't even shut the door.'

Whatever the truth, poor Petronilla was thought fair game. Her sales technique, at least in its opening stages, was

not so different from that of the whore: she was standing
still and asking a man, silently, to be interested and sorry
for her. It was a beggar's, or an idler's, ploy. 'The pears were
bad, anyway,' said her shameless assailant.

Had Adhemar known who Petronilla was, he might have
trusted her wares without testing them. That was how commerce worked, but it was a lackadaisical system that often
ended in tears. If you did not start with a healthy suspicion
of the motives of the seller, you were likely to end up *deceptus*,
disappointed in your bargain. This was a common complaint. It occurred particularly when people paid cash for
something they had not sampled, such as Petronilla's pears,
or the horse that sergeant Ramon Valeta traded with
Bernard Maurel for his own horse, and 6 ecus, in 1345. 'I
say,' Valeta recalled himself saying, almost as soon as the
money had changed hands, 'that horse you've given me isn't
as good as I thought it was; you give me back mine and I'll
give you back yours.' But the trade, once made, was usually
impossible to unravel again. ('Traitor' Valeta and 'Swindler'
Maurel challenged each other to a duel, which was called
off at the last moment.) The note of sadness in the word
deceptus was much like that applied to women (or men) who
had slipped from their former standing: better had been
supposed of them, but the gullible would not be caught that
way again.

This style of commerce prevailed all over Rodez, and it
was by no means always the buyer who was deceived. People
bought goods on credit, had the debt recorded, and hoped
to settle up when they had managed to get money. It was a
formula that was easily abused. When Guilhem Grefolieyra
bought 100 sous' worth of spices from a shop in the Bourg
square during the winter fair, all the surety he needed was
his name, which he provided readily: 'Bernard Sanorel of
the castle of Cordes in the Albigeois'. He promised to pay
when he had sold his goods at the fair, and before he left

town. Flushed with this scam, *mala malis accumulans*, he went on to another shop to buy two pieces of cheese. 'Name?' 'Phelip de Gualhac. I'll pay you before I leave town.' Neither seller saw Grefolieyra-Sanorel-de Gualhac again.

At the Bourg corn-stone, too, where the millers bought their grain and the bakers their flour, transactions were based more on trust and friendship than on weights and measures. Wheat and rye were weighed by the sestier, and each sestier paid a denier in tax. But procedures were fairly relaxed. 'If the *leudarius* [the man who raised the count's food taxes] isn't there, the seller says how much he has, on his oath, and then the buyer is understood to pay his tax for him,' read one court document. Sometimes not even the oath was necessary: the sack was accepted, plumped down where it was. 'I brought in two sestiers of oats', said Guilhem Marti once, 'and Peyre Segui just asked me whether there were two sestiers there, and I said yes.'

At the City stone, the sestier seemed to weigh less; the tax was an obol, or half as much as in the Bourg; and the City consuls, rightly suspicious that a little sharp practice was going on, kept coming over the border to check. In 1369 they found that the Bourg sestier-measure used for oats contained two measures more, eight instead of six, and that as a result the Bourg was cornering the muleteer and pack-horse trade. They demanded equality of measures to stop the 'cheating'. But as it turned out, few people expected the measures of City and Bourg to be equal anyway. Besides, if you knew the name Marti, or Segui, or Rostanh, that was usually good enough for the Bourg customers. *Fama* — that ubiquitous word that meant reputation, gossip, hearsay and common knowledge all in one — commended them; it was a guarantee of probity and quality, no matter what corners were being quietly cut.

In the same way, when Alumbors sent Peyre to buy meat at Maurel's stall (the neighbours reported that he went,

rather than she, presumably because the butchers' quarter
was not a place for a woman of sensibility), she trusted that
Maurel would keep to the regulations that were shouted out
publicly in the square. He would tell Peyre whether that
strange pinkish flesh on the slab before him was goat's or
unclean pig's meat; he would not try to sell him meat from
animals 'that did not come into town on their four legs',
meaning that they had dropped dead of disease or of old
age. Butchers in the Bourg were supposed not even to
breathe on the meat; every so often two inspectors, hands
no doubt clamped over their noses, would try to catch them
at it. But Alumbors would have trusted Maurel because their
houses were close and their families were close, and the
Maurels were consuls. They had reputations, as well as coun-
ters, to keep clean.

If goods were defective they were confiscated and given
to the poor; and a sample was burned in the square, with
the same announcement that accompanied hangings and
floggings: *Veras la justicia*, 'see what justice is'. These burn-
ings too Alumbors would smell from the house: the acrid
smell of old meat, or the scorch of felt hats. Once the effigy
of a forger, Marti Riquet, was dragged through the Bourg
behind a horse; it was burned at the edge of the square,
sparks of burning straw flickering in the wind as they fell
away towards the river.

This basis of trust, this reliance on *fama* and a good name,
was true even of the tavern in the corner of the square
where the stallholders drank and out of which they sometimes spilled, fighting and cursing. This tavern was run by
another Maurel, Johan, who, true to his trade, never became
anything in town government; but high standards were still
expected of him. His measures were to be *bos e lials*, good
and true. The price of wine was fixed (in the Bourg, in
1342, at 9 deniers a quart), and Maurel could not raise it,
'even when selling to foreigners'. If he tried to adulterate

the vintage with eggs, chalk, salt, meat or any other nasty mixture, or to water it down, his stock would be seized, wine and jugs alike, and given to the poor.

Some regulations implied more subtlety in cheating. White wine and red were never to be mixed together, and Maurel was forbidden to hold a cloth or towel over the bottle to hide it from his customers. The people of Rodez, counts and consuls apart, were not wine buffs; but they could tell by colour and by territory whether a vintage was likely to be good or not. Marcillac and Gaillac were the wines they knew, and white wine (which was not local) was considered rather a specialised taste. Alumbors and Peyre had once built up a cellar of wine of the best local provenance, from their terraces at Marcillac. Again, the name was enough to recommend it; but those terraces had been sold long ago. A man's reputation could go sour as quickly as wine could.

In Rodez, too, hard work was assumed to produce rewards. If you were seen on a downward path, you must have slackened. Among the virtues attributed to men chosen as administrators, *diligencia* came second, between 'goodness' and 'niceness'; even a humble locksmith, providing a dowry for his daughter in 1358, specified that she was to marry 'a worthy working man'. Those who did not work were bound to be poor and probably disreputable. That was why, according to one neighbour, Johan Sedassier, the poor were buried in the Bourg square, a place already dishonest and dishonourable; although he felt bound to add that two of those poor, whose names he knew, 'were said to be relatives of mine'.

Sympathy and charity were reserved for the very poor, those who could not do better. Their debts, usually on tiny tax ratings of a half or a quarter of an obol, were usually remitted 'for the love of God'. In some cases, extreme cases, poverty and godliness clearly went together. In the parable of Dives and Lazarus, Lazarus, the beggar full of sores at the rich man's gate, was the man with whom the pure of heart were meant to identify.

Laymen who were touched by the plight of the poor could become brothers or nursing sisters in the Peace Hospital, wearing cloaks marked with a blue cross, pledging their persons and possessions to the hospital in perpetuity and 'caring for the poor men and women of Rodez, feeding the weak and old as the resources of the hospital allow'. Sedassier's poor relations were among their charges, laid at last in unmarked graves among the dice-players and the market stalls.

Richer men, those tagged with the Dives label, assuaged their guilt a little with this hospital. The consuls of City and Bourg regularly inspected it, even tweaking the rough brownish linen on the beds as poor men slept in them or lay impassively watching; climbing to the upper floor to check the kitchen and the crockery; reprimanding the chaplain and the cellarer for not buying candles wholesale. They elected the master who ran the place, so that in 1380 Jorda Segui, then a consul, found himself in the hospital chapel with Johan Guisardo, Galhart's brother, witnessing the new master's oath of office and offering the traditional, slightly curious remark: 'Good luck to you and good luck to us.' In their wills, merchants asked to be carried for burial on Peace Hospital beds; and pious or unemployable younger sons, like Girma's Johan, were made brothers there with wine and feasting, while the consuls presented them with thick wax candles specially engraved with flowers.

The word for charity, *pitansa*, was closely related to pity, the sort of pity that was supposed to reign in the hospital as the brothers bent over their charges; but even genuine pity could be tinged with irritation. *Pitansas* usually came down to cash payments; charity sometimes became a right that the poor claimed assiduously, and the better-off resented. The very poor were cared for, being passive with illness or old age. The uppity poor, demanding hand-outs, were a different matter.

The best example of this clash, rights against resentment, occurred in Alumbors's own family. Her younger sister, Isabella, had married Ramon Fort. The Forts, by long tradition, had a claim to the cups, bowls, linen, spits, knives, scissors and uncooked food left after the bishop's banquet on his first entry, and to the food left over at the bishop's palace at Christmas, Easter and Pentecost. They sent their peasant-tenants to collect it (making sure that any precious stuff was first stowed in an iron-bound chest in a locked room) and then shared the food with them, spreading the bishop's charity over quite a number of households.

The tenants were impressed. In 1398 Peyre Campanhac of Borranhet farm, then about seventy, remembered going 'in Bishop Ramon's time' with two of the Forts and two other tenants, to the bishop's house. (Although it must have seemed like a palace to them, they did not call it one; spades were spades.) 'We got bread from the bishop's officers for the Forts', said Campanhac, 'and the rest of the uncooked meat left over from the morning, good mutton and pork and chicken: that is, two hens, uncooked, with all their feathers on. This was enough for all the Forts. I myself carried away a barrel of wine that the bishop's butler gave me.'

Peyre Campanhac's unmarried niece, Sobeyrana (Queenie), who was sixty, remembered her father going to the bishop's house and bringing back bread and other things, 'feasts and leftovers', as she put it, that were being prepared there for lunch and supper. 'I can remember eating food from these banquets,' she said; 'well, my father called them banquets. It was charity and it was from the bishop's supplies.' Sobeyrana made no particular distinction between feasts and crumbs from feasts, for both were good;

and on her lips that word *pitansa* seemed to have no edge of sourness, for her family had come to expect it as a right that had become gloriously extravagant. In fact, one year when there was some doubt about it, Campanhac went along with a lawyer's writ and waved it in the bishop's very face: 'and he ordered the officer to give the food to us'.

At the time the jug of gold turned up in Peyre and Alumbors's shop, at the time the Diviner of Serra was summoned to do her work, hundreds of men and women were crowding into Rodez in the same expectation of a windfall, if only from public charity. These war refugees were often too weak to labour for masons like del Cayro on the defence works, and were too poor and anonymous to pay even tiny taxes. Many simply lay in the street, or huddled wherever a wall could protect them.

The consciences of some were touched by this. Berengar Natas, for example, who had shown a certain sympathy towards Marques, was indirectly involved in the running of a hospital set up by his brother Huc, where the poor were to be given meat pâté and pies on Easter Sunday, and porridge was provided for infants at the breast. When paupers died in the hospital, the Natas family was obliged to provide a shroud, four candles and a penny wax cross. But even these hopeless poor were not entirely to be trusted, as Galhart Ebrart found when the 'sick' of his hospital, some years later, decamped with the blankets and sheets.

The burden of helping to feed the poor with contributions of cash or corn fell on tax payers of a certain bracket and above, who already had plenty of calls on their money. The grain was ground into flour; the flour was made into half-pound rye-and-barley loaves by a cohort of women who were paid in wine for their services; and the loaves, having been blessed by the priest, were handed out at the door of St Amans from a basket lined with a white cloth on Sundays and feast days. But it was not always done cheerfully. 'Item,' read one council decision of 1375, 'there are many paupers in Rodez, and we're afraid the town will get a bad reputation if they stay here. We think there should be a very strict and careful watch night and day, and that the poor men who are already here should be thrown out.' Occasionally in these years the Bourg consuls made a loss on the corn charity, 'because there are more [poor] people here than there used to be, and those who owe the corn say they will pay no more than the record says they must'.

Among those who owed grain to the charity was Marques himself. He gave three measures of rye a year. The action was not spontaneous so far as he was concerned; the contribution went with his house, a hangover from his uncle's more comfortable days. None the less, he paid it. Duran de Monferrier, the most illustrious of Marques's creditors, the man who had formed such a golden impression of Alumbors's son-in-law, owed charity too, and tried not to oblige. His mother was an eminent benefactor; her will, in 1372, left money to all the town hospitals, a measure of rye to all the Bourg confraternities (lay religious associations) and ten sestiers of rye 'to be distributed as bread to the poor of Rodez on the day of my burial'. Her son did not follow her example.

Duran was rich enough to lend money in quantity and to put up the highest bids to farm the count's fees at the main weighing station; and he was also down to give the Bourg charity, each year, a bushel of rye. Sometimes he did not pay at all; sometimes he paid late, when the baking had already started. Sometimes the sergeants would take a blanket or a tankard from his house to speed matters on, but Monferrier was not about to miss that sort of thing. Huc Farcel, Marques's builder-friend, who was also a sergeant, was once arrested for stabbing Monferrier with a knife, perhaps a sign of the frustration officials were reduced to. Monferrier even managed to avoid the charity collectors shaking their boxes outside the doors of St Amans, until the consuls came down on him for more than 60 livres, a considerable sum, in back-payments.

Monferrier, of course, did not like idleness. His evidence in the Marques case showed that feckless behaviour was not something he wished to subsidise. His own will, written in 1403, left 65 sous for an obit in the cathedral every year, with a morning Mass with deacon and subdeacon and all other usual solemnity, to be said for the salvation of his soul. He left only 5 sous to the three offertory bowls 'for feeding, clothing and providing shoes for the shameful poor of Christ'. The word 'shameful' (a convention which most testators left out) seemed to sum up Monferrier's attitude; and that of many others less rich, less busy and less important, who brushed alongside Alumbors as she went to beg Monferrier for more money or more time.

This ritual embarrassment became the pattern of Alumbors's life. The first demand for payment of a debt, the *citacio*, would be delivered by a servant to the house. Marques would put it in a corner and forget it. Alumbors would find it, and would try to negotiate an extra period of grace. If she failed, or the writ was lost, or Marques did not answer, he was publicly denounced and excommunicated by the priest in church. Since Marques was eventually in debt to creditors all over the Bourg, this happened many times; so often that it seemed to notary Porret, who drafted many of his quittances, that he had been excommunicated 'for almost the whole time I've been in Rodez', and that he had never seen him anything but poor and publicly condemned by his creditors.

When Marques still failed to pay back his debts, the usufruct of the shop was sold to Valeta. For Alumbors, this was another peculiarly public disgrace. First the Bourg crier, standing carefully on the southern side of the flat stone in Sant Stefe, would shout out that the shop was to be sold 'with all its entrances and all its exits and all its rents and all its rights'. Then, on the day of the sale, the auction would be cried through all the main squares of the Bourg, the auctioneer going first with his sing-song gabble, Porret with his quill and papers struggling after: 'The said usufructs are rated for the present at fifteen livres, and I'll give them away for fifteen livres if no-one offers me more, say the first word and I'll say the second, and so on and so on until we get to the highest bidder, they're at fifteen livres of Rodez for four years, at fifteen livres of Rodez . . . ' If there were no bids on the first circuit, auctioneer and notary would keep on going round the town until a bidder appeared; and it was not unknown, in the end, for the desperate footsore auctioneer to buy the usufructs himself.

Smaller possessions seized for debt were sold after a week if the debtor did not pay. They were sold 'at the house' — perhaps at the meeting house, but possibly too at the house of the defaulter. In 1338 Agnes Mercieyra had been forced to sell the clothes that had formed her dowry 'if she still has them': a green cloak, a ring of gold or silver set with a precious stone, and a silver crown studded with pearls that her husband, Bec, had given her on their wedding day.

Yet there was sometimes no alternative to selling, unless it was to borrow. For Alumbors, that meant begging from those rich and reputable souls who, not so long ago, had been her equals. By all accounts she hated this more than anything. She could not set off for the creditor's office without moral support from a friend or a relative. Sometimes Canac went with her; presumably in that case, since the creditors knew him and thought well of him, he did most of the arguing. He was with Alumbors when they were both forced to run after Johan Girma in the street, pulling at his sleeve and pleading for grace. But generally it was

Alamanda Fromenta, her old friend, who went with her: 'sometimes to settle up and sometimes to be let off and get more time to pay'.

Private creditors like Girma were humiliating to deal with, but at least they were relatively flexible. They did not resort immediately to the authorities, and neighbours did not always see the negotiations; a measure of face was kept. This was not the case if a man defaulted on his public taxes. Then the sergeants were sent round as a matter of course. Their remit was broad: they could seize anything except the debtor's clothes and those of his family, his bed and bedding and the tools of his trade. At worst, they could put defaulters in the stinking prisons (the Castles, as men called them) of either the City or the Bourg, where they were shackled to the damp walls. The shame of prison was so acute that one jailbird, giving evidence about another, would admit only that he had 'often seen him', and 'eaten with him', in the Castle, as if on a social call.

Yet the lesser torments inflicted by sergeants were bad enough. They sealed up Amalvi Mercier's barn, with the hay and hissing geese still inside it, with red wax seals (which Mercier, in a fury, promptly broke again). A troop of them went down to Dona Guizas's lime quarry, when that doughty lady failed to pay her taxes, and saw that nothing was dug or stacked for a few days. They took a sack from Gerald de Panat's house, somehow failing to notice that it contained two hundred dried herrings. They locked up workshops and warehouses, chalked a cross on the door or on a window, and took the keys away; they seized pieces of furniture from houses; they took doors off their hinges, leaving private quarters open to the street.

Alumbors seems to have taken care that this sort of thing did not happen to her. But it had recently happened, if only posthumously, to her uncle Berengar. Every family, no matter how prosperous, seemed to have one member who

struggled to stay afloat. Berengar had worked for a time as
a deputy consul in the City, helping to draft the 1355 tax
register. He was paid 'a good florin' for this, meaning one
of relatively sound silver, 'because he is a poor man and
does not have enough to live on'. In 1357 and again in
1359 the consuls found more florins for him, for small jobs
or 'help', always recording the payments rather carefully
and diplomatically, for this was clearly long-term charity
going on; and, goodness knows, there was not much money
or inclination for that. But it did not go far. In 1367, after
Berengar had died, his nephew Galhart — Alumbors's
brother, and the custodian of Berengar's children — faced
an order from the creditors that sergeants should seize all
Berengar's property.

Galhart's first instinct was to panic on his own behalf:
'I've got nothing movable that belongs to those children.'
His second impulse was to remove himself as far as possible
from the properties which bore the disgrace. He recommended that the sergeants could seize, as 'least damaging
and least useful to the children', a house and garden on
the steepest slope of the hill at Santa Catarina outside the
Bourg — 'though I've no idea what rent they carry or who
owns them'. And there the sergeants went to do their worst.

They seem to have done so with the grim dedication of
bailiffs in all ages. Most people agreed that there was such
a thing as 'acting like a sergeant', independent of the uniform a man wore or the insignia he carried. Sergeants were
a bossy and brutish lot, and not the most intelligent. They
tended to hold craftsmen's jobs; and as they sat at their lasts
or cutting tables they would keep their official sticks prop-
ped in a corner, ready for emergencies. Sergeants did not
usually go armed, but their status was in their staves, which
had the shields of Bourg or City fixed to the top. As long
as they carried them, they were invulnerable; they could not
be resisted. An attack on a sergeant was an assault on all

town authority, shocking, living long in the memory. Although a debtor might feel he had been insulted or humiliated, the weight of insult was all on the other side.

A century before, just near Alumbors's house, one such awful attack had occurred; one of her forebears, Huc Rostanh, had witnessed it. It was a Tuesday in the summer, in 1280. Peyre Corbes, carrying his rod of office, was going about his duties in the Bourg square. On his way he was attacked by the de Petra brothers, Andreas, Ramon, Huc and Bernard. Bernard and Huc were apprenticed to the cloth trade, Andreas and Ramon (so they said) were in minor orders; so all were young yobs, the youngest possibly not much older than ten. They lived in a house that was so tumble-down that the count actually considered his honour damaged by its presence. And, having started out badly, the de Petras were in trouble with sergeants for the rest of their lives; thirty years later, Huc, his inheritance squandered, was found crouched in the church of the Dominicans to seek sanctuary from his creditors.

The reason for the attack on Corbes, according to Rostanh, was that Huc had gone that same Tuesday to La Cadena, the favourite hanging-out spot, and had found Andreas crying. 'What's up?' he asked him. 'What's wrong?' Andreas replied, sobbing, 'Corbes hit me.'

What followed was described by another boy of about ten, Peyre Combas junior, who watched the fight with his father. His father was a sergeant, and he was to become one himself; his account was full of barely suppressed pride in the office, as well as a small boy's energy. 'Huc de Petra told Corbes, "If you don't put the stick down, you'll really catch it,"' he said; 'and Corbes put it down on the Camboulases' counter [the square was crowded, everyone at their stalls and shops]; and then the sergeant suddenly drew a knife to defend himself because the brothers were attacking him.' They pelted him with sticks and stones until a senior officer, the

Bourg baile, came up and stopped it. Peyre Combas's father, standing beside him, remembered remarking to a neighbour: 'It's a shame you didn't shout for help when such a great wrong was being done to the town.'

What did Combas senior mean? He did not mean the whole town: he meant one half, taken as the whole (it was a common usage); and one man, as the whole community's representative. And that man had been hurt. Combas senior clearly felt it; he was a sergeant too, after all. The spectacle of officers fighting was shameful. Their rod was supposed to keep them out of trouble; it represented nothing less than the honour and authority of the count and the Bourg, wrapped up in one. Once a sergeant put it down he was an ordinary man, relinquishing his office. Huc de Petra said he had actually heard Corbes say, 'If this stick I'm carrying wasn't the count's, I'd knock you down'; and understanding precisely the import of that, the brothers made sure Corbes put it down before they laid into him.

Sergeants took their duties seriously, the more so because they worked in a town where they could sometimes invoke two lords, rather than one, to back them up. The power-sharing arrangement of 1316 had combined the civil courts of bishop and count and their court officers, especially in matters of debt collection, which often (like Marques's debts) straddled the border. But much of this work was still done by separate sergeants from either side, City or Bourg, wearing their lord's badge over their hearts and carrying his arms on their staves. Many led a double life, attached to one side as well as to the common court; and they could say they worked for one lord, or two, more or less as the mood and the circumstances took them. Two, being more irresistible, was usually preferred. If anyone in Rodez could twist partition or co-operation to their own advantage, sergeants could.

Several of them gave evidence at an inquiry of around

1350. Ex-sergeant Ramon Valeta (last seen as the disappointed trader of a bad horse) made a typical statement of loyalty: 'What I have, I hold from the lords of Rodez and under their jurisdiction.'

Q. Could they order you to do good or evil?

A. Of course they could order me. It's common knowledge ['*es fama*'].

Q. What do you mean, common knowledge?

A. (with a strong hint of exasperation): Common knowledge is when someone does a thing and goes on doing it and from that people say, 'So-and-so's doing such a thing.'

Sergeant Peyre Combas, son of the small boy who had seen Corbes attacked many years before, also gave evidence at this inquiry. He was then about forty-five, and had been a sergeant for twenty years. 'I carried out many orders for my lords,' he said (that 'my' was especially familiar); 'I captured criminals and put them in prison or escorted them to punishment and execution, and I did other things that were part of my job as sergeant.' Not content with that, the prosecuting lawyer went back over the same ground.

Q. Are you an officer for the lords of Rodez?

A. I'm a sergeant, as I said before.

Q. Do you hold anything from them as a vassal or a tenant?

A. No, but I certainly live under their jurisdiction.

Q. Could these lords, or their proxies, order you to do good or evil?

A. Yes.

Q. And you'd have to obey them?

A. Yes. But [sharp fellow, this] in my evidence I've only told you the truth.

Several other sergeants, asked the same question about good and evil, responded: 'Certainly they could order me; but if they ordered me to do something bad, I wouldn't believe them.'

Sergeants, in short, were not to be trifled with. Moreover, in Rodez, they not only invoked the power of multiple lords but also descended in swarms. Typically, the job in hand would be done by a sergeant from either the City or the Bourg; and he would be reinforced by yet another man from the common court who came along as a joint representative *per companho*, to keep him company, like a chaperone at a dance.

This happened to Grigori del Cros, a wealthy neighbour of Johan Gasc's in Sant Stefe, in the City, as he was unloading a delivery of wine one day outside his shop. Some time before, he had been excommunicated in the bishop's court for failure to pay court charges, allegedly for heresy. (One wonders what on earth he can have done, or said; he invoked God vividly enough when the law turned up.) Three sergeants, two of whom he knew, approached him; but two were bishop's sergeants, and one, Johan Brau, in his grey-and-blue uniform tunic, was from the common court. They treated separately with him, but annoyingly (he was a busy man, after all, trying to unload a cart) they each said exactly the same thing: two of them speaking for 'the Official and the bishop' and one, Brau, speaking for 'the lords of Rodez'.

The burden of what they said was one and the same too: they had orders to arrest him and put him in the bishop's Castle. For a small consideration, they might forget about it. (This part was left out of the sergeants' deposition to the court; there, del Cros simply 'refused to co-operate'.) Del Cros said he had no change, and could promise only to have the money tomorrow. The sergeants insisted. At that,

he ran away, back into his house. The sergeants, in the course of duty, climbed the steps after him, but Grigori and his wife locked the door at the top of the stairs and refused to open it, saying 'God's blood, you're not coming in here!' One of the sergeants tried to get in, but the accused slammed the door on his finger and drew blood. Then he threw wood and stones and other things down the stairs at the sergeants, who might have been badly hurt if they had not run away. Thus they left without carrying out their orders.

With the episcopal and the common-court sergeants already round Grigori's neck, worse was to come. The judge's lieutenant, Deodat Carlat, a Bourg official, came to his house to collect a debt of 3 gold ecus. He said they were gold ecus; Grigori, typically confused, said they were 'gold ecus called *jordi*'. But at least he opened the door to Carlat's knock, and asked what he wanted. When Carlat said, 'That money you owe', Grigori said he had none. Then he rather grudgingly went away and fished out what he called 'an ecu penny' from somewhere. Carlat handed it straight to his servant; the servant went off to weigh it and, on his return, said it was good. Grigori then saw Carlat off, following him out into the street.

'If you don't pay the rest of that money you owe, I'll make you pay it,' Carlat was saying.

'Look here, Deodat, you've got no right to go on like this. I'll pay you the rest, I just haven't got it.'

'God's blood, you're in for it now. I've got a firm promise from you of the amount you're obliged to pay me, and by

God's blood I'll get you put in the Castle until you've paid
it.'

'God's blood, you liar, I'm not obliged to go in the Castle
on your account and you've got no power to put me in
there.'

'God's stomach, I have and you'll be going there. Right
away, in fact.'

Grigori then chased Carlat back to his office at sword-
point, wounding him in the hand; but, said the coin-crunch-
ing servant who gave this evidence, 'this happened in the
Bourg and isn't important.'

It was important to Grigori. He had everyone on his back:
not one court, but three. He, of course, maintained he
had been perfectly polite: asking permission to go upstairs,
closing the door nicely ('We didn't think we had injured
the sergeants because we could close the door'), talking
about the money 'not angrily' to Carlat. But he ended up
missing his summons to the common court because he had
been arrested in the Bourg for beating up Carlat, and there
is a note of satisfaction in his statement to that effect.

Del Cros offended doubly, running up debts on both sides
of the border; Bernard de Manso, a City hotelier, offended
once (although he, of course, maintained that he had not
offended at all) by not paying his tax for repairs to the old
walls in 1347. But again, two sergeants turned up: Johan
Brau, who had gone after del Cros, in his grey and blue,
and Duran del Verdier, the City tax collector. It was mid-
August, round the feast of the Assumption, as de Manso
remembered it. He was upstairs, above the shop; the
sergeants came in and asked for 36 sous. If he did not pay,
they said, he would lose the doors of his hotel.

De Manso said he had paid most of the money already to
somebody else: in fact to Ramon Gabriac, the brother of
the man who, two months earlier, had refused to open the
Sant Stefe gate to the Bourg men trapped on the wrong side.

The sergeants were quite unmoved by that. They started the usual routine for default, taking the small inner door of the hotel off its hinges. De Manso's protests at this point caught neatly the common dread summoned up by sergeants: Alumbors's dread, of exposure and humiliation.

Brau: I'm taking this.

De Manso: Don't, please. If you want to take something, I've got better things inside.

Brau: The door of a place like yours might as well stay open. Anyway, I don't want any of your other stuff.

De Manso: I'll get robbed if it stays open. There are robbers everywhere in town these days. I'm really worried it will happen to me. Johan Floretas's workshop was burgled just the other day —

Brau: Are you saying I'm a robber? Is that it?

De Manso: No, but I've seen other sergeants of the court who are.

The officers took his door. He did not get it back for three days, 'and I suffered very great inconvenience'. 'Did you call the sergeant a robber?' asked the court. 'Not as far as I remember,' said de Manso. 'If I did, I didn't mean any injury to the lords or the court of Rodez.' Not much, anyway.

The sergeants did not care what they took; they were doing a job. When Aymeriga Mansaga fell behind with her taxes they took her private treasures — a silver cup, a silver belt, a crystal rosary — and kept them for five years. From the houses that were kept on either side as tax dodges (in the Bourg, houses owned by absentees like Marques's colleague, Bernard Claustras), they carried away an unimpressive haul of blankets and frying pans: camping gear, in fact. Most pathetic of all, they seized a pledge of a lantern and a pewter pot from Guilhema, the lantern-maker, who paid her rent in lanterns too; they were worth together 4 sous 3 deniers, and were all she had of value in her place. They were taken anyway. No-one, unless desperately poor, was allowed to get away with it.

As it happened, one of this dutiful breed of sergeants was also one of Marques's tenants. His name was Pons Aldebal, and he was an officer of some acumen. In 1366 he had been sent to the count, then at the Black Prince's court in Bordeaux, to explain how the Bourg was trying to resist the prince's taxes: 'We asked him to do the best he could for us, and Aldebal was eight days at Bordeaux waiting for a reply.'

Aldebal seems to have been a cloth-worker as well as a sergeant. In 1370 he was in charge of the cloth hall in the count's mansion, collecting fines for defective manufacture and probably jostling Canac, among others, in the crowds handling the material. He was later to become the Bourg castellan and to have 'English' captains in his lock-up, but for the moment he was a tenant of fairly plain words. As he told the inquest, he knew 'that Peyre asked for the rents on his workshop and other properties before payment was due and before the time was up. He did that from Peyre Fabre and from other tenants of his, and the reason was his debts.'

Aldebal knew that Marques, far from being a grasping landlord, simply needed cash at once. His sergeant's eye noticed that sort of thing: the way men blustered, became importunate, made up excuses, when they were in a hole over money. And he had plainly discussed Marques with other people, like Fabre, and speculated about the financial state he was in. He may not have done so unkindly; he called him 'Peyre', as if he was a friend. But it was clear that

Aldebal did not miss much, even in his unofficial capacity. He was a tenant who paid over his money to Marques and simultaneously, as he pressed the coins into his palm, understood that he himself was the man in the superior position, the one who could really hurt his landlord if he failed in his obligations.

How many others knew as much of Marques's troubles and Alumbors's shame? Fourteen of the eighteen witnesses in court had heard Marques denounced and excommunicated for debt, at his creditors' request, from the pulpit in St Amans. The parish priest was required to read out the list of excommunications after every sermon, and to say what they were for. As he did so, the lights would be doused in church, the missals laid on the ground and the bell tolled, as if for a funeral. It was meant to be an awful moment, even if dulled by frequent repetition and missed by those who, as the custom was, slipped out for a quick drink before the Consecration. And Porret, who knew his law, said that when Marques was excommunicated it followed that Alumbors was too, as the joint owner of the property and possibly the guarantor of the loans; though none of the creditors, and only one of the neighbours, mentioned that.

No-one mentioned, either, the shaming technical details of buying back grace. At the end of his longest period of disgrace, and perhaps on other occasions too, Marques stood in sight of the congregation in the crowded and untidy church, in an unbelted shirt, bareheaded and without his shoes, holding one of the same thick candles he carried, sometimes, on watch duty. Hot wax dribbled down the sides of it to set on his hand and arm. After a while, his arm ached. He looked like a man who had been pulled out of bed and out of some moral torpor. Most of the neighbours, sympathetically, tried not to moralise about this penance; but some did. The longer a man remained excommunicate, seeming not to care, the more people queried his adherence to his faith as well as his solvency. Huc Farcel and Bernard Porro, both building workers and friends, thought that Marques became 'like any good and hard-working man' as soon as he was absolved and received communion again.

Inside the parish, therefore, there was no escaping the publicity of debt. Most of the evidence in the Marques case came from Bourg creditors and tenant-neighbours, especially those who lived under Alumbors's very roof: 'right-next-door neighbours' as they described themselves. Little escaped them. Coming in and out through the shop, crossing Alumbors in a tantrum at the top of the steps, sniffing the wood-smoke and cooking-cabbage smells of the family's meal-times, they knew more than enough to judge the household. But the judgments of most of Peyre's tenants, whether under-the-roof or outside it, were not those of the creditors, haughty and censorious: they were often made in envy and curiosity, rather than rebuke.

When the case of the jug of gold came to court, Canac's lawyers asked the witnesses whether Peyre was poor, 'and whether his poverty, especially in movable goods, was known to everyone in Rodez'. As far as his tenants were concerned, the answer was plainly no; Marques gave charity, rather than received it. He was their landlord; he owned more than one house, more than one workshop; in some cases he provided, in his own house, the materials they worked with, the rooms they worked in, their benches and long cutting tables. Everything, they agreed, was well-kept and in good condition; they were there on his sufferance, and were not about to criticise him.

Their sharp eyes rested on Alumbors, too. It was the wife who spent money from day to day and had to see that the children were presentable. In this at least she seemed to succeed: neighbours commented that the children, Johan and Guilhema, looked well fed, with proper shoes and tidily combed hair, and that Alumbors herself managed to keep a good table with salt meat and wine and that enviable sign of sufficiency, 'two sorts of bread', coarse black and white.

It was her women friends, especially, who noticed how the table was set. They mentioned salt meat, not fresh, because fresh meat was a luxury. The salt version, with a thick brown rind and a stripe of lean between two layers of fat, was called *baco*, a word the men of Rodez had borrowed from the English; it was the cheap staple the mercenaries bartered for, good for journeying and camp cooking, a hard slab that would last for weeks. Yet Guirbert Engles had also seen Marques going to buy fresh meat from the butchers, and mentioned that both he and Alumbors looked 'good and plump' on it.

Their diet may not have varied much. Fruit was costly, as we have seen from Petronilla's pears; a full basket, nicely arranged, took a day's wages for a skilled man. A tray of eggs cost a third as much; soft cheese, young *cantal* that could almost be spread like butter, was an expensive present. Rye bread, hard cheese, bacon and greens were what filled most people's plates; but Alumbors could clearly do better than that. The neighbours and tenants, in general, thought she and Marques had an abundance of 'rich things'.

We might well ask what those rich things were, besides white bread, fresh meat and good shoes. Every so often objects of startling beauty, studded with pearls or inlaid with gold, turned up in the houses of people in Rodez: even people who could not or would not pay their taxes. Occasionally townsfolk indulged each other with gestures that seem strangely luxurious or extravagant, like the sweet-eating that went on in the meeting houses, or the moment when the Bourg barber, 'as a friend', placed a garland of garden-grown roses round the head of one of his customers. These incidents give hints of a way of life that was sometimes softer, or lighter, than we might expect.

There was a royal wholesale tax, a *gabelle*, on luxury goods as on almost everything else: and these luxuries included figs, raisins, almonds, large wax candles, eau-de-vie, pepper and spices. It may have been something from this list that caught the fancy of Alumbors, or the notice of her neighbours. Or perhaps she often dressed in green; for green was the fashion-shade of the moment, always mentioned in inventories, and to lose a green coat or a green hood was plainly thought worse than losing one of any other colour.

Yet the tenants and neighbours more often talked in terms of 'necessities'. Peyre and Alumbors were said to have plenty of those, but the neighbours never said what they were. It was too obvious. In guest-houses, necessities meant pewter bowls and drinking cups, pillows, towels and table-cloths; in hospitals, they meant bedsteads, sheets and wine of good quality, which was watered down except on Sundays. 'Necessary' clothes, to judge by the items that were handed out by the City consuls to eighteen poor men each year, were a shirt, an overcoat of Rodez cloth, a pair of thin white stockings, a pair of sabots and a hat. Somewhere between those necessary things and those rich things lay the sort of household Alumbors kept.

If other tenants besides Aldebal noticed the struggles over money, they did not say so. Andreas Formis, a napper of cloth, had rented a house from Marques for fifteen or sixteen years. It seemed to him that if Peyre was simple, 'it was a good sort of simpleness, because he ran his household without doing wrong or injury to anyone . . . I always found him perfectly straightforward.' He admitted that Marques used to ask for his rent in advance, but this merely reinforced his respect for his landlord. 'I sometimes pay him a florin or a franc before payment day comes round', he admitted, 'to keep him in a good mood and to make sure he doesn't throw me out of the house.' This may have been Formis's little joke; it was the only suggestion of bad humour in Marques that anyone related. Aymeriga

Guasanha was impressed, on the contrary, by the fact that Marques did not always demand his rents on the dot. 'Sometimes I'd be having dinner with him and he'd give me a bit more time to pay what I owed for the part of the house we rented from him . . . if he wasn't rich he wouldn't have done that.'

Of all the tenants, the Guasanhas knew Marques best. They were virtually members of the family. The part of the house they rented was not just their workshop but, as we have seen, their home too. The father, Ramon, was a tailor. His daughter Aymeriga, a teenager, seemed to be round the house most of the day with sewing to do. Marques apparently liked her; he often took her into his confidence, complaining about his bad luck or letting her watch the diviners tapping the shop floor. Invitations to the family to eat with him and his family upstairs were transmitted through Aymeriga, as were his occasional offers to waive the rent for a while. Her father thought the rents were pretty high in any case, but Aymeriga seems to have been impressionable and grateful. 'Peyre kept a good table, with a lot of food,' she said, 'just as a good and wealthy man would.'

To these people, then, Marques was rich. There was sometimes even a note of awe in it, as when Peyre Bolas, the curtain-and-shroud man, said he had never seen Marques anything but prosperous and thriving. But this was little comfort to Alumbors, who naturally gazed up the social ladder rather than down it. She may have gained more comfort from those who, for one reason or another, knew little about Peyre and even less about herself.

Parish news — fortunately for Alumbors — stayed in its tight circle. Even people who were close to Marques might not know he was excommunicated if they attended a different church. Guirbert Engles, a cobbler who had rented his house from Marques for sixteen years, did not know that on several Sundays of the year Marques was at home all day.

'I belong to the parish of St Blaize in the Bourg', he explained, 'and that's where I hear the Mass and the sermon. Peyre is from the parish of St Amans.' The explanation was sufficient for his hearers. Bernard Rigaldi, who had been a next-door neighbour for four years, went to St Amans but was out of the town much of the time on business, clerking for Master Bernard Viguer; he knew nothing of the state of Peyre's health or finances and had not heard the denunciations, 'because, as I say, I've been away a lot'.

Yet it was only accident that kept these folk from hearing and, when they had heard, from judging Marques. Others who reserved their judgment were prevented by something altogether less natural: the fact of the town's partition. Among the citizens who gave evidence in the case, only Father Griffe knew Marques; and he, as his manager, assessed him gently, with none of the impatience of the Bourg businessmen who had struggled year in and year out to deal with him. Griffe tried to be fair, the fairness of a man brought in from outside to smooth over bad feelings between men who had known each other almost too closely and almost too long.

The other citizens knew nothing of Marques and his circumstances, and no more of Alumbors. Guisardo, that inveterate border-crosser, did not even know whether Marques owned the house in the Plassa de l'Olmet or whether he lived there. He had heard about his rich uncle; he had heard that Canac was 'a good man, well-spoken of, good reputation'. 'But that's about it,' he said; 'I can't add anything to that.' Indeed, no other citizens knew anything about Canac or could make the usual painful comparisons.

As for del Cayro and Cayrosa, the two masons knew much more about the drain — how it lay, where it ran, the subsidiary pipes — than about the man who owned it. And, even more surprisingly, they had no notion that gold had been found there. Del Cayro, asked whether Marques was poor or not, fell back rather lamely on the physical appearance of the people he had seen round the drain: 'Well, the family looked well-dressed.' And, like Guisardo, he remembered the rich uncle. 'Peyre should have that property still, unless he's sold it. I'm not sure about that, but he certainly doesn't look like a pauper now.'

The effects of division could be even more subtle. Bernard Claustras, for example, did business with Marques, had been born in the Bourg and had a house a stone's throw from Marques, on the corner by St Amans; indeed, he knew Marques well enough to call him *tu*, at least at first, when he caught him crying. But the screen of partition, so natural in Rodez, still came down: he told the court he could not talk about Canac finding the coins or confirm whether everyone knew that he had kept them for himself, 'because I'm all the time in my workshop in the City and not in the Bourg'.

And then there was Johan Gasc. It was probably no coincidence that both Alumbors and Peyre kept telling Gasc they trusted him 'more than anyone else who's here': more than Marot, whose eye was on the best chance of money, but also more than Marti Barbier, who came from the Bourg. Gasc did not seem to know the family at all; they had lost no face with him; he could not (and did not) judge them. And he did not go home to add his impressions to some fund of neighbourly gossip, for gossip did not seem to cross the border.

For Alumbors, there was relief in that. On one side of town, at least, Marques was still a man who, as far as anyone knew, was doing well. His clothes were not worn out; he was going to church, making money, meeting his obligations. Over in the City, where his uncle had been known for his wealth, some of that reputation still clung to him. Bourg creditors like Monferrier might have Marques excommunicated from the pulpit in St Amans, and might comment with a certain smugness on his lack of business sense. But Alumbors could comfort herself with the thought that in one half of town, as in the minds of the poor men who clustered for the rye bread that Peyre and not Monferrier had given them, her husband was a rich man and a benefactor, and she herself his proud and patient wife.

7

Huc Rostanh
and the service of God

O VER IN the City, however, there was one man who knew
the truth about the Marques case. Indeed, if you had
asked Alumbors's brother, Huc, what he knew, he might
well have replied, 'Too much.' As a canon of the cathedral,
he could have been removed from these scrabblings over
material things. As a citizen, he had no need to know what
was happening in the separate jurisdiction a little way down
the street. But he was dragged in anyway. He had been
in the cathedral one day, attending the sacred offices, when
Marques had accosted him. Another City priest was there
too: Father Griffe, who had recently taken over the running
of what was left of Marques's estates. Griffe reported that
the two stood there, in the half-built cathedral with its piles
of red bricks and drifting veils of dust, screaming at each
other.

Griffe did not say how the altercation had started. It is
possible that Marques had gone there only to talk about
money, or to whine, or to beg. Huc Rostanh affected some
of the poverty of a priest; he subsisted on set rations of wine

and bread and coins from the offerings left in the cathedral chapels, including the pennies Marques put down, and his half-burnt lard candles. But he was also a man of means. His house in Sant Stefe was rated for tax purposes at 5 deniers, where the average rating was 2; his vestment allowance was 20 livres a year, three months' wages for a skilled worker. He was paid in silver for the Masses and Offices he attended, and the bread in his rations was white. He kept servants, priests-in-training, to wait on him, shop for him, even to keep close to him as he sang the Office. And as much as anything, his ability to read the breviary and missal he carried raised him above the common herd.

At around the time Marques accosted him, Rostanh was trying to raise an extraordinary tax from the clergy of both Bourg and City 'to throw the English out of Sauveterre and to ransom the place'. The laymen of the Bourg, among them his brother-in-law, were facing a bill of 1,000 francs for the same enterprise, which the consuls were trying to raise hearth by hearth. Marques was having to borrow to meet it, but Rostanh was having to borrow too, because the City clergy would not pay up. He had had to ask the papal collector to stump up 150 livres for him to speed to the count's wars; and this fiscal inefficiency on his own part may have accounted for the sour mood in which Marques found him.

'Look at you!' he shouted. 'Why do you let yourself get so downtrodden and out of luck that you're excommunicated and have to mortgage your property? Why don't you spend your gold and silver? You've got plenty, haven't you? Where is it?'

According to Griffe, Rostanh said plenty more, 'thundering with anger'. It was all too much for Marques. Other people could hear, and they were not all privy to his financial affairs, as Griffe was. He burst into tears.

Sir, I've no money at all. God's blood, I hid all the
money I had . . . I put it under the floor of my shop
and I can't find it, I can't even guess where I put it or
hid it however much I do; I've prayed about it in all
sorts of places, I've gone on pilgrimages [*romanatges*],
I've done all sorts of things and they've all wasted my
money and now I'm in this state, poor and suffering. I
can't pay my debts . . . I can't keep my reputation, or
tell people the truth as I always used to . . . I don't
know whether I'm coming or going. I'm afraid I'll lose
my wits and become barmy, or mad, or something . . .
I don't even want to speak about the money, because
it makes me so angry and so ashamed.

We do not know how Rostanh responded to this; Griffe
did not say. He was not a man without compassion. He had
already put aside a house he owned in La Teulada, at the
top end of the Bourg square, to be used after his death to
shelter poor men in simple beds with sheets. 'The Hospital
of the Holy Cross' was the name he had chosen for it. He
had earmarked annual rents of rye and wine to keep up a
little chapel there, and to pay the board of the woman who
was meant to look after the sick. He also gave alms regularly,
handing out bread on the second, fourth and sixth weekdays
in Lent to all the poor of Christ who came to the cathedral.
But this did not mean that he placed his brother-in-law in
the same helpless category.

When Marques called himself 'poor and suffering',
Rostanh probably discounted it, much as he would have
discounted that wheedling 'Sir'; his words to Marques showed that he thought he ought to be able to take charge of
his life. In other words, he sympathised no more than the
consuls did when people got themselves into trouble, or
than Bernard Claustras did when he found Marques weep-
ing over an essentially avoidable mistake. Although Rostanh

too spoke in terms of *malastruc*, bad luck or bad stars, he also blamed Marques for letting the bad luck happen to him through sheer disorganisation.

Rostanh's own life hardly allowed for that, even if it had been in character. His days were circumscribed at almost every point. He was subject first to the long list of rules which he had sworn to obey at his institution, between his formal embracing and kissing of his canon-colleagues and his first formal seating, in tunic and hooded cape, in his own stall in the choir. These rules were written up and posted by the choir, near the roster board for services. He was bound to read the breviary every day, and to sing matins, vespers and compline — when the wooden peg beside his name announced it was his turn — 'distinctly, with care and devotion'. When he said Mass, that too had to be done carefully, at nine o'clock sharp, with no gabbling or ad libbing. Special attention had to be paid to the passage between *Qui pridie quam pateretur* ('Who, the day before He suffered') and *in Mei memoriam facietis* ('Do this in memory of Me'), when the bread and wine became the Body and Blood of Christ; when he received the wine himself, mixing it with water, he was instructed exactly how to place his fingers over the chalice. The wheat used for the Host had to be clean, and the wine from grapes only, preferably red, 'because that looks more like blood'; but that was not Rostanh's department.

He himself had to worry more about punctuality. If he arrived at Mass after the end of the epistle, or crept into the Divine Office after the second psalm, he lost a day's rations. Only illness, or medical treatment such as a bleeding, or a business trip, or (curiously) study in the library would excuse him. If he claimed 'bodily necessity which could not easily be deferred', he had to make sure that the excuse was genuine, 'or he will not be given his rations and will not avoid the penalty'. His servants had to be there, too, and they were fined if late: 1 denier if late for Mass, 2 deniers for matins. Lastly, again on pain of losing his daily rations, he was not supposed to wander round the church holding conversations.

Beyond that came the long list of chapter rules, openly displayed 'so that no-one can say he is ignorant of them'. Rostanh could not come in with falcons or hunting dogs, or let out a curse. He was to be kempt and reverent and clean, and conduct himself with pious devotion. He had to abstain from gluttony and drunkenness, water down his wine, avoid taverns unless the visit was really necessary, avoid cards and dice, and abjure reins, saddles or spurs of gold.

This last was a sly reminder of how Rostanh could have flaunted his wealth, had he been allowed to; for he was also a businessman. Membership of the chapter offered impressive opportunities to advance in the secular world. The chapter was a great owner of property, reporting 134 houses and gardens in the tax list of 1355, besides its own corn-measure and weighing place. The canons had also negotiated the use of the bishop's estate at Combret as the result of a mournful letter, sent in 1347, that lamented how 'the City of Rodez, being in such a cold high place, has few vines and poor wine, and the chapter has to bring in its own supplies from far away and at great expense'.

The houses owned by the chapter were inalienable properties, a quarter of them in Carrieyra Nova, the richest of the City streets; they were rented mostly to laymen. Fifty-seven other properties were rented out by the cathedral chantries or the Office of Works, most of them within the bounds of the cathedral building site in Terralh, the priests' street. Terralh was full of goldsmiths and artisans and taber-nacle-makers, paint and hammering and gold-glinting dust. It was here that Fontanier Broa made his ceremonial shields, and here that Guilhem Bournazels and Johan Marti, a carpenter, paid rent for their house to the office next door where honeyed stacks of candles were sold for funerals.

Priests and laymen therefore lived cheek-by-jowl, and frequently under the same roof. In the 1355 tax list, thirty-four citizens held parts of priests' houses. The clergy were known as an improving class; indeed, when people explained why the City was a better place, most said it was because it had more priests and they had done their houses up. In fact, priests were forbidden to buy houses in their own names or the names of their relations; but the chapter, for one, included several individuals who put chapter funds to private purposes. In 1325 the canons voted chapter money to a colleague, Berengar Mercier, to buy a basement and courtyard in a street called Bonaval, evidently for trading; Mercier told them he planned to find as much of the purchase price as he could and to shout out his bids, or have them shouted for him, at the public auction. The next year another canon, Bec de Penavayra, purchased a meadow near the leper-house 'as a private person'. Rostanh's house in La Teulada was obviously his to dispose of as he liked.

Priests could therefore be expert at managing property, as Rostanh was — and as Father Griffe was. At the very time he was managing Marques's estates, Griffe was having a brand-new house built for himself in a smart street called Penavayra. A typical priest's house, though smaller than Rostanh's and possibly smaller than Griffe's, was described in a contemporary deed of purchase: it had a hall and kitchen, built-in cupboards and winepresses (suggesting there was a suburban vineyard attached) and, in an upper room, clerical vestments folded in a chest. Most were close enough to the cathedral to be battered by the sound of bells. Such houses had often been owned by priests previously and stayed in priestly hands, which meant that, virtually as a matter of course, they did not pay tax.

The privilege of avoiding lay taxes, lay jurisdiction and lay punishments — *privilegium fori* — belonged to any man who had taken the tonsure, at whatever stage in his life or however casually; and it had been bitterly fought over in France, as in England, for most of the previous two hundred years. War expenses kept the controversy going. By the 1350s the consuls had made their point that since the new town walls were going to protect the clergy too, they ought to help pay for them. But they were a long time prevailing. The 1355 tax register is full of clerical fiddles or attempted fiddles: two parts of a meadow owned by Brother Guilhem Pons, a Franciscan, 'and that meadow is assigned to a chaplaincy for ever and therefore nobody can be assessed for it'; Father Bertran de la Fon's half-share of a house with his layman brother (the brother pays); Father Sicart Alaman's reluctant offer to pay for his house in Balastieyra 'saving his rights and privileges'. In all, out of sixty-six clerical properties listed, only twenty-five were declared for tax. One was Rostanh's, which was presumably inherited, and in which he lived in spacious splendour without tenants, with only a servant or two for company.

These houses, in effect, were often tax-free colonies of priests and their servants. The servants were sometimes young clerks in minor orders, like the unfortunate Bernat Teldes (eventually a canon and a colleague of Rostanh's) who got caught one day, as a teenager, failing to pay for meat he had bought for his canon-uncle; and sometimes they were women. The position of these female servants was ambiguous, perhaps even to themselves. The tax assessors, coming across a grey little woman (or a slim-hipped young one) scouring pots at the door of a priest's house, usually spared them. Father Duran Roquier had two helpers in his house, a cook and someone he called his sister, who was spared tax 'because she is Father D's servant for the love of God'. In 1378 Father Peyre del Fraysse acquired a woman, Ramunda, who was assessed for a quarter of a denier in tax;

in 1375 Father D. Carrada paid an eighth of a denier for his. Some women servants were taxed as residents, some not; we do not know why. But in 1375 two priests were listed with bastards, who were certainly assessed for tax.

One court case of 1337 opens a small window into that hidden world. Berengaria (she was not given the courtesy of a surname, being too poor) was once a priest's servant, doing the cooking and cleaning for the chaplain-curate of St Amans, in the Bourg. Her story began with a casual remark. Berengaria was working in the kitchen of Astruga Guirlarda, her new employer, on the day that the chaplain of St Amans was carried to church for burial. The small room was full of women: not only Astruga but Finas, too, her daughter-in-law. 'May his soul rest in peace, he was a good man,' said Astruga to Finas as the coffin passed. Berengaria butted in: 'He isn't a good man and he never was. He shut me up one time and locked the door and laid me.'

Astruga told this to the court; her evidence went no further, and its abruptness suggests that a shocked silence greeted the remark. Yet what was one to make of Berengaria? She was poor ('If she wasn't, she wouldn't have to be a servant', as Astruga tartly put it), and whereas Finas had married her Bernard with a dowry of 180 livres, Berengaria, according to Astruga, would have been hard-pressed to find a hundred sous or even fifty. Before she had worked for the chaplain she had been around, living in various run-down parts of the suburbs. Her two sisters were thought to be honest — Johan Combret, a neighbour, supposed they were, because they had married and 'had some money'; but Berengaria had moved in for at least a month with a couple of prostitutes, Petronilla and another Berengaria, who lived in Le Monastère.

Among these women, a certain pride attached to claiming that their numerous bastard children had fathers of standing. Petronilla said that her latest addition, a boy, had been fathered by Aulric Saumah, the messenger of some lord. And Berengaria freely put it about that Peyre Guirlart, Astruga's other son, had raped her and ought to do right by her. As Bernard Molenier testified, 'she said it in front of me and Huc Cabrespinas and plenty of others'.

But she was just as willing to accuse a priest. For Berengaria, a priest was a man like any other; and men wanted only one thing. Astruga Guirlarda, on the other hand, was shocked by that assumption. In her ordered and decent life, priests were better than other people. The Guirlarts lived, and made shoes, just beside the Peace Hospital. Many of their neighbours were clergy, brothers and nursing sisters working beyond the hospital wall, rarely seen, sustained by alms and rations of mutton and barley bread. These people were close to sainthood; in the hospital, the worst sin recorded was the stealing of scraps from the table after supper. For Berengaria, however, a priest was her employer, her oppressor, and a rich man, like all the rest.

Others felt the same way. The chapel of the Holy Slipper in the cathedral, just by the scene of Marques's meeting with Rostanh, had once been the setting for an even keener show of resentment by a layman against a priest. It had happened around Christmas in 1348, when Bernard Perier, the priest-in-charge, went into the chapel (informally known as *lo Soc*) to pay his respects to the relics. He loved the new cathedral: in his will, made a few years later, he especially asked to be buried 'inside the new church and in front of the chapel of St Lawrence, if the chapter will allow it'. A service was in progress but Perier, although he had his vestments on, was not taking it; possibly he was pottering about in his realm, opening cupboards, clearing little stalactites of wax from the candle-holders, revelling in his importance. As he was doing so, Guilhem Castanhier, a City butcher (whom we have already met, sealing up the sack of money that Bernard Gasto had thoughtfully removed from his partner's house), came in and struck Perier with the flat of his hand on the throat. He would have gone on, and beaten him up thoroughly, had not the worshippers intervened to pull him off.

The lawyer who wrote the charges laid it on thick, saying Castanhier had been 'prompted by the devil' to commit 'a double sacrilege, attacking a holy man in a holy place'. Worse, he had done it in the presence of the faithful gathered to hear Mass. Everything about Perier at that moment — his robes, his gestures, where he was — separated him from ordinary men. Yet to Castanhier, who rented his butcher's bench from the chapter, priests were also his landlords; and he had some secular grievance, which we can only guess at, that he wanted sorted out.

Besides, churches and services were not held in awe. People stood for the Mass, jostling each other, talking with barely lowered voices, dropping litter. The devout would wander round the walls, kissing the painted images or praying aloud, while small children relieved themselves behind the pillars. When churches were dark, they became useful places of assignation. Castanhier later became a sergeant and an officer of the common court, suggesting that his sacrilege did not weigh against him for long.

The line between priests and laymen was, in fact, very thin in some ways. Some tonsured clerks were mere children: one, ten years old, was accused of the accidental death of another boy 'in a childish game out in the fields, playing darts'. Curates of smaller churches (the 'holy-water benefices' to which most Rodez schoolboys passed on eventually, most with a mere fuzz of beard on their cheeks) had only the flimsiest knowledge of reading, Latin or how to sing the Office; they subsisted on small offerings for gabbled Masses, and frequently went into partnerships in trade to try to make ends meet. Between 1355 and 1385 seven City priests were listed for shops where they worked, and two of them, Canon Johan Codonat and Father Guilhem Cantal, kept stalls in the butchers' quarter, the lowest part of town. Indeed, all twenty butchers' benches and the tiny rooms behind them were owned by the chapter, and the rough red hands of a butcher like Castanhier were placed between the white palms of a canon like Rostanh with each change of ownership.

The synodal rules were not mute on the subject of butcher-priests. Rectors and chaplains were supposed to denounce all butcher-and-tanner priests for three consecutive Sundays during High Mass, and to insist that they abandoned their trades within two months or lost their status as priests. They were also forbidden to wear anything that was the *dernier cri*: overcoats or tabards, stitched-together sleeves, peaked or laced-up shoes, anything in red or green, or short cloaks which allowed their under-garments to be seen, 'since such clothes suit a secular soldier better than a soldier of heaven'. The admonitions seem to have fallen on deaf ears. Butcher-priests kept their short clothes, more practical to slop through the *mazel*; and their profane voices can be heard loud and clear in the evidence given by Gerald Marro, a layman, to the common court in 1338.

Marro, a man of some wealth, kept a butcher's stall in the City *mazel* with his brother Ramon; next to them was a stall manned by Gerald de Vernholes, a clerk in minor orders, who had his son to assist him. Marro tells the tale:

It was last Thursday. We were on the stall. We'd sold this chap a piece of meat — don't know who he was — when Gerald de Vernholes chipped in and said to the man who'd bought the meat, 'That meat's rubbish. It's not worth that price.'

Then my brother Ramon and I said, 'You're lying through your teeth. It's good stuff.'

Then Gerald took his sword out and came up to me

and put it to my throat, and called me a liar. So I got
up and I seized a spit that was out on the stall [for spit-
roasted chicken], and I threw it at him, and I think I
got him in the face.

It was developing into a grand little brawl, when suddenly
Vernholes played unfair. Dragged before the common court,
he said he was a priest 'and had a priest's habit and a priest's
tonsure, and therefore should not be tried in that court,
but in the court of the lord Official of Rodez'. He had
papers to prove it, too. The proctor of the common court
looked at his haircut and his clothes, agreed that they were
clerical, but insisted he should be proceeded against as a
layman. It took the *baile* — the bishop's man on the common
court — to intercede for this clerk, as he languished in the
City jail, and have him sent to the bishop's court for sen-
tence, Marro's bruises still livid on his cheeks.

Disappointed expectations of goodness coloured many of
the stories of clergy in Rodez. Then, as now, priests were not
supposed to be tempted as laymen were. They were meant
to keep men straight, to act as guarantors of good behaviour:
even, as we have seen, of something as elementary as handing in lost property. And, not least, they were meant to be
neutral agents in a divided place.

The basis of the 1316 power-sharing arrangement, and its
first clause, was the setting up of a joint perpetual chantry
where two chaplains, one from each side, would pray unceas-
ingly for the souls of those who had died in the rioting the
year before. This assumed that prayer was non-political, a
way of cooling the temperature. It was not. Rodez was partitioned in these matters, as in everything else. Laymen often
resisted it; in their wills they would leave money to all the
churches *infra aquas*, as if they saw the whole town included

intact in the cradling embrace of the river. But in the minds of the authorities, one side was always more Godly than the other; and a priest, like a layman, could live on only one side of the dividing line.

There could be no doubt, in a canon's mind, which side was better. It was the side to which the men and women of either side, City or Bourg, brought their tiny red-faced children, in proper caps, for baptism; the side with the cathedral. This was being built in the latest Gothic style, or the closest Rodez could get to it, with more than a touch of the fortress churches built against the Albigensians farther south. Bishop Ramon de Calmont had laid the first stone in 1277, signing it with the sign of the Cross, but a century later the cathedral was still unfinished; indeed, much of the nave was still a building site, with the ruins of the previous church left where they had collapsed 'with the hugest crashing of bells' at the end of the thirteenth century. The apse and side chapels had been built and decorated, with a liberal use of bright blue paint, gold stars and the City's red shields, but less than half the vaulting had been done in the choir. More than a century later, in 1495 (how poor Rostanh's jaw would have dropped to see it), a sketch-map of the City still showed the cathedral with two cranes poking from the roof.

The project was enormously, almost disastrously, expensive. Rostanh had spent many a chapter meeting discussing where and how funds could be raised to pay for it. The Office of Works had tried everything: seizing the revenue of vacant benefices, special collections, papal indulgences for a hundred and then for four hundred days, bishop's letters encouraging people to become Friends of the Cathedral in return for large annual contributions; even sales of building stone that were surplus to requirements. But the war drained everything away. The bishop blamed *sterilitates et mortalitates, turbines et tempestates*; but it was equally logical to blame taxes, which now even peaceful priests were pursued for.

Rodez sat on one of the main northern routes to the shrine of St James at Santiago de Compostela, but the pilgrim trade had never caught on as the chapter had hoped. A small pilgrims' shop had been set up in Terralh, the priests' street, right by the cathedral, to sell cheap metal souvenir badges brightened with a dab of paint. It was run (for the transfer fee of a bundle of reeds) by the Broas, who also made candles and, as a sideline, painted red shields for the City's border markers in the soggy meadows down by the river. Possibly Marques's *romanatges*, his 'Roman journeys' of piety, had amounted mostly to a step down to Broa's and a handful of small change left in the chapel of the Holy Slipper, a few yards from the place where he and Rostanh had quarrelled.

The Holy Slipper and the Holy Veil were the most precious objects in Rodez. The slipper, of black leather embroidered with silk, was said to have been worn by the Virgin and brought to Rodez by St Martial, who had seen Christ and supped with Him after the Resurrection. The veil, of linen, was supposed to have been used by Mary to cover the lower parts of Christ on the Cross. Most people in Rodez seemed to think that the veil had covered her head; but it did not matter. It was Our Lady's, and she was the friend and helper of all men, the one they called on when they were in deepest trouble.

When the count, back in 1315, was first told that some of the bishop's men had been killed in the Great Riot, his reaction was 'Sancta Maria! Any of ours dead?' (He added, typically enough, 'Holy Mary, grant that this Rodez trouble doesn't mean bad luck.') When Brenguier Affaros struck Bernard de Condat, a surgeon, with his sword in the Bourg square, everyone heard Condat cry *Sancta Maria mort ma mort ma* — 'Holy Mary, my death, my death!' — and recognised it as a speed-version of the Hail Mary, not a curse, but a commendation of his soul. When children wept with fear — as the Fornols boys wept when, a long way out of town by the river, they were bullied by youths and had their nets stolen — they sobbed 'Mother of God!', *Mayre de Dieu*, because they sought a mother's softness and safety.

Men swore by God and by His Body and Blood, as Marques swore even in the cathedral; but to Mary they stretched out their hands. The Bourg meeting house had a wall painting of the consuls, her vassals, kneeling at her feet. But the image Marques would have known best was in the brightly painted chapel dedicated to her in St Amans, where the priest-in-charge was ordered to keep one candle burning continually and two on feast days, and to guard 'the fees and prayer-money and things' with his life; and there Marques would have put down his pennies and knelt, with one petition in his mind.

Yet everything in the City was better done; and the City, with Rostanh in prominent place, honoured Mary tremendously. The City accounts began with the words *Ave Maria* even before 'In the name of God' — at least they did when the scrupulous Bocart kept them. The Virgin's picture was on the monumental cross by the fairground from which the 1315 rioting seems to have taken its direction: but, because this was such a baldly political use of her, the image was sometimes removed or broken by parties unknown, and a Broa would have to be brought in to mend or replace it.

In May, on the Feast of the Relics, the slipper and veil were taken in procession through the City, with musicians and trumpeters and a huge garland of flowers going before them. The City square was covered with green branches and set with benches and a portable pulpit. Barricades and ropes had to be put up to keep back the press of the crowd, and afterwards the veil was exposed above the cathedral doorway, guarded by two canons, as if it were the consecrated Host

itself. The excitement could be measured by the breakages.
Even stone walls were knocked down 'when Our Lady went
up'; in 1358 the marquee ropes got lost; and one year a
black-silk cope and an amice were torn to shreds. Occasionally, everything would be soaked with unexpected snow. In
the City accounts Our Lady appeared as a personality in
her own right, demanding, coquettish and expensive, and
enthroned in the hearts of men.

The chapter kept the Holy Slipper in a silver box, wrapped
in a piece of embroidered silk, alongside the veil and a phial
of the Virgin's milk, buried in three lead vessels inside the
high altar. Few people had seen these things at close hand;
but Rostanh was familiar with them all, for the chapter
regularly took them out for reverential stocktaking:

—two silk veils of Our Lady, or most of them; one red,
the other multi-coloured with several blood-coloured
spots . . . and this one, at the suggestion of Henry,
Count of Rodez, was decently placed in a vessel of silver
and crystal specially made for it.

—two glass phials, one containing milk of the Virgin
and another which seemed to contain blood.

—two nodules from the tree of Our Lord's Cross, and
a little piece of wood in a vessel with an inscribed stone.

—a fragment of the jaw of St Blaize, attested by continu-
ous and longstanding public recognition, which was
placed decently in a silver head.

A complete inventory for 1321 also listed a Majesty of Our
Lady, 'magnificently encrusted with jewels and gold, with
three garlands worked in silver and precious stones about
her head, and a crown laden with jewels and silver'. This
treasure was frequently displayed: Rostanh would have

carried it, and Marques would have glimpsed it, on the chapter's occasional forays into the Bourg. There was, besides, 'a new veil, as much new as old' (in other words, patched up); quantities of silverware and vessels and brass candlesticks; a processional cross ('but the pole has no cross in it'), and the crucifix containing the wood of the True Cross ('from which crucifix three stones have been removed or have fallen out, and gold decorations are missing in various places'). Constant moving, building and use had battered these treasures about; but shabby manufacture played a part, too, and several pieces were not quite so precious as they seemed. An inventory made when the treasure was seized from the church to be melted down during the Revolution, in 1795, noted that most of the 'jewels' were bits of coloured glass.

But there were other treasures, too. When the sacristan unlocked his cupboards, full of the testamentary bequests of past bishops, Rostanh would see an extraordinary profusion of vestments, plate, embroidered altar cloths, silk covers for the Gospels, a shoulder cape with four large pearl buttons, white sandals, shimmering lengths of white silk 'worth 200 francs' to make a cape, a red silk cover for the bishop's throne, a new missal ('and I believe there is not one more beautiful in all Languedoc') and an enormously heavy iron clock 'in a case, without chimes'.

Few benefactors added to their wills that dampening phrase 'not to be sold or otherwise alienated'; so from time to time, to meet chapter expenses, pieces of plate and chalices would disappear. As Rostanh would have emphasised, these were usually in pledge; they could be redeemed again. Only the episcopal cross was sold outright. Times, after all, were hard. The clergy were being taxed, and the new cathedral, built to the glory of God and the Virgin, was soaking up money like a sponge. Besides, the wealth to be found in the sacristan's cupboard almost begged to be invested or, as it were, distributed.

It was extraordinary for such a poor place. Out in the surrounding villages, according to the records of a pastoral visit in 1418, even the most basic equipment was lacking; and that was probably the case in the smaller churches of Rodez, St Blaize, Santa Martra, Santa Catherina, and the rest. In the poorer streets, as out on the wild hills and in the deep wooded valleys beside the pelting streams, the churches were crumbling; priests' houses were in disrepair, adjacent cemeteries full of rubbish. The naves were cluttered with chests, bundles of clothes and flitches of bacon, stowed there for safety in case the English showed up. Most of the baptismal fonts needed lead basins to hold the water. The pastoral list ran on:

Monjaux: Get a lantern for taking Viaticum to the sick by the first Sunday in April. Repair the broken windows by the octave of Easter.

St Martin de Cormières: Make a silver reliquary for the parish relics, or at least a gold-plated copper one, before Christmas.

Villefranche: Get an Ordinary and a synodal book [the standard book of conduct and behaviour for priests]. This last is very important ...

Sévérac l'Eglise [where Marques had vineyards]: Remove the chests, etc., from the nave.

Sebazac: Sell an engraved altar candle, and use the money to buy a missal.

St Peyre de Naucelle: The prior must appear in person before the bishop's Official to explain why he kept the

Sacrament in a wooden box in a scrap of dirty linen, as if it were unconsecrated.

Worse was to come. At Concourès, in the tabernacle with the Sacrament, the bishop found two caterpillars. The church had already been found to lack lead, glass and a breviary, but this had been forgiven and forgotten 'because the prior served dinner'. Now poor Bernard, the curate, was summoned to Rodez to be fined by the bishop's proctor on pain of excommunication. We can imagine him struggling in, one man among the crowds that flocked to the Official's court on judgment days, to quote the City's propaganda: marvelling at the cathedral with its raw red brick and, once inside, agape at the decorated altars. No other place could compete with it: except, of course, the one down the hill.

To Huc Rostanh, the Bourg's fierce sense of spiritual rivalry would have seemed daft. The whole place was known to be obsessed with commerce; matters of the spirit were virtually crowded out. If his sister Alumbors was involved with notorious usurers like Natas, it was because burgenses lived that way. Almost every Bourg merchant of note, including Girma's and Natas's fathers, had been named in royal letters against usury that were sent to the town in 1338; the buyers and sellers in the Bourg square had been excommunicated *en masse*, early in the century, for trading in a cemetery; and the whole church body of St Amans itself, besides numbers of named parishioners, had had to be formally absolved by the bishop from charges of trafficking with the English in 1366.

The chapter, it was true, lent money occasionally; indeed, it could provide extraordinary amounts of cash almost instantly. In 1369, just before Rostanh was appointed to raise the clerical tax, Estol Aribert (then consul, still living in the partitioned house in Sant Stefe) was acting as chapter treasurer. He lent the consuls the huge sum of 195 livres, in two instalments, to go towards troops for the war. He insisted on repayment within two months, but seemed to charge no interest. The chapter professed not to profit by lending, and in any case always muttered repentance. 'We of the church, you understand', read one self-justifying letter, 'would rather lose the profit of the world than the grace of God and the salvation of our souls.'

The Bourg, it seemed, simply did not think that way. St Amans itself was hidden down the hill, half-buried behind stalls laid out with pastries and meat and fish, virtually draped in awnings like the central tent at a fair; and the monks of that church, who were supposed to follow the Augustinian rule, lived lives of shocking negligence and lack of order. When the abbot of St Victor of Marseille, their mother-church, paid a diocesan visit in 1347, he had to remind them of the most basic rules of priestly behaviour: the curate to reside in person, Mass to be said on the usual days at the usual times, church roof and windows to be repaired, a wax candle to be kept burning before the tomb of St Amans. By 1370, when Mass and Divine Office, at least, seem to have been regularly said, the roof and windows were still full of holes. It was almost appropriate that Marques should have to perform his public penances for bad management in a church where services were still somewhat casual, and rain dripped in on the congregation.

During the 1350 inquiry about the Bourg square, some pointed questions were asked as to whether the Bourg was really a Christian place. Oh yes, chorused the witnesses, 'from time immemorial'. A more doubtful note was sounded by Johan Fabre, a royal notary: 'It's seemed Christian enough for as long as I've been there, but I've only lived there eight years.' On the hard rock of Rodez, the cover of religion sometimes seemed a little thin: so that Alumbors Marques, sister of a canon, could resort to witchcraft, and then go to church placidly, like any Christian woman.

On the other hand, Christianity in the Bourg was reputed to be ancient. The church of St Amans was older than the cathedral; St Amans, the first bishop, had presided there, baptising the faithful in his own stone font. People believed, whether it was true or not, that the first Christian temple in Rodez had been built on its site. And the Rostanh family had a close connection with it. The Rostanhs, after all, had once lived in the Bourg; and in the 1340s, when that damning report had been drawn up, one Guilhem Rostanh had been the St Amans chaplain-curate, the priest who should have been in residence and was usually elsewhere. The chapter had also had to summon him on a charge of usurping the cathedral's parish pence: collecting 'up the hill', in the City, for the various St Amans charities. Guilhem Rostanh, confronting the canons in the cathedral, denied it fiercely: 'I've never done or countenanced any such thing.' But it was an old trick; indeed, as Huc Rostanh knew, it still went on.

The City, being the richer side, was the better place for alms; the Franciscans always swore by it. But the Bourg's main church, lacking the pulling-power of the cathedral, made up for it in guile. Collectors for the Bourg *bassinas*, the alms for the souls in Purgatory, came rattling their collection boxes into the City on Sundays and feast days, just in case unthinking citizens would drop their money in. On several occasions, too, the sacristan of St Amans obtained letters from the bishop authorising a collection 'for candles in Rodez'. His candle-money collector then went through the City streets, gathering deniers and obols, and ordinary folk, according to the official protests made later, 'were confused by his ambiguous title, and gave their money believing it was going towards lights in the cathedral'. Afterwards, when the cathedral collectors came round, 'they said they had given already'.

The scam did not work so well the other way about. In

1294, collectors for the cathedral building fund ventured into the Bourg; and raised a little over 4 livres, as against more than 78 livres on their home territory. There is no record that they tried it again; if the City wanted to flaunt the cathedral, the City would have to pay for it.

For their part, Rostanh and his chapter colleagues went down to the Bourg three or four times a year on an errand that was ostensibly religious but was, in fact, political: to show the glittering Majesty of the Virgin in that squalid square, by that squat church, to prove the City's superiority of devotion. They also carried the great cross; and it was no coincidence that they sang the *Vexilla Regis*, as if they were marching into the land of the infidel under a crusading banner. These little shows, however blessed by incense or gold paint or invocations of the saints, were in fact political and territorial.

A little before the Great Riot, at the beginning of the century, one of these displays had been disrupted in a way the clergy vividly remembered. The bishop, the canons and the City priests had all gone in procession to stop a jousting tournament which the count was holding without the bishop's permission. They had gone down Santa Martra (the same border street!) with the majesty of the Virgin in front, the great cross bobbing behind, and a train of people following in humble devotion. The priests were in their surplices; a litany of Our Lady was sung. But midway through the exercise, the count's men attacked them. The bishop was chased into a house; some of the clergy, terrified, crammed in behind him; the worshippers fled. When the bishop, ruffled and furious, eventually blustered out of the house again by the garden gate, the clergy saw the count's son riding nonchalantly near the hanging elms, 'as if he was out for a promenade'. This injury too was remembered in the catalogue of Bourg crimes.

One canon, Peyre de Scoralha, a bishop's attendant who

had been a monk in Marseille, stayed behind in the street alone to keep the Virgin safe. We do not know what his thoughts were as he stood there, in the suddenly silent street, with the beautiful heavy treasure in his arms. But it was he who made that tentative remark that the scrapping lords of Rodez might love the other side more if they got to know it; and he also said, later on, that it was only because canons were 'bound to love the honour of the bishop and the church' that they were drawn into bitter political disputes that good men left alone.

But drawn in they were; and the liturgical calendar sometimes provided even better excuses for rivalry. Palm Sunday was one test, when the canons would process among the border gardens at the top of Santa Martra. There, as the feast demanded, they would bless whatever branches they could find: gnarled apple with the pink buds barely forming, still-dead brambles, or plum with blossoms as fragile as the snow. In and out of the Bourg they went, through wicket gates and on the wrong side of walls, thorns snagging their surplices, as the litany died away raggedly behind them.

The delegation went down too on Rogation Days, when the boundaries — both external and, in Rodez, internal — had to be blessed. The Rogation processions continued for three days; on the third day, Rostanh and his colleagues went in procession to sing Our Lady's praises through the border streets of the Bourg and up to St Amans itself. While they were about it, they would linger in the Bourg square to say the Office of the Dead and give absolution, sprinkling holy water over the 'tombs' among the market stalls. Nothing was cleared for them: the hucksters still sat in their accustomed corners, the smell of cheese and sheep and salt fish all around them; but the brass sprinkler was dipped into the brass water bowl and shining, holy drops shaken out, as the canons bowed deeply and made the sign of the cross.

The burgenses made quite a good show of not understanding what was going on. As one of them pointed out,
the square did not look like a cemetery. 'In the cemetery St
Amans', he said, 'there are usually pots of water beside the
grave-mounds, and there are crosses on the mounds and
tombs which are sculpted out of stone. I haven't seen that
in the square . . . By St Amans, there are little wooden crosses
too and pots of holy water.'

Very few people, besides, could distinguish what exactly
the City clergy were singing. This would probably have been
true of Marques and Alumbors as well, had they raised their
heads to listen. They were meant to know the *Pater Noster,*
the *Ave Maria* and the *Credo*; in confession the priest was
supposed to test them, but there was probably not much
time (or inclination) for that. And what priests did was
often mysterious. During the processions in the square most
burgenses seem to have kept on working, heads down. When
the cathedral clergy went past, singing psalms, 'I don't know
which ones they were singing,' said one man; 'I'm not very
learned.' 'I didn't understand them,' said another. Barto-
lemi Terissa, a merchant of thirty-three, said he didn't
understand them either, 'but I think they were holy.'

These remarks suggest that whatever the cathedral clergy
thought they were doing, it could be taken as pure provo-
cation. The Bourg priests, with simple cross, stole and holy
water, buried the dead; the cathedral canons paraded
through with singing and statues, not stopping, making their
point. In Rostanh's case, this may have been as close as he
ever came to comforting his sister and brother-in-law in
person with his prayers.

He came past sometimes, too, to claim the dead. Huc
Serras's house marked a sort of frontier post, the boundary
between the main parishes of Bourg and City. Serras was
the man with the Saracen remains in his cellar; his garden
was in the dividing ditch, right by the Peace Hospital, and

in 1358 he was paid for crenellating his own house as part of the border defences. (He did it so shoddily, with odd bits of wood, that by 1360 it had fallen down again.) Outside the door of his wine-shop there were often distressing scenes: mourners and clergy arguing about funeral fees or the proper destination of the body, while the bier with its coffin or white-sheeted corpse stood in the street, deterring customers.

Matters came to a head in 1392, when a man dropped dead in the street beside the Peace Hospital. His name was Gerald Lagomia. (The notary, for some reason, gave his name first as Gerald Canac, and then crossed it out.) Lagomia had fallen just inside the City as he died, but he had wanted to be buried in the Bourg. Priests from St Amans could not come into the City to collect him from his house, where his corpse was washed and laid out in winding-cloths; equally, priests from the City could not take him to St Amans. So a compromise was made: a priest from the cathedral would accompany Lagomia's body as far as the Ebrart hospital, where he would hand it over to a clerk of St Amans. The clerk would provide and light the great wax candles, toll the bell, and take the body on for burial.

Eventually, the residents of nineteen houses to the north of Serras's house (including, just to be on the safe side, the Sant Stefe gatehouse and the watch-tower beside it) were understood to worship in the cathedral while they lived but to belong to St Amans when they died. The agreement contains a street map, a precious little sketch of the debatable land on either side of the ditches, with the houses arranged in eccentric perspective, some flat, some dimensional, round the divided criers' stone in Sant Stefe. Each house is numbered, but the numbers are not consecutive: number 2 is beside 5, 1 beside 13; Serras's house, number 19 on the list, is not on the map at all. Passing under the Gate of Peace the artist has drawn a small track, a dotted line, to give depth. It suggests footsteps: the footsteps of weary Gasc returning from work, of Rostanh in procession with the Cross, of men carrying coffins. It is a map that speaks volumes about the cares of partition, which were mixed up even with the care of souls.

This competition for the dead was strictly financial. The living gave their offerings; but the chapter could claim from the dead and their relatives 8 deniers for an *obit*, or service of the dead, 8 deniers for the burial of children in the cemetery behind the cathedral, and the beds (complete with hangings, pillows and mattresses) or the value of the beds of anyone over ten who was brought to be buried in church. When Johanet, the man who had painted the royal arms for the shields that had just gone up in the City, buried both his children in the same week, it was worth 16 deniers to the chapter and the cathedral building fund; though the City consuls, out of charity, paid for small shrouds for them.

A canon like Rostanh would naturally assume that the cathedral was the better place to be buried; but the burgenses, including his sister and brother-in-law, treasured their dowdy church, and scraped and saved to keep it in repair. Marques kept St Amans going not merely with the pennies he left for lights before Our Lady, not merely with tithes of his oats and wine when he still had them (for which priests were supposed to nag their parishioners at least eight times a year), but also with the annual fee of 6 deniers and a measure of rye expected from every head of household for the upkeep of the church. Between them, the confraternity members looked after the fabric and kept the chapels lit, 'so that God may enlighten the living and absolve the dead'; and if His enlightenment sometimes seemed reluctant, that was not for men like Marques to question.

Calls on his money were frequent. The two rival churches had to be kept up not only for the glory of God, but for the besting of each other. The arms of the Bourg were everywhere inside St Amans: engraved on the chalices, sewn on the chasubles, stamped on the four chained books and, not least, painted on the shields held up by two angels on the columns of white stone that separated the sanctuary from the choir. The church was a small sanctum of Bourg pride, a pride that could seldom be shown to the same effect outside it.

The church almost seemed to furnish itself from the generosity of Marques's rich neighbours: Guilhem Maurel's cloth of gold, ornamented with Bourg shields, presented in 1369, or Astruga Robberta's silver chalice 'with my name on the foot', bought with the profits of the tavern that was built on the bones of the dead. But the church did not mend itself. In 1370 the churchwarden was charged to get three tilers to re-roof the whole building at public expense. And one year, the Rogation Day invasion by the City clergy called forth a defiant response: payment to workmen 'to make the square beautiful on Rogation Tuesday'.

The relics inside St Amans were also in the consuls' charge. In 1313 they were produced for consular inspection; some were queried, like the knife wrapped in a piece of blood-stained silk, or 'an odd bone with an odd tooth, found inside the altar'. But whereas the City could claim, besides its pieces of the jaw of St Blaize, only an arm of St Andrew and certain remains of St George, the Bourg had 'a big bit' of the head of St Lawrence and three of his teeth; a rib of Peter and a rib of Paul; an elbow of St Vincent; a tooth of St James (in a glass); a bone 'from the foot or the hand' of St Innocent; and a bone from the knee of St Amans himself. This last relic was kept inside a silver-gilt container in the shape of a seated figure of 'My Lord St Amans', covered with gold decorations, pearls and tiny Bourg shields. When necessary, this glittering body was repaired by small diversions from the royal wine tax. The light that burned in a bowl before him was maintained by the Bourg shoemakers, who required each apprentice and new member to leave a pound of wax there.

The Bourg too had a piece of the True Cross, which was set in 1367 in a cross of gold decorated with precious stones, with the arms of the Bourg in enamel at all four points. The consuls paid the goldsmiths 60 sous for each mark of silver worked, 76 sous for each mark of gold; and the money came, presumably, from the same taxpayers who were struggling in the same year to pay for the war against the English. Lastly, most competitive of all, in a glass phial, came the Virgin's milk.

In a hardscrabble town, the consuls made awkward keepers of gorgeous things. Thus in the 1370s, when they became custodians of a processional cape with fringes embroidered with images, another cape, funerary, of black satin, six little silver bells and two annotated prayer books, they gave them immediately to the sacristan, rather than lose them among the lead and sling-shots in the meeting house.

Not all the sacristans, however, could be trusted. That 1347 visitation by the abbot of St Victor of Marseille, when Guilhem Rostanh was chaplain-curate, had turned up a curious arrangement. The sacristy of St Amans was being part-run by Peyre and Andreas Catel, from a notorious family of money lenders, and a silver chalice was missing. This was perhaps already melted down into some of the false *guianes* pennies which Huc de Pineto was palmed off with that year when he went to change a gold florin in Astruc Catel's office, under the gate leading into the square.

Astruc ('Lucky') Catel also sold jewels; in the 1330s numbers of men from outlying hamlets, who had come into Rodez for the fairs, found themselves in debt to him for those and arraigned in the bishop's court. Since only one register for fair debts survives, we cannot tell how unusual this was, or how often jewels were on offer. But we may wonder, certainly, where these sparklers had come from, and indeed whether they were really jewels at all.

In 1370, matters were rather the same. This time Guilhem Natas was sacristan, the brother of Marques's creditor and honorary uncle, and one Huc ('Groats') Martel was living in his workshop. A few years before, notary Bernard Fonfrega and sergeant Gui de Podeo had been ordered to carry out a night raid on this workshop; they found a sackful of false Breton pennies stuffed in a mattress. Martel put up a fight and denied that the money was his, but the count's treasurer's lieutenant had seen him before, 'putting down a Breton penny for a *patate*, though it wasn't worth one'.

Martel was subsequently jailed for circulating false coin, sentenced to the loss of all his goods and banned from public office. Yet most of the time money-chisellers and people of repute, including priests, worked easily enough together. The Catels even became consuls. The sight of Natas, Martel's landlord, walking in the church or the cloister with his arms full of vestments and chalices, might have confirmed Marques in his feeling that some families had all the influence and all the luck; and were not only forgiven their sins, but given the chance to expand and improve on them.

Forgiveness of sins was evidently something that weighed on Marques's mind. His miseries over his money were leading him into bad ways: he was starting to cover up, to tell lies, to feel ashamed. His excommunications regularly cut him off from grace. He had appealed to God in all the ways he knew how, and God had not helped; evidently more expiation was needed. Rostanh had yelled at him as if his mortgaging of his property was a sin in itself. But Marques could not think what else to do, other than to throw himself on the mercy of his brother-in-law.

It was no longer the job of Rostanh, a canon, to hear confessions. That was the job of parish priests. None the less, he knew the formula; and if a man had come to him, desperate, or away from home, or afraid that his own priest would spill the beans, he was bound to accommodate him. In that case, he had to hear the confession in an open part of church, not hidden in some corner, with his stole about his neck and his hood up, covering his eyes. He was bound to look away from the penitent, especially if a woman; 'and if he learns of some ghastly sin he must not spit, or turn his head this way or that, or make any sort of gesture, but must speak words, informally and kindly, which will bring the sinner to loathe his sin'.

Marques's visit to Rostanh may well have been intended as confession; where the confidant was a priest, there were inevitably overtones of that. Yet, if it had been so, Father Griffe would hardly have reported it in court. It is likely that Marques expected something similar, but different: a blend of spiritual and practical advice. If this was what he wanted, Rostanh failed him, at least at the outset. He showed, instead, his rage and contempt. As a man of affairs, he scorned Marques for his lack of drive and organisation. As a relation, he scorned him for the difficulties in which he had plunged his sister. And, not least, as a chief exponent of the City's pride, he scorned this shabby specimen of the community 'down the hill': forgetting that he, Huc Rostanh, canon, citizen, businessman, success story, was also representative of the mercy of Christ.

Drawing the moral

FOR SEVERAL WEEKS, the witnesses gave their evidence. They came into the count's hall each afternoon, singly or in groups, pushing their way through, to make their depositions in the presence of the notary. The notary got tired; in the special registers dedicated to the case his writing grew larger and larger, spreading and sprawling. His quill split, his ink ran out; again and again he trimmed, refilled, and bent his aching hand to the task. In the end, the judge made his decision; but there history gets the better of us. We do not know what it was.

Like any crowd of folk encountered on a journey — Chaucer's pilgrims too, or Langland's folk, their contemporaries — the characters in the Marques story disappear where we cannot follow. Yet we do not lose sight of them entirely. Other documents allow us to pursue them just a little further into the darkness and to surmise, as best we can, what may have happened in the case of the jug of gold.

The Segui shop, once drained, prospered: in later years, with widow Seguina still in robust charge, the City consuls went there to buy *violet* of Moustivilliers for their robes. But we hear no more of the shop next door. We see that Johan Marques, Peyre's son, appears in the 1380s renting a house from the count in Barrieyra, the second-best Bourg street, and a meadow from the bishop quite close to the centre of town. He was making small but useful loans to the count and the consuls, including the loan of his horse for a trip. In 1385 he was *levador* of the Bourg wine tax, the man who did the donkey work of going from shop to shop collecting the money for the man who had farmed it. In 1386 he put up a bid of 300 francs to farm the tax himself, but did not get it. He thus failed by a slim margin that test of being *bo e sufficiens* that tax-farmers, as well as consuls, had to pass. The next year the *gabelle* was farmed by Guilhem de Carlat, son of the man Johan's father had challenged over his inheritance.

If Peyre Marques won the case (and his story, all along, suggested that the money was his), his victory may not have done the confused old man much good. And Alumbors seems to have died before the case came to court. If Canac lost, he would have had to pay the legal costs. But he did not seem to stumble; in 1394 he was taking charge of an order from the count for sumptuous clothes of wool and fur 'which he had brought down from Paris' in several trussed bundles and trunks.

To the medieval mind, however, the man who won was not necessarily exalted, and the one who lost might not be left comfortless. The weak man, the loser, could still sometimes triumph over the strong. The natural order could be reversed. The deer could hunt the hound; the trout could entangle the fisherman. If it happened seldom in life, it could happen in poems, jokes and dreams; and in that world, there were no social or financial limitations.

Inside the covers of the City and Bourg accounts, at the end of the thick paper pages beautifully inscribed with records of incomings and outgoings, small sketches appear. A fanciful squared-off castle with turrets; a siege machine; ornamental crosses; plump fish, fatter than any the artist could have pulled from the Aveyron; and in one, from the Bourg in 1375, a sketch of a cat with prominent genitalia, head twisting round fiercely, while a bird pecks under its tail. 'This bird is pecking the cat's arse and eating the — ' runs the legend. *Ita est.* 'That's right.'

The cat (*catel*) may have been only a cat; or it may have been whichever Catel, of the family of money-chisellers, was giving trouble at that moment. The bird may have been only a bird, a long-beaked scrawny-legged creature; or a man with a grievance that he worked out in ink on paper, the only means at his disposal. This man, as if proud of his work, has signed it with his name in Latin, underscored with a decorative line and a second, even fancier, line patterned with circles filled with ink: Johan Guisardo, Galhart's brother.

Inside the back cover of a tax register for 1363, someone else wrote a poem. It may well have been the man who wrote the register; he seems to have been a semi-trained lawyer. This was not his only effort. Two short verses in the same hand appear in the register for 1364:

> Look and hear
> What folk say to you;
> Watch what you do:
> You'll soon be buried too.
>
> Be good
> Don't fear
> If you're good
> God the Father will hear
> If you don't do well
> You'll go to hell.

His more ambitious piece, in the 1363 register, starts with a lawyer's preamble in pretty bad Latin: *Noverint universi presentes pariter et futuris hoc presens plublicum* [sic] *insturmentum* [sic]: and goes on:

> The poor people weep and sigh
> Every day to God they cry.
> Pay some heed to what they say,
> Poor and rich, from day to day;
> You should put it in your heart,
> What they say on either part.

The next verse begins with *Volias saber*, 'Know that', the formal lawyer's opening of public announcements made in the vernacular at the flat stone in Sant Stefe. In one poem, therefore, the two most typical bits of lawyer-jargon were used to point a contrast: on the one hand the overbearing law-backed official, on the other the ordinary small-voiced man in the street. Lawyers always won on earth, that much was plain; but that was not the end of it.

> No-one listens any day
> To what the poor man has to say.
> Watch that you don't judge him so,
> You will go by this way too:
> God the judge lets judgment fall
> On who has served Him best of all.

Which side of the stone was our poet shouting from? Did he shout to the north, towards the City, or to the south, towards the Bourg? As it happens, he came from the City. He shouted north. But what he had to say was universal; it was something any man or woman of Rodez would have

sympathised with, if they had ever had to answer to a
sergeant or tug at a creditor's sleeve. The human aspirations
of the townsfolk, their deepest hopes and anxieties and
sorrows, were utterly without division.

From his great cold height, therefore, God the judge looked
down on the town. He saw Huc Rostanh in the choir, singing, his book before him, his robe blown by the cold draught
that found out the gaps in the cathedral walls. He saw Johan
Maurel, the publican, turfing out a band of customers, their
steps unsteady, into the Bourg square, and saw the women
cabbage-sellers move away from their groping hands. Under
the gateway He saw Andreas Catel setting out his false
money, counting it, burnishing it, laying it out again; and
laid a finger of conscience on the back of his neck. In the
courthouse He saw Johan Brau, in his grey and blue, swinging his sergeant's stick as he recounted some act of civil
disobedience; and Helias Porret, half-hidden among his
bundles of yellowing paper, listening with a corner of an
ear.

Beside St Amans, under the red earth, He spied out the
bones of Alumbors Marques lying straight, but ready to
scramble out again, still nagging, at the last trumpet call.
He saw Gerald Canac unloading his pack-horses, shaking
out the folded cloth, with the purposefulness of a man who
has learned to live with the guilt of a sin committed long
ago; and, in another street, searching for something that he
cannot quite remember, but searching because the act of
looking stops the buzzing in his deaf old head, Peyre
Marques.

All would be gathered, citizen and burgensis, so many
soft-eyed souls, like creeping chicks in the Almighty robe;
all would be lifted higher than the dividing walls, higher

even than the English-haunted hills, to the Last Judgment, where accounts would be set straight.

The town was Rodez; the river was the Aveyron. The year was 1369 or 1370, though nobody can say for sure.

Epilogue

Yᴇᴛ ʜɪsᴛᴏʀʏ is not a box we can lock, or a book we can close, and then forget. It continues into the present, sometimes with surprising force. Incidents from long ago, if they were vivid enough, can overwhelm much more recent memories. And that is true, too, of this story.

The war that was being fought in 1370 still echoes in the hills round Rodez. It is there in the political geography, the echoes of tricks and sieges and defiantly fortified places. But it has crept into the culture, too. One of the most useful sources for my research was the wonderful annotated edition of the City accounts by Henri Bousquet. The second volume, printed in 1943 at the height of the Second World War, contains this curious 'announcement' just before the preface:

> History is the great teacher of peoples . . . but we do not listen to it. Even after the experience of several centuries, too many people today consider it odd to question England's claim to be France's best friend. It

is possible that England loves France, but in the way
the wolf does in the story of Little Red Riding Hood.

So the war has gone, but left behind the horror of war;
and the internal walls and ditches in Rodez have long gone
too, but left their shadows. I found they had been replaced
by drab municipal car parks; but those too were neutral and
rather unsatisfactory spaces, suggesting that the two parts of
town could not naturally amalgamate their housing patterns.
And indeed the town, in character, was still two towns.

The City square marked the centre of one half, surrounded by tall grey buildings, bookshops and robe shops
and sellers of funerary urns. The Société des Lettres,
Sciences et Arts met in the City in an upper room, where
the grand old men in berets, leaning on their canes, would
stoop to admire the ancient vellum volumes displayed under
glass, like still fish in water.

Just as in the fourteenth century, the City had a sense of
space and dignity and a more upscale, tidy market, domi-
nated by the gleaming motorised stalls of cheese-sellers and
meat-sellers. The king of the stallholders was Crémafix,
whose silver van was always parked in the shade of the plane
trees at the east end of the cathedral, and whose wares
included Cantal cheese of every conceivable age, peasant
bread with a black crust, sweet doughy *fouaces* as large as
wheels, and fresh butter slapped with a knife on to squares
of waxed paper. On the other side of the square was the
Café de la Paix, a place lined with ornate mirrors. In front
of these, on market days, the peasant vendors could be seen
eating their home-made sausage out of pieces of foil; but
they seemed slightly ill-at-ease there, as though they
belonged in that other place, down the hill.

And down the hill, in the Bourg, there was still that
second-best feeling. The square was cramped and small;
where the City had the cathedral, the Bourg had only

Molenier's hat shop, with a rusty model of a Napoleonic tricorn that creaked in the wind. This market was the peasants' place, or the place of the people who sold cheap clothes out of the backs of vans; or the preserve of the grand-mothers with their paper-lidded pots of preserve and their live hens, which were pushed on to the big scales in a frenzy of feathers and fear. Those ignorant of the town's history might well conclude that this was just a quaint subsidiary neighbourhood. Those who knew it understood that it had been that way, though fighting against it with all the pride at its disposal, for 800 years.

Other things had not changed, either. Then, as now, there were scarcely any foreigners in town. Rodez had no black faces. A few Algerians lived in run-down apartments in a miasma of cooking smells and washing. I met one of their women once, in the entry to an apartment block, tearing up lottery tickets she had found in the mail box; she was wearing a scrap of material as a veil, which she plucked across to escape my eyes. The menfolk squatted on the corner at the bottom of the main hill, by the pharmacy, in anoraks and woolly hats, hands pressed under their armpits. In the window of the pharmacy was a guide to mushrooms and toadstools one might find in the woods: also strange and dangerous, found in dark corners, known by their smell.

From the southernmost edge of the Bourg, or from the ramparts under the west face of the cathedral, the landscape lay as immense and almost as empty as it had ever been. There were green tongues and ridges of woods; but dry naked plateaux formed the horizon as far as the eye could see. And the wind, inevitably, blew and blew. It was often too chilly to sit and stare for long; but in the lee of buildings, or of the cathedral, old men would sit in little groups, identically dressed in the black clothes they wore for coming into town, smoking and spitting and cursing life.

I had met these men before. Indeed, I kept meeting them,

not only in my documents, but in the sort of books that Dropy and Fournial in the archives would draw my attention to, in their twittering or lugubrious way, feeling it important that this English woman should be educated. There was a character that remained, even if the centuries had altered the town. There was a soul that did not change. And here it was, described by a nineteenth-century writer and quoted in Henri Affre's *Dictionnaire du Rouergue et des Rouergats*, from a few decades later.

The man of the Aveyron . . . is full of bitterness, mistrust, stubbornness, torpor; but also full of strength, delicacy and reflection. He is sober, charitable, steadfast in love and in hate; he is trained in patience by back-breaking work, a thin soil, a harsh climate; but independence is always the most distinctive mark of him. He hates to feel the hand of authority. You must know how to drag what you want out of these people; and, even then, you may never get it. You may think them won over because they do not revolt, but active resistance is a violent state that does not suit their dourness; their form of revolt is inertia. If you spoil them, they jib at it; if you push them, they stop, and you will find them unbudgeable. 'Sir,' said the mayor of Rodez to one of those ancient bishops who was picking a quarrel with the town, 'dig down just six inches here, and everywhere you'll find rock.'

A court case in Rouergue goes on for ever. It is a veritable heritage that the prosecutors and the lawyers bequeath among themselves; but it is not the love of disputing that drives it, but the hatred of giving way . . .

The men of Aveyron are not vain, or curious, or frivolous; they never flatter. I have said that the Rouergat is litigious because he is opinionated. I could have added, because he hopes he will get something out of it; and he hopes for that because he is poor. But, at the same time, he is charitable. Avarice is unknown to him. This vice is the consequence of wealth; to be avaricious, you must first possess something.

In the early spring of 1975 I said my goodbyes at the archives. Shy Monsieur Delmas came from his office to shake my hand. Madame Fabre shed a tear; after all the ingratitude in her life, gratitude was hard to take. Noël, offering me his bristly beard, told me to convey to Britain my congratulations that it had seen the light under *les socialistes*. Dropy, taking out the little rattling tin, offered me a last aniseed drop for the journey. I did not see Fournial; I suspected he was still in his hotel room, lying on the bed with his tie askew, stomach gently rising and falling, asleep.

As I left Rodez for the last time, the train described its usual long loop round the base of the hill. My notes filled five folders; my suitcase was stuffed with bottles of *vin de noix*, tins of thrush pâté and pressed flowers from the high moors. Half a Roquefort cheese, in a badly-insulated polystyrene box, sat in a bag at my feet. The town, with the cathedral bell-tower at its centre, moved out of view. I settled back in my seat, began to read. But the train was still circling; some minutes later the town swung back in front of me. For a moment I thought we were returning; for a moment, too, I wished I was. The five folders of information were not all I had brought back with me. An unexpected affection, partly for the medieval place, partly for the modern, had slid its way into my heart. It is still there.

Notes and Sources

These notes are not exhaustive, but refer only to the most important events, incidents or quotations. Readers requiring the source
of something that is not listed are most welcome to contact the
author. Suggestions for further reading on the period are on page
238. Documentary sources referred to in the notes are listed on
pages 239–43.

REFERENCE NOTES ON THE CHAPTERS
References to original sources are given as they are registered in
Rodez and Montauban. A *liasse* is an unbound bundle of different
documents, usually related by subject. In registers, fo stands for
folio; *recto* (r) denotes the upper or right-hand side of the folio,
verso (v) the under or left-hand side.

Henri Bousquet's excellent printed and annotated version of the
City accounts, *Comptes Consulaires de la Cité et du Bourg de Rodez.*
Première partie: Cité (1350–1358) [Archives historiques du Rouergue vi] (Rodez, 1925); *Deuxième partie: Cité (1359–1388)* [Archives
historiques du Rouergue xvii] (Rodez, 1943), has been used where
it provides an easier reference.

THE PLACE, THE SOURCES AND THE STORY

The Marques case is contained in two different registers, both incomplete and both undated: Fonds d'Armagnac (henceforth F d'A) A219, in Montauban, and C1444 (ii) in Rodez.

1 HUC DEL CAYRO AND THE TOWN AT WAR

Shepherds and spirits: *see* G. Mollat, *La vie et la pratique religieuses en France au XIV siècle* (Paris, 1963), p. 207

St Amans and the broken pitcher: *see* H. Bonal, *Histoire des Evêques de Rodez*, ed. J. Rigal (Rodez, 1935), p. 327

Catarina's lament is cited in a slightly different version in the *Anthologie des Chants Populaires*

St Amans and the idol: *see* Bonal, op. cit., p. 353

State of the cathedral: *see* L. Bion de Marlavagne, *Histoire de la Cathédrale de Rodez* (Rodez/Paris, 1875), pp. 26–43. A later sketch of the cathedral with its crane is reproduced in H. Benoit, *Le Vieux Rodez* (Rodez, 1912)

Del Cayro's story: F d'A A219 fos 240v–241r

The trip to Paris: Henri Bousquet, *Comptes Consulaires de la Cité et du Bourg de Rodez; Deuxième partie: Cité* (Rodez, 1943) (henceforth Bousquet, *Comptes*, ii), pp. 106, 111

Spying: Both City and Bourg kept special sections of their accounts labelled 'Espias', with full listings of where people were sent and what they were meant to be doing. *See* CC200–215 *passim*; Bourg CC126, 128

The watch: Bourg CC126 fo 89r; Bousquet, *Comptes*, ii, pp. 9–11. The watch was started in 1348; a proper roster was drawn up in 1362

The scare of 1355: Bourg CC125, *passim*; Bousquet, *Comptes Consulaires de la Cité et du Bourg de Rodez; Première partie: Cité* (Rodez, 1925) (henceforth Bousquet, *Comptes*, i), p. 241

Castelmary expedition: Bousquet, *Comptes*, ii, pp. 80, 85 and n

Encounters with English, real or imagined: e.g. J. Rouquette, *Le Rouergue sous les Anglais* (Millau, 1887), p. 125; Bousquet, *Comptes*, i, pp. 225–6; Cité C 215 fo 40r; English 'in the woods', Bousquet, *Comptes*, ii, p. 164

Guerrilla nicknames: H. de Gaujal, 'Rôle ... de la revue passée à Rodez le 3 de janvier 1386 ...', *Mémoires de la Société des Lettres, Sciences et Arts de l'Aveyron* (1837–8), 189 ff

Merigot Marches's reminiscences (Froissart calls him Aymerigot

Marcel): *Chronicles*, ed. M. le baron Kervyn de Lettenhove, Tome XIV, 1389–1392 (Brussels, 1872), p. 164

Grape-pickers: Bousquet, *Comptes*, ii, p. 100. Consuls always announced the start of the grape harvest

Grain exports: G 59 fo 20r (Gaffuer case). Gaffuer maintained he had not exported grain at the time the ban was announced: 'only afterwards'

Definitions of 'foreigners': *see* e.g., Legal memorandum, Bourg FF1 no. 7; C1418 fos 10v, 11r, 12r, 24v

Guiralda's eggs: C1414 fo 28r

The royal order about walls: Bousquet, *Comptes*, i, p. 94

Routier deal: Bourg BB3 fo 1v

Wall-building: Bousquet, *Comptes*, ii, pp. 23–31; Cité DD1 m 4; Cité CC199–200, *passim* (damage to property)

'Throw the foreigners out': Bourg BB3 fo 9r. For their worthlessness, see the City arrears book of March 1385: Cité CC53 *passim*

Rules about Jews: E. Martène and U. Durand, *Thesaurum Novarum Anecdotarum*, iv (Paris, 1717) (henceforth TNA), col. 769 (Synodal Statutes of Rodez, 1289). The Bonhome case: C1414 fo 49v

Richard Ardit: Bousquet, *Comptes*, i, p. 213

The City and English taxes: Bousquet, *Comptes*, ii, pp. 40, 419. The quittances give the rate of exchange into sterling (*esterlins*)

The Bourg and English taxes: Bourg CC127 fos 2r, v, 5v

Bourg resistance to French taxation (especially hearth taxes): Bourg CC125 *passim* (1340s); Artières, *Documents sur la ville de Millau* [Archives Historiques du Rouergue vii] (Millau, 1930), pp. 111–12 (1350s)

Birth of Richard II: Bourg CC127 fo 7v

The City's reversion to the French cause: Bousquet, *Comptes*, ii, pp. 62, 419; J. Artières, op. cit., no. 318

Privileges negotiated in Paris (both copies remain): Bourg BB2 fo 31r; Bousquet, *Comptes*, ii, p. 109

Inquiry into royal power (c. 1352): F d'A A216 *passim*

Deals with *routiers*: Bourg BB3 fo 80r

Toulouse and Carcassonne: C1418 fo 10v

Del Cayro's account (Witness 15): F d'A A 219 fos 240v–241r. *See also* C1444 fo 32r, v; F d'A A 219 fo 244r

2 JOHAN GASC AND THE PRIDE OF PARTITION

'Master': *see* A. Gouron, *La Réglementation des Métiers en Languedoc au moyen âge*(Geneva, 1958), pp. 241–2

Res publica: C1444 fos 87r, v (Gasc), 47v (Barbier), 66r (Marot)

Descriptions of the Bourg square: 2E12.212, *passim* (an inquiry of around 1350 into whether the square was a sacred place and the purposes it was used for)

Superiority of the City: C1418, fos 10v–12v; Legal memorandum, G481 (c. 1320)

Burials and games in the Square: 2E 212.11, *passim*

Saracens: ibid., fos 6r, v, 13r; Cité CC1 art. 1134

Gasc's story: C1444 fos 93r–94r

Minting: C1209 fo 14v. Minting was always the second of the count's rights to be listed, after his coronation. For the notional worth of his coinage, see ibid., fo 23r, v

Black Death: Bourg CC125 fo 82v. It was referred to as *tan gran mortaldat*

The Seyrac case: G59 fos 7v, 10r–14v

St Amans and the walls: Bonal, *Histoire des Evêques*, pp. 356–7

'Walking down the street like anybody else': C1414 fo 84v

First partition of the town: F. Bosc, *Mémoires pour servir à l'histoire du Rouergue*, 2nd ed. (Rodez, 1879), p. 191

Treaty about Sant Stefe: Bonal, *Histoire du Comté et des Comtes de Rodez* (Rodez, 1855), p. 206

The drain and the pear tree: Cité DD1 m. 4

Town crier's rules: Bonal, *Histoire . . . des comtes*, p. 205

Bonifaci house: Legal memorandum of 1331, G28, un-numbered; Bourg DD1 fo 3v; Bourg CC125 fos 92r, 138v; G164 fo 128v; G28, *liasse*

Maurel house: CC1 art. 1183; Cité CC208 fo 7v; Cité CC1 art. 1183; Cité CC29 fo 13r; Cité CC30 fo 25r and CC tax registers *passim*, under *Sant Stefe*

Border evidence: G 481 *liasse*, Cité CC1 art. 1176; E98 m. 13; Legal memorandum, Cité FF23; Bourg DD1 *passim*, Cité DD1 *passim*; Legal memorandum of 1352, G492 no. 8

Border markers: Insignificant party: Bourg DD1 fo 5v. Large party: Cité DD1 m. 6

Johan and Agassa: C1416 fo 33r, v

Fishing rights: C1414 fo 50v; C1209 fo 16v; Cité DD1, *liasse*, art. 31; H Bousquet, 'Droits de pêche dans l'Aveyron au moyen âge', *Procès-verbaux de la Société des Lettres, Sciences et Arts de l'Aveyron*, xxxii (1931–4)

Fornols case, G59 fo 9r, v

Pontier case: Cité FF23, *liasse*

Border building regulations: Cité CC19 fos 4or, v, 9or–91v, 98v, 101r; E1192 fo 100r

3 GERALD CANAC AND THE LORD'S DEMANDS

Gasc's story, continued: C1444 fo 73v, 94r, 99r

Canac is mentioned as a vintner in the 1380s' tax lists: Bourg CC series, *passim*. However, witnesses at the earlier inquiry knew him as a cloth merchant; he was trained as one; and he is found dealing in cloth later (*see* Drawing the Moral). The two trades were not mutually exclusive

Earth and air: *De cel entro terra* was the phrase. *See* tenants' recognisances: Fonds d'A A92 *liasse*

Counts' funerals: *see,* e.g, Bourg BB2 fo 66v (1375); Bourg BB3 fo 12v. The consuls wore black and had a Mass said, which was considerably cheaper than having one sung

Counts' oath: Bonal, *Histoire . . . des comtes*, pp. 143–6; C1209 fo 14r

Count's first entry: Legal memorandum, Bourg FF3, un-numbered. See also Bonal, *Histoire . . . des comtes*, p. 24

Bishop's first entry: AD G42 fo 4or (Entry of Peyre de Castelnau, 1324). E. Baillaud & P. Verlaguet, *Coutûmes et Privilèges du Rouergue* (Toulouse, 1910), pp. 42–51

Count's mansion: Repairs: C1331 fo 76r; C1330 fo 58r. For a description of the *sala* in its surroundings, see the count's rent book for 1385: C1266, *passim*

Cloth manufacture: Baillaud & Verlaguet, op. cit., pp. 165–6; Bourg FF3 *liasse*. For revenues from the cloth hall, *see* C1234 fo 53v (1386–7)

St Martial Gate dispute: G485, *liasse*; paper book; Legal memorandum, Cité FF3, un-numbered

Privileges of Bourg and City: Affre, *Lettres sur la ville de Rodez* (Rodez, 1874) pp. 20–9; Baillaud & Verlaguet, op. cit., pp. 99–100; Bourg AA3 *liasse*. For the bishop's restrictive clauses, see Bonal, *Histoire des Evêques*, p. 232; Bousquet, *Comptes*, ii, p. 81. For the count's, see Bourg AA6 no. 6

Count's revenues: C1330 fos 7v, 32v (1366–7); C1234 fos 4v, 5r, 31r; C1330 fo 66v

Camboulas case: C1414 fo 19r, v

Conduct of the fairs: E98 *passim* (the case of a young sergeant accused of brawling). Fair regulations, Cité FF2 no. 17

Lord's love: C1418 fo 26r

Count's demands: For the most blatant among many examples, *see* C1335 122v (1381); Bourg BB4 fo 44r (1393); Bourg CC125 fos 73v, 82v; Bourg BB3 fo 75v; Bourg CC128 fo 9r. For thrice-washed sheets, *see* Bourg CC129 fo 12r. For breakages, *see* e.g. Bourg CC126 fo 57v; Cité CC220 fo 32v. Spices and mules: C1331 fo 68v; C1335 fo 158r

Fripperies: Bourg CC125 fo 73v; Bourg CC126 fo 52r

Excuses for raising taxes: Bourg BB3 fos 61r, 75v, 77v, 90r, 105r, 122r

Plenacassanha's library: G. Mollat, 'A propos du droit de depouille', *Revue de l'Histoire Ecclesiastique*, Tom. xxix (1933), pp. 316 *et seq.*

Petrarch: Bonal, *Histoire des Evêques*, pp. 186–7

Flores Sanctorum: Bonal, *Histoire des Evêques* , p. 580; G482 fo 23r

'I'll be in touch tomorrow': Baillaud & Verlaguet, op. cit., pp. 57–9

4 HELIAS PORRET AND THE WEIGHT OF THE LAW

Canac's career and character: F d'A A219, fo 320v; C1444 fos 2v, 3r, 35v, 66v, 107v. *See also* Johan Riol's evidence, C1444 fo 35v; Huc de Trayssac's, ibid., fo 85v; and the statement of their case by Canac's lawyers, ibid., fos 2v, 3r

Marques's complaints: F d'A A219 fo 25v; C1444 fo 94v, 97v, 120v; about the English, ibid., fo 97v

The silver chains: C1414 fos 49r–52r

St Amans and the thieves: Bonal, *Histoire des Evêques*, pp. 325–6, 355, 358

Gasto case: G59 fos 108v–109v

Count's fines and punishments: C1335 fos 5r, 52r; E98 m. 5, 17

Hangings: see, e.g. G482 fo 32v; C1418 fo 27r (smell of the gallows); C1433 fos 18v, 29r, 48r; 2E212.12 fos 6r, 22r; Legal memorandum, G480, un-numbered; F d'A A216 fos 8v, 29r

Porret's job and his watch duty: C1444 fos 106r–109r; Cité CC207 fo 35v. Rules of his job: see Bonal, *Histoire . . . des comtes*, pp. 216–18; Cité CC17 no. 17; Cité CC19 fo 80v ('charges set by the late count', which also applied to the common court. His house, F d'A A92 *liasse*; Bourg BB4 fos 56v, 57r

Marques's garden: Bousquet, *Comptes*, i, p. 59; Cité CC28–38, *passim*

Riot inquiries: C1418 *passim* (bishop's witnesses); G482 *passim* (count's witnesses)

Helis Montes: C1418 fo 19v

Father Charay: G 482 fo 36r

Huc Sandral: C1418 fo 18v

Guilhem Caissac: G482 fo 35v

Actual killings: C1418 fos 18v, 36v

Bourg bad behaviour: C1418 fos 33v, 34r, 35v

Compensation: Pariage (G480 no. 13) clauses 1, 2 and 3; C1418 fos 33r, 36r

The burned house: *see* the City tax lists for 1366; Cité CC1 art. 1552; F d'A A216 fo 29r

5 PEYRE MARQUES AND THE WILL TO SUCCEED

Gasc's story: C1444 fos 97r, v, 98r, v

Bartelemi's standing: F d'A A219 fo 248r; C1444 fo 135r; Bourg CC9; Affre, *Lettres*, p. 46 (1335–6 and 1342–4); Bourg CC125 fos 75r, 91r

The sickly cousins: C1406 fo 61v; Bourg CC125 fo 130r; Bourg CC126 fo 79v; Bourg CC126 fo 4r; C1444 fo 135r; C1406 fos 61v, 62r

Criteria for consular office: Cité CC1 *passim*; Bourg CC125–128 *passim*; Cité CC33–50 *passim*

Bourg and City *mayos cominals*: Affre, *Lettres*, pp. 29, 99–100; Bourg DD1 *liasse*; Cité CC205 fo 28r; C1444 fo 171v; Bousquet, *Comptes*, i and ii *passim*, esp. pp. 51, 112; Cité CC204 fo 24r

'Democracy': Bourg BB2, 3, 4, *passim*, esp. Bourg BB3 fo 51v; BB4 74v, 81r, 94r; Bousquet, *Comptes*, ii, pp. 192, 497–8; Bourg CC126 fo 115r

Grumblers (in order of grumbling) 2E212.12 fos 9v, 20v, 30r, 15v

Mayo stocktaking (City): Bousquet, *Comptes*, i, pp. 178–83

Lost keys (Bourg): Bourg CC125 fo 108v. The Bourg also lost the *vidimus* of its privileges in the 1340s and the consular seal in 1359. (Bourg CC126 fos 54r, 118v)

Bocart's remarks: Bousquet, *Comptes*, ii, pp. 60, 64*n*, 84*n*; on chiselled money, ibid., p. 60; Peyrasmortas's fees, p. 81*n* and 85*n*

Claustras's evidence: F d'A A219 (second foliation), fo 10r

Evidence of friends and neighbours: F d'A A219 *passim* and C1444 *passim*, fo 20r

Paris charges: Bousquet, *Comptes*, ii, pp. 106, 111

Coderc case: Legal memorandum, Cité CC366 no. 9 (i)

'P. Rostanh': Cité CC48 fo 62r

Guisardo's contract: C1405 fos 98r–99r. His mistakes: Bourg BB3 fo 12r, v; Bourg EE1 *passim*; Bourg BB2 fo 42r

His evidence in the Marques case: F d'A A219 fos 290r, v; 291r; 292v; 294r

6 ALUMBORS MARQUES AND THE SHAME OF DEBT

Diviners: C1444 fos 94v, 95r

The hermit: Bourg CC126 fo 59v

Prostitutes: *see* the little colony in F d'A A235 fo 55r

The leper-house: Bousquet, *Comptes*, ii, pp. 74, 76–80; Cité CC200 fo 1r; Cité CC199 fo 11r; Cité CC200 fo 24v; Bourg CC125 fo 10v. Duran Monferrier's father had provided *bru* for a dress for Biatris in 1355. (Bousquet, *Comptes*, i, p. 204)

Poisoning the wells: C1433 fos 34v, 35r (inquiry of 1365)

Witchcraft: Synodal statutes of Rodez, 1289: *see* TNA, cols 693 and 733

Bad luck: F d'A A219 fo 25r

Housewives in the square: 2E212.12, *passim*, esp. 4r, 13v

Regulation of prostitutes: *see* Cité FF2 no. 17 (ordinance about the fairs); Bourg regulations concerning *putanas publicas de bordel*, Baillaud & Verlaguet, op. cit., p. 174

Molenier's story: F d'A A235 fo 57r

Court fines and punishments for rape: C1335 fos 5v, 52r, 94r, 159v, 193v; C1338 fo 5v

Petronilla's pears: C1414 fo 42r

Valeta's horse: F d'A A216 fo 18v

Grefolieyra's deceptions: G59 fo 8r

Meat regulations: Baillaud & Verlaguet, op. cit., pp. 33, 172–3

Wine regulations: Cité FF2 no. 16; Legal memorandum of 1302, Bourg FF8, un-numbered; Legal memorandum of 1342, Cité FF2 no. 16

Peace Hospital: G442 no. 6 (1323 agreement on administration); Cité CC19 fo 32r; E1127 fos 24r–26r; Affre, *Lettres*, p. 302; will of Bernard de Ramis in 1360: E1594 fo 43r; Cité CC199 fos 6v, 5v

The Fort case: E970 fo 17v (Isabella's will, 1361); P. Cabaniols, 'L'Entrée à Rodez de Pierre Castelnau, Evêque', *Mémoires de la Société des Lettres, Sciences et Arts de l'Aveyron*, (1841–2); G42 fo 67r, v, 68r (evidence of the tenants)

Complaints about the corn charity: Bourg BB2 fo 87r; Bourg CC129 fo 12r (1386)

Marques's payment: Bourg BB125 fo 120v

Auctions: Legal memorandum of 1395, G485 no. 35; Legal memorandum, Cité CC371 no. 19

Pleading for grace: Peyre Malamosca, a notary, witnessed this scene. C1444 fo 126v

Corbes case: C1414 fos 59v–69v

Sergeants' statements: F d'A A216 fos 20r, 24v, 26r

Del Cros case: G59, fos 44v–70r

De Manso case: ibid., fo 18r

Excommunication ritual: Mollat, op. cit., p. 75; G28, un-numbered

Roses: C1414 fo 2v

'Luxuries' list: Bousquet, *Comptes*, i, p. 378

'Necessary' furnishings: Bousquet, *Comptes*, ii, pp. 277, 297, 339

'Necessary' clothes: Affre, *Lettres*, p. 326

7 HUC ROSTANH AND THE SERVICE OF GOD

Rostanh and Marques: F d'A A219 fos 24v–26r

The Sauveterre tax: Bousquet, *Comptes*, ii, p. 147; Bourg BB2 fo 28r, v

Canons' rations: AD G384

Rules of priestly conduct: TNA, cols 706, 708, 725–6

Rules of the chapter: 3G9 fos 15v, 16 r, v, 17v, 19r

Berengaria's story: F d'A A235 fo 53v–57r

The Castanhier case: 3G9 fo 17v; G59 fos 95v–102v

Rules about butcher-priests: Cité CC62 fo 33v; Cité CC37 fo 30r; Affre, *Lettres*, p. 169; TNA cols 727–8

Marro case: G59 fos 105v–107r

Cathedral building: L. Bion de Marlavagne, *Histoire de la Cathédrale de Rodez* op. cit., pp. 18, 26, 36–7, 41, 43

Cathedral decoration: *see* the redecorating accounts of 1385: Bousquet, *Comptes*, ii, pp. 289–90

Lists of relics: L. Bion de Marlavagne, op. cit., p. 278; E959 fo

7r; 2E212.12 fo 19v; Verlaguet, *Ventes des Biens Nationaux dans l'Aveyron*, Tome i, (Millau, 1931): Treasure seized from the churches in Rodez, 14 Pluviose An III (February 2nd 1795)

Inventories of relics, 1321 (E959 fos 6v, 7r) and 1323 (ibid., fo 40r, v); inventory of objects given to the cathedral by Pierre, cardinal-bishop of Ostia (E1126 fo 34r, v)

Pastoral visit of Bishop Vital de Mauléon, 1418–20; *Revue Historique du Rouergue*, 1914–15

Abbot's visit to St Amans, 1347: Bourg GG35 no. 4

Is the Bourg Christian?: 2E212.11, *liasse, passim*

Disrupted procession: C1418 17r, v

Order of processions: G47 fos 10v–13r

Canons in the Bourg square: 2E212.12 fos 1r, 3r, 8r, 15r, 29v

Border burials: E1071 fos 122r, 124r

St Amans relics: Inventory of 1313. Printed in *Revue Historique du Rouergue*, Tome ii (1917–19), p. 128; Affre, *Lettres*, p. 208

Register of fair debts: G964 *passim*

Rules for hearing confession: TNA, cols 693–5

DRAWING THE MORAL

Cat cartoon: Bourg BB3 fo 1r

First poem: Back of register, CC37; *see* Bousquet, *Comptes*, ii, p. 41

Second poem: Inside back cover of the register, Cité CC36; Bousquet, *Comptes*, ii, 40

SUGGESTIONS FOR FURTHER READING ON FOURTEENTH-CENTURY FRANCE:

F. Braudel, *L'Identité de la France*, vols 1 and 2 (1986; English translations 1988 and 1990)

P. Contamine, *La Vie Quotidienne pendant la Guerre de Cent Ans, France et Angleterre* (Hachette, 1976)

— *La France aux XIVe et XVe siècles. Hommes, mentalités, guerre et paix.* (London, 1981)

G. Duby, *Le Moyen Age de Hugues Capet à Jeanne d'Arc, 987–1460* (1987)

— *Love and Marriage in the Middle Ages* (Eng. translation 1994)

J. Favier, *La Guerre de Cent Ans* (Paris, 1979)

R. Fédou, *Les Hommes de loi Lyonnais* (Paris, 1964)

E. Forestié, *Les Livres de comptes des frères Bonis* (Paris/Auch, 1893)

Bernard Guenée, *Un Meurtre, une Société: L'assassinat du Duc d'Orléans, 23 novembre 1407* (Gallimard, 1992)

B. Guillemain, *La Cour Pontificale d'Avignon* (Paris, 1966)

— *Essays in Later Medieval French History* (London, 1985)

E. Le Roy Ladurie, *Les Paysans du Languedoc* (Paris, 1966)

— *Montaillou, village Occitan de 1294 à 1324* (English translation available in Penguin paperback)

E. Levasseur, *Histoire des classes ouvrières et de l'industrie en France* (Paris, 1900)

P. S. Lewis, *Later Medieval France* (London, 1968)

G. Mollat, *La vie et la pratique religieuses en France au XIV siècle* (Paris, 1963)

J. B. Russell, *Witchcraft in the Middle Ages* (Ithaca, 1972)

P. Tucoo-Chala, *Gaston Fébus. Un grand prince d'Occident au XIVe siècle* (Pau 1976)

P. Wolff, *Histoire du Languedoc* (Toulouse, 1969)

— *Commerce et marchands de Toulouse (vers 1350–vers 1450)* (Paris, 1954)

SOURCES

General sources used for this book are listed below.

ARCHIVE MATERIAL USED

(1) *Archives Départementales de l'Aveyron*

Série C (Comté du Rouergue)

C 1027, 1069, 1466, 1523–29: farm receipts, quittances and appeals concerning the Seneschalcy of Rouergue, 1351–4 and 1385–9.

C 1234–39, 1266, 1276–84, 1329–44, 1354–5: rents, *lauzimes*, receipts and expenses of the County of Rodez, 1321–42 and 1366–1400.

C 1379–80: Notarial minutes ... Bernard Gui (1282–3)

C 1381–94: Notarial minutes ... Adhemar and Johan Catel (1286–1346)

C 1395: Notarial minutes ... Brenguier Malet (1292–4)

C 1405: Register of acts ... Bernard Viguier (1354–99)

C 1406–7: Notarial minutes ... Guilhem Fornier (1360–66)

C 1408: Notarial minutes ... Bartelemi Serras (1374–80)

C 1414–16, 1418, 1424, 1433, 1457: registers of proceedings, appeals and inquiries concerning the county court in session at Rodez, 1280–92, 1325, 1343–4, 1365.

Série D (Collège des Jésuites de Montauban)

D 51–2, 430–3: ordinances and memoranda concerning the administration of the Hospital of Santa Martra, City of Rodez.

Série E (Titres de Famille)

(A) Family Documents and private land purchases

E 20	... Andreas, 1343–52
E 44	... Bastida, 1322
E 52	... de Bessoles, 1316
E 98	... Combas, 1296
E 118	... Daurlhac, 1344
E 127	... Delcros, 1330–45
E 130	... Ebrart, 1355–1438
E 188–9	... Gaffuer, 1325–82
E 254	... La Parra, 1383–4
E 382	... Monferrier, 1336–1426

(B) Notarial Registers, Rodez

E 794	... Peyre Adhemar (1400–31)
E 908	... Peyre Boeri (1386–92)
E 959–67	... Huc Canac and successor (1278–1366)
E 968–71	... Guilhem Canac (1344–75)
E 1070–1	... Bernard de la Porta (1369–1402)
E 1072	... Ramon de Saurs (1383–92)
E 1074, 1473	... Peyre de Vaurs (1396–1410)
E 1124–9	... Guilhem Longuofon (1371–91)
E 1192	... Peyre Prohet (1336–43)
E 1221–2	... Johan de Roffiac (1338–60)
E 1224	... Guilhem Roqueta (1370–3)
E 1470	... Adhemar Catel (1319–22)
E 1594	... Bernard Viguier (1352–63)

Série G (Diocèse de Rodez)

G 1, 34, 47, 143: episcopal cartularies, papal bulls, registers of liturgical procedure and admission to benefices, 13th and 14th centuries

G 9: Register of episcopal acquisitions in Rodez, 1118–C15

G 144, 997–9: episcopal receipts from the temporalities and the diocese, 1320–8, 1392–5

G 384, 501–16, 736–9: episcopal grants and *reconnaissances* for properties held from the bishop, 1254–1408

G 42, 442, 495: ordinances and memoranda concerning episcopal jurisdiction in the City, C14–15

G 59, 964: registers of proceedings in the common court of Rodez, 1330–1 and 1346–8

G 472, 479–81, 483–5, 487: memoranda of agreements between the count and the bishop, C12 onwards; letters and royal mandates concerning the Pariage, mainly copies, 1316–50

G 10: Negotiations between the bishop and royal officers about a projected Pariage involving the City and Villefranche, 1309–16

G 26, 28, 31, 75, 475, 492, 965*bis*: royal mandates and tax ordinances, appeals against them, and memoranda of disputes between the bishop of Rodez and the seneschal of Rouergue, C13–15

Série 3G: Chapter documents

(2) *Archives Communales de la Cité et du Bourg de Rodez*
(A) *Cité*

AA 1: . . . privileges granted to the City by the bishops of Rodez, 1218–1419

AA 2, 3: . . . royal letters confirming the City's privileges, 1364–1494

AA 4, 5: . . . agreements between the bishops and the City consuls about the detail of privileges, C14–15

CC 1, 3, 4: . . . *cadastres* of the City, 1355 and 1397

CC 17, 19 . . . *reconnaissances* made to the consuls and sales concerning the community, 1298–1398

CC 28–68: . . . registers of tax contributions, 1352–1400

CC 199–227: . . . consular accounts, 1350–1403

CC 365–8, 371–2: miscellaneous letters and agreements about tax payments, 1253–1399

DD 1, 2: . . . boundary disputes and agreements, 1331–1404

DD 3–5, 8–11: . . . sales and purchases concerning the consuls, 1270–1399

EE 1, 2: . . . letters and orders regulating City defence, 1351, 1400

FF 1–5: ... disputes about community privileges, 1310–95

FF 14, 21: ... consular disputes with the Chapter and others about tax payments, 1099–1499

FF 22, 23: ... City objections to royal taxes and royal mandates, 1294–1382

GG 17–19, 21: ... records of the Confraternity of Notre Dame

GG 20. ... records of the *Bassi de Purgatoria*, 1335 onwards

GG 23, 24: ... records of the leper hospital, 1204–1489

HH 1: ... farm of City offices, consular inspections, 1306–38

(B) Bourg

AA 1, 5, 6: ... confirmation and extension of Bourg privileges by the counts of Rodez, 1214–1519

AA 2, 3: ... royal letters confirming privileges, 1291–1445

AA 7: ... agreements on administration between the consuls and the counts, 1346–C15

BB 1: ... creation of new consuls, 1268–c15

BB 2–4: ... consular deliberations, 1365–1411

CC 9: ... register of tax arrears, 1361

CC 106, 108, 111, 124: agreements between the counts and the consuls about town finances, 1321–1415

CC 125–9: ... consular accounts, 1342–3, 1348–9, 1351–2, 1359–60, 1364–7 (expenses for negotiations about English taxes), 1383–6

DD 1: ... boundary and property disputes, 1364–1529

DD 2, 3: ... sales to the consuls, 1256–C18

EE 1, 2: ... letters and orders from count and king about town defence, 1369–C16

FF 1, 3, 4, 5, 6, 9: disputes between consuls and counts about town privileges and administration, 1307–1471

GG 34–5, 50: administration of the fabric of St Amans, 1280–C15

GG 38–40, 42–6, 52–4, 57–9: revenues and administration of Bourg hospitals, charities and chantries, C13–16

HH 1: ordinances regulating fairs and cloth manufacture, 1369–C18

II 1: inventory of documents in the *mayo cominal*, 1389